A FRIEND OF THE DEVIL

A FRIEND OF THE DEVIL

The Glorification of
the Outlaw in Song
from Robin Hood to Rap

JOHN KRUTH

**Backbeat
Books**

An Imprint of Hal Leonard LLC

Published in 2017 by Backbeat Books
An Imprint of Hal Leonard LLC
7777 West Bluemound Road
Milwaukee, WI 53213

Trade Book Division Editorial Offices
33 Plymouth St., Montclair, NJ 07042

Printed in the United States of America

Library of Congress Cataloging-in-Publication Data

Names: Kruth, John author.
Title: A friend of the devil : the glorification of the outlaw in song from
  Robin Hood to rap / John Kruth.
Description: Montclair, NJ : Backbeat Books, 2017. | Includes bibliographical
  references and index.
Identifiers: LCCN 2017016602 | ISBN 9781617136719
Subjects: LCSH: Outlaws in music. | Popular music--History and criticism.
Classification: LCC ML3470 .K78 2017 | DDC 781.5/9--dc23
LC record available at https://lccn.loc.gov/2017016602

www.backbeatbooks.com

For Steven "Sparky" Brick, Eric von Schmidt,
and Martin Jack Rosenblum:

We'll meet again one day,
In the sweet by and by,
And sing the old songs,
'round the campfire in the sky.

"Once you stand up against the norm,
you can't ask for mercy."
—Peter Rowan

CONTENTS

INTRODUCTION

The inspiration for *A Friend of the Devil* first struck ten years ago while I was writing my second book, *To Live's to Fly: The Ballad of the Late, Great Townes Van Zandt*. Having conducted a series of interviews with Van Zandt's family, friends, and sidemen, I discovered, while gathering hundreds of memories and anecdotes about the legendary troubadour's life, that his quintessential outlaw ballad, "Pancho and Lefty," has continued to haunt the imagination of nearly everyone I spoke with. It turned out that Van Zandt's inner posse of songwriters and drinking buddies, Guy Clark, Rodney Crowell, Steve Earle, and David Olney, were all still ruminating over the meaning of the song's lyrics and its enigmatic ending, thirty-five years after it was first released in 1972. Contemplating Van Zandt's opus inevitably led to a broader discussion of the outlaw ballad genre in general. Nashville songwriter David Olney has been particularly immersed in the form, creating a number of brilliant sonic portraits, including those of Jesse James and John Dillinger. Contemporary artists, from Richard Thompson to Taj Mahal, Dr. John, John Prine, Robin Williamson, and Peter Rowan (many of whom I'd interviewed for previous books and magazine articles), had either sung, written, or recorded great outlaw ballads themselves, and not surprisingly possessed an enormous passion for and knowledge of the subject. So I interviewed many of them again, along with dozens of other songwriters, musicians, and authors, and began compiling a new taxonomy of bad man (and woman) songs that not only reached back to the early "rapparee" (outlaw or highwayman) ballads of Ireland, Scotland, and England but delved into more recent recordings by artists such as Beck, King Missile, KRS-One, and Jolie Holland.

As an itinerant musician for the last three decades (playing mandolin, banjo, and guitar), I have had the good fortune to work with a myriad of singer/songwriters and bands (from Eric von Schmidt to Violent Femmes) whose repertoires always featured a tune or two recounting the misadventures of various brigands and murderers. While listening to (and writing about) such songs stirs one's sympathy for these doomed desperados, actually playing them provides a more profound understanding. Melodies work like tattoos that get under your skin, touching something deeper. Lyrics become engraved in your brain, like initials passionately carved into tree bark. You suddenly begin to see these tragic heroes in a different light, apart from their respective myths. Although many committed desperate and brutal crimes, we can understand how outlaws like Earl Durand, the semi-feral mountain man of Wyoming, had sadly become a victim of his own making. There is often a paradoxical relationship between the love we feel for a familiar song and the reprehensible actions of the criminal depicted within its lyrics. Whether inspired by the singer or carried by the song's melody, we sometimes find ourselves singing along to songs like "Hey Joe" or "Down by the River" that describe unjustifiable acts of violence.

Over the centuries the song form employed by early griots and troubadours has changed very little. The enduring framework for these ballads has typically been basic three or four-chord progressions supporting a simple rhyming lyric that, more often than not, trivializes the gritty reality that outlaws commonly faced, while glorifying and even sanctifying their misadventures. It wasn't until the advent of rap in the mid-1970s that things began to change drastically, as an all-pervasive beat became the prime catalyst for free-styling rhyme. Overnight the bard waxing poetic about the lives of notorious bandits seemed antiquated and obsolete and was quickly replaced with the actual culprits themselves (as in the case of Foxy Brown and many others) standing before an adoring throng while spitting the résumé of their badass ways.

The outlaw as a heroic figure, and the narratives that lionize him, is a global phenomenon stretching back before the days of Robin Hood gallivanting through the "green, green trees" of Sherwood Forest. But it is with the "Hood," who first forged the stereotype of the noble brigand, that our journey begins. Today, these ballads remain alive and well in the twenty-first century, found in a myriad of styles and cultures—from folk and country to reggae, Afro-beat, and rap. While there is always some compulsive historian digging up dusty nuggets of a forgotten past, there will always, hopefully, be cutting-edge artists continuing in the tradition: writing, singing, and rapping a new mythology befitting their own era.

While the outlaw ballad is found in every country around the world, *A Friend of the Devil* primarily focuses on the West—America and the UK—along with various forays into Europe, as well as Jamaica, Brazil, Mexico, Nigeria, and Australia. As a cultural curator, I have assembled a rogues' gallery of concise mug shot–like histories of each criminal, along with the songs that glorify them. They are grouped together based on themes evoked by the title of each chapter, as well as musical style and, whenever possible, a linear timeline.

Songs can be deceptive. Built on rhythm, rhyme, and metaphor, they rarely offer a precise portrayal of people or events. Charged by the singer's emotion, they become something else, beyond reportage or journalism. Songs don't always fit neatly into particular categories, whether because of their mix of musical styles, or because they contain more than one point of view: songs are often written collaboratively. So how does one categorize a work with such fuzzy borderlines? As with the best DJs, whose flow is based on knowledge, impulse, and intuition, my aim is to create a mix that is simultaneously smart and fresh, while knowing that I can't possibly "spin" every song and legend of the outlaw genre and that there are more than a few unworthy of repeated listenings. Good, bad, or ugly, outlaws, and the songs exalting them, have become ingrained in our culture.

My mission with *A Friend of the Devil* (as Sam Shepard wrote of *To Live's to Fly*) is to track the backstory "like a manic bloodhound, without spoiling the mystery of the man." Enjoy the ride!

John Kruth
New York City
February 2017

1

MYTHS AND LEGENDS

Over the centuries, the image of England's most famous outlaw, Robin Hood, has become deeply ingrained into the Western psyche. An extraordinary swordsman, ace archer, and irresistible charmer of fair ladies, Robin, whether avenging the corrupt Sheriff of Nottingham or wooing Maid Marian, would never have considered standing before an adoring throng, bathed in bling, crowing his résumé of valiant deeds. It would have been considered poor taste, and besides, that's what minstrels were for, to compose and sing praise songs to glorify heroes. It's a tradition that harks back to the traveling troubadours of medieval Europe and griots of West Africa, who regularly lavished tribute upon the village chiefs in exchange for the privilege of freely traversing their territories. They often literally sang for their supper and, upon occasion, for their lives. In return, the itinerant musicians were temporarily granted the noble man's hospitality for honoring his generosity, wisdom, and great accomplishments, in rhythm and rhyme. Besides, what sort of chump would stand before a crowd stroking his own ego? English society, from lowbrow to proper, simply wouldn't stand for such nonsense. Transplant one of today's rappers, boasting of all the loot and booty he's tasted and wasted, back to a medieval tavern of yore, and he would undoubtedly have been showered with mead and pelted with boar bones, if not winding up on the rack for a serious attitude adjustment.

Since its humble origins on the streets of the Bronx in the mid-1970s, rap has razed a number of musical traditions. Melody was immediately disposed of, along with any notion of romantic love, which has been popular music's greatest inspiration for hundreds of years. A bone-crushing mechanical 4/4 beat became the vehicle for the blunt verse of the self-styled gangsta. The roots of such narcissistic odes are not only found in the syncopated rhythms of West African hand drums, koras, and balafons (marimbas), but in bawdy ballads from the dank musty pubs of medieval Europe, as well as the competitive poetic traditions of ancient China, home of the original poetry slam. In the eighth century C. E., a showdown took place between two brilliant wordsmiths, the wandering poet Li Po and his friend/rival Tu Fu (also known as Du Fu), over who could spontaneously compose the greater verse. After downing several cups of plum wine, Li Po allegedly derided Tu Fu, claiming he was lucky if he could write a sonnet in a week's time, while purportedly mocking him within his enduring verse:

> How thin, how wretchedly thin, you have grown!
> You must have been suffering from poetry again.

Robin Hood's posse were known as "a band of merry men." They courted fair ladies and battled the king's men with verve, self-confidence, and plenty of style to spare. As portrayed in ballads, bedtime stories, and Hollywood films, from Errol Flynn's quintessential celluloid hero to Mel Brooks's ridiculous 1993 movie, *Robin Hood: Men in Tights*, the Merry Men were a righteous crew who never took themselves too seriously. Through his gallant acts of philanthropy Robin was not only a great provider to his people but offered an important service to his adversaries that they never fully appreciated nor understood—he divested them of the burden of their wealth.

Although seemingly pragmatic, the Hood was a jazz man down to his goatee and uncanny ability to live in the moment and think on his feet, while forever improvising new and clever ways of foiling his foes. Robin's reward was neither the hoard of gold nor the willing harem but the exhilaration of meting out justice to the corrupt Sheriff of Nottingham and his gang of spineless toadies.

There are many varied, and sometimes fanciful, explanations for the mythological Robin Hood's name: it could be from the garment; it could be from his lifestyle ("robbinghood," like "knighthood") or his place of residence; it could even be from a Celtic word meaning "magic" or "devil." Today the word "hood" has its own connotations, being short for "hoodlum," a thug who's quick to oblige you with a knuckle sandwich for simply identifying him as such. Yet while most hoods are sleazy, the original Hood had style. His name became synonymous with a color; like James Brown with Black Power or Joey Ramone with black leather, Robin Hood owns the color green, deep green, the shade of his beloved Sherwood Forest, a righteous hue.

The outlaw ballad in the days of "Robert Hod," as he was known in the thirteenth century, was originally sung by bards and troubadours as an ode to the man's noble deeds and egalitarian attributes. Here, with an excessive usage of vowels, is one of the earliest known verses recalling the "gentylman" and "good yeman Robyn Hode."

> Robyn was a proude outlawe,
> Whyles he walked on grounde.
> So curteyse an outlawe as he was one,
> Was never none yfound.

Robin Hood's story became such a part of the English identity that, in recent years, the University of Nottingham has offered a master's degree in the lore and legend of the charming criminal's life. Perhaps one day we'll find out for certain if he actually existed. The earliest surviving story about Robin Hood is something of an action thriller, entitled "Robin Hood and the Monk," written circa 1450 and preserved at Cambridge University. Taking place in Nottingham, the story recalls the details of Robin's frequent skirmishes with his nemesis, the town's wicked "Shryff." Twenty-five years later, "A Gest of Robyn Hode" collected the many tales of the dashing outlaw that had been passed on orally over the previous 200 years into one long continuous narrative. It wasn't until the seventeenth century that a minstrel by the name of Alan-a-Dale was credited with singing the first broadside ballad recounting Robin's daring adventures in song. The earliest ballads based on "A Gest of Robyn Hode," began to appear in the early sixteenth century with the advent of the printing press in England. Originally Robin was nothing more than a common yeoman (land owner), but by the end of the century he was elevated to the status of nobleman and given such aristocratic monikers as the Earl of Huntington, Robert of Locksley, or Robert Fitzooth.

Robin's love interest, Maid Marian (originally known as Clorinda, the Queen of the Shepherdesses), came along much later, with the intent of promoting heterosexual romance at the annual May Day festivities across England. After all, the Merry Men spent a lot of time together, cavorting in the forest, and falling in love with some girl was a surefire way of breaking up the old gang.

There's no such thing as a definitive history of Robin Hood. His legend is rife with vagaries and discrepancies. Early ballads often mention a "King Edward" but with no clarification whether he was Edward I, II, or III. While most scholars speculate that Robin Hood probably lived between 1270 and 1370, most of the songs and stories that celebrate him were written in the sixteenth century and are set in the era of King Richard the Lionheart, who left his throne in the twelfth century to fight in the Crusades. To further add to the confusion, it is believed that the troubadours of Eleanor of Aquitaine's time (1122–1204, before Hood was allegedly born) had already given the man and his myth a serious makeover, toning down the criminal gang element of Robin's life while emphasizing his chivalrous love affair with Marian, and essentially molding him into "King Arthur Lite." By the eighteenth century, Robin's legend was de-clawed and adapted for children's stories. While maintaining a modicum of adventure and keeping his reputation as a staunch philanthropist intact, these tales portray Hood as an antihero who no longer posed a threat to British convention.

The legend of Robin of Locksley would hit rock bottom in 1964 with *Robin and the 7 Hoods*, a musical set in prohibition-era Chicago, where bows and arrows were replaced with clattering Tommy guns. Essentially a vehicle for the Rat Pack, the film starred Dean Martin and Sammy Davis Jr., with the "Chairman of the Board," Frank Sinatra, in the title role of "Robbo," a good-hearted philanthropic gangster who steals from the rich and delivers the loot to the local orphanage. Alan

A. Dale (Bing Crosby), the orphanage's director, tips off the newspapers to Robbo's big-hearted gesture, which immediately gains him the overwhelming sympathy and support of the public, as enjoyed by the fabled Hood. Upon being pronounced free, Robbo thanks the members of the jury with a rousing rendition of "My Kinda Town." Marian (played by Barbara Rush) is hardly the pure-hearted maiden of yore, but is rescripted as a prime manipulator, who, after seducing and framing nearly all of Robbo's "Merry Men," sets her sites on the do-gooder, Alan A. Dale. The populace of Sherwood Forest, had they lived to witness this perversion, would undoubtedly have had the film's director, Gordon Douglas, drawn and quartered.

The myth of the hero (or most often the antihero in our case) is integral to Celtic folklore and found in various cultures worldwide. And we soon discover the figure of Robin Hood reborn as a ladykiller from the deep woods by the name of "Black Jack Davy," who has been hailed in song for centuries by Scottish folk singers before finding his way into the repertoires of twentieth century folk revivalists such as the New Lost City Ramblers, Bob Dylan, the Incredible String Band, and Dave Alvin (of the Blasters), as well as the White Stripes and bluesman Taj Mahal.

Beyond his romantic gypsy allure, Davy is an obvious symbol of class and race warfare. Stealing the lady of the manor away from her lord and spiriting her off into the "green, green trees," the debonair kidnapper soon converts his captive to the romantic life of the forest-dwelling outlaw. She, "fair Eloise," falls so hard for Gypsy Davy that by the time her husband arrives to retrieve her, she objects, claiming she'd rather sleep on "the cold, cold ground" with her new beau (a man of the people) than live in a gilded cage with him (a stuffy old aristocrat). Fair Eloise, we're told, even forsakes her baby. While we cheer for our heroes and their hot new love affair, the payback is swift in coming. In the version of "Black Jack Davy" sung by the Incredible String Band (a pair of eccentric young bards from Edinburgh, Scotland, who, along with their fellow Scot, Donovan, created some of the best psychedelic folk of the mid-1960s), the song ends on a high note, with the gypsy and his fair Eloise riding off defiantly to live happily everafter, "singin' through the green, green trees." But the tale most often told bears little or none of their twee hippie optimism, and in some instances ends in a bloody retaliation at the hands of the vengeful, jilted husband, said to have been one John Kennedy, either the fifth or sixth Earl of Cassilis.

The earliest version of "Black Jack Davy" (a.k.a. "Blackjack Davey," "Black Jack Davey," and sometimes "Black Jack David") is a song from 1624 recalling the exploits of a charismatic gypsy king by the name of Johnny Faa (a common Romany surname), who, along with seven of his band, was rounded up and brutally executed in Scotland. Faa was guilty of enticing the Lady Jean Hamilton (a young, bored, upper-class mother of two) away from her manor to elope with him, for which he was unceremoniously hanged by the neck, while she wound up imprisoned in a lonely wooden tower, pining the rest of her life away for her dead outlaw.

Originally entitled "Gypsy Davy" and sung as everything from "Gypsy Laddie" to "Wraggle-Taggle Gypsies," the song was first published in 1720 in *The Skene Manuscripts*, a book of Scottish genealogy. In 1808 the Scottish bard Robert Burns quoted the song in his book *Reliques of Robert Burns: Consisting Chiefly of Original Letters, Poems, and Critical Observations on Scottish Songs*. By the beginning of the twentieth century, English folk song revivalist Cecil Sharp had created a popular arrangement of "The Wraggle Taggle Gypsies O," which captured the imaginations of British school children for generations as they sang of the exploits of Black Jack Davy. The blues yodeler/steel guitar picker Cliff Carlisle introduced the tune to the American record-buying public in the 1930s. Despite various lyrical twists, "Black Jack Davy" has remained the prototype for nearly every outlaw (or rock 'n' roller) who's ever come down the pike, whether on a milk-white steed or in a shiny new Ford Mustang, and stolen the heart (and frequently, the virginity) of some young lass, only to hit the road once again before the cock crowed. He regularly reappears over the centuries in a variety of guises, reincarnating as Mississippi John Hurt's "Candy Man," as well the notorious lady's man Mr. Earl, from the Cadillacs' 1955 hit "Speedo," a romantic hustler who "don't never take it slow."

Bluesman Taj Mahal, while staying true to the song's lyric, reworked its rhythm on his 1974 album *Mo Roots*, giving the song a funky, chugging reggae feel. With his smoky soulful vocals, Taj ultimately made "Black Jack Davy" sound "black."

A year later the British folk-rock revivalist band Steeleye Span, with their layered modal harmonies, rock-solid rhythm section, and intricate string arrangements (which together forged a new genre that could be considered "prog/trad"), fashioned "Black Jack Davy" into something of a four-minute mini-opera. Steeleye Span, along with Pentangle and Fairport Convention (which at one point featured vocalist Sandy Denny and Richard Thompson on guitar and mandolin) made traditional music hip for a new generation. While the song's melody takes a few unexpected twists, Steeleye Span's version of "Black Jack Davy" for the most part sticks firmly to the script. The band's lead singer, the mellifluous Maddy Prior, sings of a "bonny brown steed" that "the squire" rides "down dales (and) over a many a wild high mountain" until at last he comes upon his young wayward wife, "cold and wet and weary." Once more she rebukes him. A "goose-feather bed" has little or no appeal to her now that she has slept "on the cold hard ground" with the likes of Black Jack Davey.

> Then I'll kick off my high heeled shoes,
> Made of the Spanish leather,
> And I'll put on my lowland brogues,
> And trip it o'er the heather.

Bob Dylan cast "Black Jack Davey" into a minor key on his 1992 acoustic folk roots album *Good as I've Been to You.* His trademark rough vocals and supple guitar chops were the perfect vehicle for this traditional ballad. Whether or not Dylan decided to leave Davey's fate a mystery by ending the tune before filling in the details of the gypsy's gory death, we'll never know. Dylan has always been something of an enigma himself, as well as a benchmark for all singer/songwriters. So it's not surprising that Jack White, while reworking traditional material, would look to Dylan for his arrangement of the old Scottish folk song. Although a rocker of the first order, White has always kept one foot in Americana, performing and recording strong renditions of songs by Son House and Dolly Parton as well as producing rockabilly queen Wanda Jackson. White's version of "Davey," recorded in 2003 with his band the White Stripes, brings a hard, crunchy electric Jimmy Page/Led Zeppelin feel to the tune. Meg White's simple drumming put a galloping beat behind her former husband's fuzz drenched riffs, driving the lyrics, which describe the forlorn lord of the manor as he rides his horse through the gloaming, desperately in search of his young, runaway bride, who was "just 16."

While the band's clever use of dynamics makes the version of the song memorable, White (keeping true to Dylan's version) also fails to take the ballad to its ultimate conclusion. Instead he leaves the husband (who represents "the Establishment"), his wife, and her gypsy lover (embodying the image of young romantic revolutionaries) standing by a riverbed to sort out their tangled affair. One can only assume that the carefree couple happily then run off into the woods together, leaving behind her overbearing husband, a needy baby, and all that household drudgery. After all, she is only a teenage girl! But as we know, this is not how the story ends, and Davey and his fellow "wraggle-taggle gypsies" wind up dead—whether hanged or displayed in the middle of town with their heads atop poles, depending on which earlier version of the story you hear.

"That song has an element of class consciousness, as many traditional folk songs do—lust, babies, and horses. What else do you need?" asked singer/songwriter/guitar-slinger Dave Alvin. Alvin released a soulful acoustic version of the tune as the title cut of his 1998 album *Blackjack David*. "I first heard the [Woody] Guthrie version, then the 1920s Vernon Dalhart record and then the fifties Warren Smith version. It has an interesting historical take that could be true, but the essence of a bored gal running off with the mysterious stranger goes all the way back to Greek mythology and probably all the way back to Eve and that no good, lying snake in the Garden."

The heroic figure of Robin Hood is mirrored in Hispanic culture in the legend of Joaquin Murrieta. Considered a patriot by some, he was no more than a ruthless bandit in others' estimation. His name (like that of Zapata or Che Guevara) has for many Hispanics come to symbolize political resistance to the prevailing Anglo powers in the state of California. Born in 1829, (although there is still some debate whether he was originally from Chile or Mexico) Murrieta, a Spanish landowner, was said to have had a Cherokee mother and was known to be highly sympathetic to the plight of Native Americans.

Joaquin first came to California during the Gold Rush of the 1850s. According to a novel written by the end of the nineteenth century, Murrieta and his family were brutalized (in some versions, his wife and/or sister were raped while his brother was hung) by a gang of Caucasian miners, said to be jealous of his new found wealth.

Joaquin, along with his friend Manuel Garcia, also known as "Three-Fingered Jack," organized a gang of angry hombres who became known as the Five Joaquins, to take revenge on the greedy gringos. Soon every crime in the territory, from robbery to cattle and horse rustling and murder, was added to their names, yet Murrieta's ragged band of desperados found support, sustenance, and sympathy among Anglos and Hispanics alike.

By May of 1853, California Governor John Bigler had hired the ex–Texas Ranger Harry Love to round up a posse and hunt down the Five Joaquins, along with Three-Fingered Jack. They were all well paid and before summer's end had cornered the outlaws, killed them, cut off Garcia's hand along with Murrieta's head, and preserved them both in brandy. Not only did they return said body parts for their reward, but more money was to be made by putting them on exhibit as curiosities, for which ghoulish spectators paid the exorbitant price of one dollar each to gaze in awe and disgust. Despite nearly twenty people signing sworn statements that the head in fact belonged to the legendary outlaw, a woman claiming to be Joaquin's sister scoffed at the absurdity, pointing to the lack of a facial scar that clearly identified her brother.

Rumors began to circulate, claiming that Murrieta was free and roaming the countryside once more. With the 1906 San Francisco Earthquake, Murrieta's head was lost, ultimately adding to the mystery of the man, while taking with it all trace of evidence that might quell any future argument. He soon became a folk hero, appearing in dozens of songs, books, and movies, and is said to have inspired the legend of Zorro and its popular 1950s television version.

In the hands of Walt Disney's studio, *Zorro* was essentially a rewrite of *Superman*. By day, Zorro was the mild mannered Don Diego de la Vega, a cowardly bookworm (like Clark Kent) until the sun set, when he donned his sleek black mask and cape, grabbed his sword, mounted his black stallion, and fought a series of greedy, corrupt commandantes and magistrados who oppressed the local California populace. Contrary to this heroic version of the legend, Murrieta, in the words of the great Chilean poet and playwright Pablo Neruda, was rumored to have drunk and slept his way through every saloon and bordello up and down California's Mother Lode.

One of the first novels to be published in California, in 1854, was *The Life and Adventures of Joaquín Murrieta: The Celebrated California Bandit*, written by John Rollin Ridge under the pseudonym of "Yellow Bird" (or Cheesquatalawny, his Cherokee birth name). This thinly disguised account of Murrieta's life was the first work of fiction published by a Native American writer in the United States. It turns out that Yellow Bird was something of an outlaw himself. After killing a man in a horse trading deal in 1849, he lit out for California hoping to find his fortune during the Gold Rush. After hitting rock bottom, he turned to writing dime-store novels, poetry, and newspaper articles. Yellow Bird may never have realized the historical importance of his work, which unintentionally provided the first real insight into the lives of Mexican-Americans in California following the Mexican War in 1848.

Today Murrieta's legend in song remains robust, whether eulogized in seamless two-part harmony over the driving rhythm guitar and effervescent accordion of the Norteno duo Luis Y Julian or in the flowing strings, cascading harps, blaring trumpets, and emotive vocals of singer/actor Felipe Arriaga.

"Back in the seventies you used to see 'Viva Murrieta!' painted on vans around southern California and New Mexico," singer/songwriter Peter Rowan pointed out. After reading a biography on "The Robin Hood of California," Peter was inspired to write and record an eight-minute epic ballad entitled "Joaquin Murrieta," which recalled the Hispanic outlaw's famous exploits.

"Either he got away to Mexico, where he became a folk hero . . . and they've preserved his saddle in a museum to this day, or, as the official government report said, he was killed by Captain Harry Love, along with a guy known as Three-Fingered Jack Garcia," Peter said, raising one eyebrow, referring to the uncanny similarity between the legendary bandito and his old friend and one-time bandmate Jerry Garcia (of the Grateful Dead), who once played banjo with Rowan in the bluegrass band Old & In the Way and had lost part of his middle finger on his right hand in a childhood accident.

Translated into English from the Spanish and published in Irwin Silber and Earl Robinson's *Songs of the Great American West*, the ballad "Corrido De Joaquin Murrieta" conveys how the ruthless outlaw made "any American tremble at [his] feet." Sung in a first-person narrative, the song recounts Murrieta's traumatic childhood after he was orphaned "without anybody to love [him]," and describes how his "brother was killed," and his "wife Carmelita was [raped and] tortured." The ballad portrays Murrieta, along with his faithful friend "Three Fingers," as great defenders of "the good and simple Indian," while "fighting with Americans" with cartridge belts crisscrossing their chests and their pistols drawn.

Born in Dublin, Ireland, in about 1806, John "Jack" Donahoe was a legendary figure, who is better known as "The Wild Colonial Boy," thanks to a folk song of that name composed following his violent death.

The song, popularized in our own era by the likes of the Clancy Brothers, Dr. Hook, Larry Kirwan, and many others, tells of Donahoe (also known as Donohoe, Donahue, Doogan, Doolan, Dubbin, and even Dowling) leaving "his native home" in Ireland as a teenager with the intent of migrating to "Australia's sunny shore." In reality, Jack Donahoe (all the versions of his name retain the J. D. initials) had been an orphan, a pick-pocket, and a thief, and was convicted of burglary in 1823. Two years later, at the age of nineteen, he was transported to an Australian penal colony aboard a ship called the *Ann and Amelia*. Arriving at Sydney Cove on January 2, 1852, Donahoe and his fellow convicts were assigned to work for private individuals. He went first to a John Pagan of Parramatta and then worked for Major West, a surgeon who owned an estate at Quaker's Hill, New South Wales, now a suburb of Sydney.

Donahoe's criminal career soon began but came to a quick, violent end. Numerous ballads celebrating his life sprang up, circulating orally. "The Wild Colonial Boy," the best-known of Australian folk songs, grew out of one of these earlier versions. It presents a vivid picture. Charged with malicious "intent to commit a felony," Donahoe faced "seven long years in New South Wales to wear a convict's chain." Clever and enterprising, he stayed behind bars "no longer than six months," before escaping, becoming "a terror" and "a plundering son." "He robbed the rich, he helped the poor, / He shot [some unlucky sod by the name of] James MacEvoy."

Further details abound in the sixteen or so versions of an equally anonymous ballad called "Bold Jack Donohue." In these the brigand disappeared into the brush with a pair of ne'er-do-wells named Kilroy (or Gilroy or Kilray) and Smith. According to the reputable *Australian Dictionary of Biography*, these were real people who were hanged in February 1828 for a robbery in which Donahoe also took part. But their sly leader escaped before the sentence was carried out. In song they are joined by, or replaced with, "MacNamara from yonder woods" and one "Captain Mackie too." Later came others, known as William Webber and John Walmsley, with whom Donahoe formed a fearsome gang known as "The Strippers," known for literally "stripping" the wealthy of their clothes, food, and money.

Whether true, exaggerated, or entirely false, these stories helped Jack and his pals become sympathetic figures to poor farmworkers of the region, who were all too happy to let him know where their employers stashed their prized possessions, while providing the outlaw and his "chief associates" with whatever clothing, shelter, and provisions they could spare.

His death, like his life, was enthusiastically mythologized by the balladeers. According to one version of "The Wild Colonial Boy," eventually met his fate one morning [September 1, 1830, in reality] while out on the prairie, riding along and "A-listening to the mocking bird, a-singing a cheerful song" when "a band of troopers" who'd been hot on his trail finally managed to track him down. Outnumbered three to one, Donahoe chose to bravely stand his ground and shoot it out rather than surrender and be forever remembered as a sniveling coward. Who would not admire the man's pluck as he mouths off one last time to the coppers before catching the "fatal ball" that lodged in his breast and "caused him to fall"? As one of the "Bold Jack Donohue" songs puts it:

"Resign to you, you cowardly dogs,
It's a thing I ne'er will do.
   For I'll range these woods and valleys,
Like a wolf or kangaroo,
   Before I'll work for Government,"
Said bold Jack Donahoe.

Finally, in the "Wild Colonial Boy" version, Jack "drew pistols from his belt [and] proudly waved them high," managing to take down some deputy named "Kelly" before "a bullet from Fitzroy's gun" suddenly pierced "his proud young heart."

Those were the facts of Donohoe's life and death according to the balladeers, writing later and glamorizing the man in tune with popular discontent. The Donohoe who appears in contemporary newspaper accounts is a quite different figure, reflecting the attitudes of the Colonial press of the day. Three days after his death, on September 4, 1830, the *Sydney Gazette and New South Wales Advertiser* reported on the police operation, stating that the "daring marauder has at length been met by that untimely fate which he so long contrived to avoid." As the Mounted Police came riding through the bush outside of Campbell Town, they came upon three bushrangers. While his companions both managed to escape, Donohoe was killed "on the spot, [with] one ball entering his neck and another, his forehead." The writer did not waste sympathy on this "outlaw of the people." His report concluded: "Thus is the Colony rid of one of the most dangerous spirits that ever infested it, and happy would it be were those of alike disposition to take warning by his awful fate."

The following Tuesday, September 7, 1830, the newspaper returned to the incident, this time in much greater detail. Donahoe (as he is spelt in this account) and his gang of bushrangers, after roaming the country, foolishly returned to their old haunts, where seven Mounted Policemen were waiting for them.

Then "Donahoe called out to the Police to 'come on,' using the most insulting and indecent epithets." There was an inconclusive exchange of fire. Finally a soldier by the name of Muggleston "took aim, fired, and, though a hundred yards distant, in less than a minute the vaunting bravo was in eternity."

Upon examing the body, they found a "horse-pistol and a fowling piece which he carried for defense." He also had a small pocket-pistol concealed in his britches. "The trowsers in which he was shot were afterwards recognised by young Mr Campbell, as those of which Donahoe robbed him, a few weeks ago, on the highway." Not quite the hero he's been portrayed to be, Jack Donohoe, died dressed in someone else's "strides."

Whatever his merits as a role model, Jack Donohoe's legend has continued to thrive over the centuries, beginning with a play by the pioneering Australian poet Charles Harpur entitled *The Tragedy of Donohue*, published in 1835. This inspired a later play called *The Bushrangers*, published in a volume with some of Harpur's poems in 1853, his only significant work to be printed in book form in his lifetime. It is a kind of inverted morality play in which Donohoe is represented by a character called Stalwart.

"The Wild Colonial Boy," probably the most popular of all Australian folk songs, was banned for generations by Australian authorities who believed its provocative lyrics might suddenly trigger an unstoppable wave of dissent. Considered Australia's first unofficial national anthem, the song was outlawed on the charge of containing "seditious sentiment." The story of Jack Donahoe, Jim Doolan, John Dowling, and all the other variants continued to grow until the real events were no longer recognizable. No matter how the authorities tried, they could not squelch the resilient spirit of the legendary hero. The myth continued to grow until it became an indelible part of Australia's folklore. Eventually official attempts to ban the public singing of the beloved ballad were abandoned.

"The Wild Colonial Boy" made its film debut in 1970, in *Ned Kelly*, sung by Mick Jagger of the Rolling Stones in a mock Irish accent to the sparse accompaniment of a lone penny whistle. While Jagger's performance managed to offend nearly everyone of Irish descent, as well as folk music fans around the globe, it was the one redeeming moment in Mick's otherwise anemic acting debut. (Jagger claimed never to have bothered watching the film. If that's any indication of how the leading man felt about his performance, it's probably not worth your time either.) His meager acting abilities helped to sink an already troubled film; Jagger's girlfriend, sultry chanteuse Marianne Faithfull, had flown to Oz intending to play Kelly's sister "Maggie" in the movie. But with the recent death of Brian Jones, the Rolling Stones' charismatic one-time leader/multi-instrumentalist, and her rocky relationship with Jagger, Marianne tried to take her life one night by swallowing a handful of sleeping pills. Thankfully she lived and wound up recovering in a Sydney hospital, while an unknown Aussie actress by the name of Diane Craig took her place.

The soundtrack album to *Ned Kelly* comprised a portfolio of country and folk songs written by Shel Silverstein (best known for "A Boy Named Sue," "On the Cover of the Rolling Stone," and his classic children's book *The Giving Tree*) and sung by Kris Kristofferson and Waylon Jennings. Also included was a tune sung by Jennings called "Lonigan's Widow." Over a punchy oompah-pah country waltz, he recounts the shooting of one of "four jolly troopers from Mansfield town," who'd been tracking the bandits through "the wombat." In a surprise attack by the brigand "Ned Kelly and his comrades three," Lonigan was killed as he was "cleaning the camp, boiling some tea," while they'd been "camped on the banks of Stringy Bark Creek." Lonigan (whose first name remains a mystery, as it is never sung) left behind a grieving widow who "walks these red hills [and] cries all night long."

Famous for his rustic outlaw image, Jennings surprisingly takes the side of the lawman and his victimized wife (there's no mention of whether he left behind any grieving children) as he sings, "They say that Ned Kelly ain't never done wrong, but tell that to Lonigan's widow."

Beyond a sympathetic portrait of the lawmen who died during the skirmishes with the Kelly gang, "Lonigan's Widow" contains a weighty message. Kelly, a hero to the multitudes who continue to celebrate him as "the pride of Australia [and] the scourge of the crown," was in reality a nefarious bushranger, better known in the US these days as a cop killer. Although hanged in November 1880, he remains a controversial figure, as witnessed by the smattering of opinions found on the Internet. "Ned Kelly was no Robin Hood," wrote one contributor to an online discussion. "The fictitious character of Robin Hood robbed from the rich and gave to the poor [while] Ned Kelly robbed from everyone. He murdered police all for his own personal gain. Celebrating Ned Kelly is akin to celebrating Jack the Ripper!"

Perhaps Waylon Jennings summed it up best as he coolly sang, "Bury the truth as you bury the dead."

Years later, during his 1988 tour of Australia, Mick Jagger would reprise "The Wild Colonial Boy" with the help of a cheesy synthesizer, in lieu of a tin whistle, and the nimble guitar accompaniment of Joe Satriani. The audience ate up Jagger's shabby stab at folk-rock, in which he sang of the adventures of "Jack Doolan" instead of Donahoe. The same name was used by Dennis Locorriere and Ray "Eye Patch" Sawyer in Dr. Hook & the Medicine Show's surprisingly passionate reading of the tune. Released in 1981 as the flipside to their single "That Didn't Hurt Too Bad," Dr. Hook's version of "The Wild Colonial Boy" was a worthy tribute to Australia's most notorious bush ranger. Sung and strummed on a twelve-string guitar by Locorriere, complete with close harmonies provided by Sawyer, the song finds the pair seeming to swoon in reverie as they croon, "A curse to every copper was the wild colonial boy." The tune quickly rose to No. 4 on the Australian charts. True to Donahoe's outlaw spirit, the money garnered from its sales was then generously donated to charity.

Whether he is perceived as a victim, murderer, or hero, the romantic image of Ned Kelly fighting off the police in his homemade iron helmet and vest has been seared into the consciousness of every young Australian over the last century, through the constant retelling of the outlaw's life in popular movies, books, and songs.

The son of an Irish immigrant father, Ned Kelly grew up in poverty in the British settlement of Victoria. Said to have once saved a boy from drowning, Kelly had "turned bad" by the age of twelve after his father John (a.k.a. "Red") died as the result of having spent half a year in prison doing hard labor. He had been caught possessing stolen cowhides and a sizeable amount of meat he could not account for. Red, in the recent past, had been forced to flee Ireland and then migrated to Australia after having been a convicted pig thief. With their father dead, and a bereaved mother and seven siblings to fend for, Ned and his brother Dan soon became the most convenient suspects whenever their neighbors' horses or cattle went missing. The fact that they were Irish, along with their father's previous reputation as a convict, caused the family to be charged with a dubious eighteen accounts of theft, and this was *before* Ned became a notorious bushranger.

At fourteen, Kelly was arrested after he allegedly held up a traveling chicken and pig trader named Ah Fook, who'd stopped outside the family home to ask for a cup of water. By age fifteen, Kelly was sentenced to three years for rustling cattle. Upon his release, he and his brother Dan immediately picked up where they'd left off, poaching whatever domestic animals could be found on or near their neighbors' farms. In short order, Ned, Dan, and their mother were all thrown in jail.

While their mother (sentenced to three years) remained behind bars, Ned and Dan managed to escape. Trailed by the police, with a reward that grew to £2,000 on each of their heads, the Kelly brothers, along with their friends Joe Byrne and Steve Hart, temporarily took refuge in Mrs. Ann Jones's hotel in Glenrowan. There was little time to rest as they were forced to take sixty hostages to keep word of their whereabouts from spreading. They planned to derail the train arriving from Melbourne the following morning, but their plot was thwarted. One captive, Thomas Curnow, who had been kindly released by Kelly as he was with his wife and daughter, revealed the plot to the railroad authorities. Rather than hijacking the locomotive, Kelly and his gang, after too much liquor and too little sleep, found themselves surrounded by the police.

It is said that the showdown at Glenrowan on the morning of June 28, 1880, in which the Kelly gang killed three policemen, nearly triggered a civil war. As the hostages fled during the mayhem, Joe Byrne was apparently shot while standing at the bar and bled to death. Dan Kelly and Steve Hart were said to have drunk poison as the hotel burned to the ground. A rain of bullets reportedly ricocheted off Ned's custom armor, said to have weighed approximately ninety pounds, as he boldly marched towards the squad of thirty policemen intending to mow him down. Ned's uncovered legs and arms endured a total of twenty-eight bullet wounds, but he was determined to take as many lawmen down with him as possible. Despite his injuries, Ned managed to escape and vanished into the bush.

Later captured and taken to Melbourne jail, Kelly was convicted on three counts of "willful murder" and received an execution sentence, regardless of a petition signed by 60,000 people. Despite an angry crowd of 1,500 protestors who'd gathered outside the prison walls, Kelly was hanged on November 11, 1880. His famous last words sounded as if they'd been scripted by Charles Dickens. "Oh well, I suppose it has come to this.... Such is life," he allegedly sighed, as they ceremoniously placed the noose around his neck and hanged him until dead.

Midnight Oil's anthem "If Ned Kelly Was King" (from their 1981 album *Place Without a Postcard*) seeks revenge upon those who continue to exploit and ravage the Australian countryside for their own profit. It takes aim not only at camera-toting tourists driving their jeeps roughshod over the outback but at all the "dreamtime developers" as well, with their "heavy machinery." Written by the band's guitarist James "Seamus" Moginie and lead singer Peter Garrett (whose staunch commitment to politics led him to occupy the chair of Australia's Minister of Environment in 2007), the song pleads for the country's infamous outlaw to return and avenge the rape of their beloved homeland. "If Ned Kelly was king," they sing, "He'd make those robbers swing."

"Peter Garrett wrote those lyrics," Moginie recalled recently. "We were homesick and recording in England at the time, so that was a way to write fondly about Australia. Ned was of Irish ancestry, and victimized by the 'squattocracy' or the landed gentry. His father died in prison when Ned was a twelve-year-old, thus his need to provide for his family as the eldest male. Forced into the life of an outlaw, he was eventually gunned down but survived just long enough to be hung in prison. Ned Kelly is a folk hero today."

Ray Cashman, author of *The Heroic Outlaw in Irish Folklore and Popular Literature*, adroitly summed up the plight of young men driven to acts of desperation by their circumstances and the need for a champion of the poor and downtrodden: "As a symbolic figure in Irish folklore and popular literature, the outlaw embodies folk morality in conflict with the self-interest and inequity of the state. In the aftermath of British colonization, the Irish outlaw is represented as more than a criminal. He provides a hero through whom ordinary Irishmen and women can vicariously enjoy brief victories and imagine their collective dignity in the midst of political defeat and its consequences."

The notorious seventeenth-century highwayman "Redmond O'Hanlon," as celebrated in song by the great Irish bard, Tommy Makem, perfectly fulfills Cashman's ideal of the gallant rapparee. Formerly a papal count, before he and his family were driven from their land following Cromwell's conquest of Ireland in 1653, O'Hanlon transformed himself into an Irish Robin Hood, who, with "loaded pistols" and "noble big black horse," merrily informed his victims they were about to be mugged "by the handsomest man in Ireland." Robbing "landlords of their silver and their gold" was not simply for his personal gain, but a deliberate act of class warfare, with the honorable intent of fairly redistributing the wealth "to the poor, to pay their rent and fee." Despite the aggravated country gentleman Squire Johnson's "handsome offer" of four hundred pounds to anyone willing and capable of capturing the scoundrel O'Hanlon, "no man in all the land" would consider the notion of tracking the notorious outlaw down to "hang him from a tree." The soldiers were soon summoned to do Johnson's bidding, but "while they slept that night" Redmond allegedly snuck up on the pitiful buffoons and, in a scene reminiscent of a 1930s Hollywood swashbuckling adventure film, "stole their guns and rode away."

A supernatural twist to O'Hanlon's legend comes following his death in the year 1681. As Makem proudly sings, "in the silence of the night" his spirit still rides "from Rathfriland [in County Down, Northern Ireland] to Forkhill" [formerly known as Foirceal na Cleire, a tiny village of about five hundred people in County Armagh, also in Northern Ireland].

African American folklore is also not without its own version of Robin Hood. Found in the "Ballad of Railroad Bill," Morris Slater, as he was known around the Deep South, was a sympathetic outlaw hailing from the backwoods turpentine camps of Tombigbee, Alabama.

As a traditional folk song, "Railroad Bill" became part of the repertoire of Hobart Smith, Etta Baker, Mississippi John Hurt, and many others during the height of America's folk music revival of the late 1950s/early 1960s. According to the various verses that immortalized him, Bill clearly had more of the badass gangsta attitude than Robin Hood, Black Jack Davey, or Murrieta before him. Famous for lighting big cigars with ten-dollar bills, he was not merely a ne'er-do-well but a wife stealer and a murderer who not only "whupped his mama, and shot his old dad" but also laid a couple of sheriffs and a deputy in their graves, along with some poor guy named McMillan on a full moon night.

Folk singer Cisco Houston claimed that Railroad Bill gained his sobriquet from breaking into boxcars and distributing the bounty to his impoverished neighbors. After living on the lam for many years, Bill was eventually tracked down by the authorities and killed in 1896. But songwriter/screenwriter/radio personality Andy Breckman's "Railroad Bill" refused to stick to the traditional script. His version stretches Slater's myth to extraordinary lengths, creating a hard-living, hard-drinking desperado who was "the baddest engineer that ever drove for the Santa Fe Line."

Breckman's saga begins with, of all things, Bill finding a kitten stuck up a tree. Just as he is about to save the cat, Bill stops and refuses to go through with the good deed, complaining, "This is a stupid, stupid song, and no folk singer is gonna make a fool out of me." Andy begs to differ with his protagonist, pointing out that, as the author, he's in control of the action. "For God's sake, I just made you up!" he sings. "I got the pen in my hand. I want you up in that tree, and I want that cat unstuck." Railroad Bill then suggests instead that it might be more fitting for a man of his reputation to "save some beautiful girl who's been tied down on the railroad track." By verse eleven, Andy's had enough. "You've pushed me too far," he warns Bill. "I'll show you I can do as I please." He then creates an earthquake that brings Railroad Bill to his knees, followed by a tidal wave and a monster from Neptune that takes a big bite out of Bill's leg. "I got the pen in my hand," warns Breckman (best known as the creator of the television series *Monk*) "I can do what I want. I'm a bright new young talent on the rise. So get your ass up that tree, or I swear you ain't gonna get out of my folk song alive."

The pair wind up rolling on the ground, slugging it out until a lightning bolt mysteriously zaps Bill between the eyes, killing him instantly. The cat then climbs down from the tree, laps up a bowl of milk, curls up, and takes a nap. "Railroad Bill is survived by a wife and three small children," sings Breckman. He finishes the song by chortling "Dear God, I love to write!"

Ishmael Reed's "Railroad Bill, A Conjure Man" (from his 1973 collection of poetry entitled *Chattanooga*) offers yet another take on the legend of Morris Slater, in the form of an epic poem. Reed recounts Bill's fateful run-in with the local sheriff. After plugging the lawman full of holes, Slater lights out for the woods, seeking refuge. A deputy soon follows and winds up dead as well. Bill finds himself sinking deeper and deeper into a quagmire of trouble and desperation by the minute.

While certainly closer to the spirit of the original folk ballad than Breckman's wild fantasy, Reed gives Bill plenty of jazzy style and endows his hero with the mystical powers of hoodoo. Even after he is tracked down and executed outside a country store, none of the locals are willing to accept that Railroad Bill is actually dead. "That's not our Bill," the townsfolk unanimously claim. So Slater continues to live on to this day in legend and song. Freed from the limitations of a human body, Bill becomes a shapeshifter, taking whatever form he chooses, from a cloud to a tree. Time, as far as Bill is concerned, is elastic, and he bounces back and forth from the past to the future with ease. By the end of Reed's poem, Bill has transformed himself into a film editor at a Hollywood movie studio, diabolically destroying some hackneyed flick based on his legend.

Taj Mahal, who recorded "Railroad Bill" on his 1973 album *Oooh So Good 'n Blues,* attempted to balance out some of the wild twists and turns the outlaw's myth had taken over the years, in its telling and retelling, by focusing on the song's enduring instrumental aspects. "I heard a lotta people playing that song in the late fifties and early sixties," Taj recalled. "It was on a lot of albums during that folk coffee-house time. I liked Mrs. Etta Baker's version of it. The way people from the sixties listened to and played that music—they would often times change it to a more standard style. Whereas if you go back and listen to the way the original melody went, it was set in a different time and place. [Taj attributed his rendition of the song to ethnomusicologist/song collector John Work III.] I was always after the original melody. It seemed like all the guts had been taken out of it by my estimation."

In many ways, Bruce Springsteen's "Outlaw Pete" (from his 2009 album *Working On a Dream*) represents the epitome of the modern day "folk process" (a time-honored tradition of borrowing and incorporating whatever available musical or lyrical motif might possibly improve a song, which, in more recent years, has been replaced by the common practice of sampling). Lyrically the tune's inspiration can be found in the opening verse to the classic song about the mythological American folk hero, the "great steel drivin' man," "John Henry." Oddly, though, the melody seems to have been lifted directly from the 1979 hit, "I Was Made for Loving You," by Kiss. It's hard to decipher Springsteen's intention, as from the start the tune seems like deliberate parody.

Although Pete Seeger must have harbored some doubt about the infant John Henry's verbal skills and self-fulfilling prophesy, he always managed to deliver the song with a sense of righteousness that gave it the gravitas that made it a classic.

> *When John Henry was a little baby,*
> *Sitting on his papa's knee,*
> *He picked up a hammer,*
> *And a little piece of steel and cried,*
> *"This hammer's gonna be the death of me."*

Not everyone was quite as earnest when it came to singing John Henry's praises as Seeger. In the Smother's Brothers' hilarious 1963 recording, "The Saga of John Henry," Tommy Smothers sang a more believable version of what might have happened when the supernatural baby "picked up a hammer and a little piece of steel, and said 'Goo goo, ga ga, goo goo!'"

The saga of Springsteen's "Outlaw Pete" recalls an unusual baby born in Appalachia; by the time the tyke turned six months old he'd already served "hard time" for robbing a bank. By the second verse Pete, now twenty-five, has turned to stealing horses—mustangs to be specific (Bruce always romanticized sleek cars, so the metaphor was immediately clear). Wherever Outlaw Pete rambled, he left women brokenhearted and men lying cold. And like John Henry before him, he too had a vision of his own doom. According to Bruce the song was "an existential fairy tale" in which he "cataloged all the terrible things that happened," including the juvenile outlaw sinking his knife deep into the chest of a bounty hunter named Dan, and leaving him in a puddle of "his own blood, dying in the sun." Pete's redemption comes in marrying a Navajo girl, with whom he briefly settles down on the reservation and has a baby girl. But Outlaw Pete was not cut out for domestic life and soon climbs upon his horse and rides off "for forty days and nights" (quoting the Bible always brings a certain to seriousness to any tale) until they finally reach a snow-capped mountain peak. Like all the best myths, "Outlaw Pete" remains something of an enigma. What drives our hero to dig his "spurs deep into his pony's side" and disappear "over the edge," or camp out "high upon that icy ledge," where he was sure to freeze to death? How, exactly, the young outlaw finally meets his death we'll never know.

"The characters are outlandish. They're not real. They're mythical. The tale is a fable," said Springsteen, defending himself to a journalist from the *Washington Post*, who wondered if the song's dark subject matter was suitable for kids, after the song was illustrated by Frank Caruso and published as a children's book in 2014.

Ridiculous as it may seem, Bruce Springsteen's "Outlaw Pete" is one of the more recent additions to the pantheon of American folklore that glorify the supernatural powers often attributed to thieves, drifters, and outcasts. Washington Irving's classic of American folklore, *The Legend of Sleepy Hollow*, is said to have its origins in a German folktale collected by author/professor Karl Musäus. The chilling tale of a nameless Hessian mercenary, whose head was blown off by cannon fire in an unknown battle during the Revolutionary War, was first published in the United States in 1819, in a collection of short stories called *The Sketch Book* (which also included "Rip Van Winkle" and was credited to Geoffrey Crayon, one of Irving's many pseudonyms).

In the wake of the tragedy, the apparition mounted a mad black stallion each night to gallop through the gloom and haunt the populace of the tiny village of Mount Pleasant, New York.

In 1865 the Irish-born American novelist Mayne Reid reimagined *The Headless Horseman* as a western. Adding the subtitle *A Strange Tale of Texas*, Reid moved the setting of Irving's story to the wide-open prairies and sweeping skies of the Lone Star State, far from the haunted, arthritic forest where the cantankerous school-master, Ichabod Crane, had met his mysterious fate. Translated into French by a young Vladimir Nabokov, *The Headless Horseman* would inspire (and manage to endure) a series of revisions, in which the phantom avenged horse thieves and guarded mines from greedy prospectors. Before Tim Burton directed the visually delicious *Legend of Sleepy Hollow* in 1999, turning Ichabod Crane (played by Johnny Depp) into an eccentric forensic specialist, Irving's tale had been adapted for a silent film starring Will Rogers in the 1920s and remade once again a decade later as a talkie in the 1930s. *The Adventures of Ichabod and Mr. Toad*, an animated Disney package film, combined two shorts, *Mr. Toad*, inspired by Kenneth Grahame's children's classic *The Wind in the Willows*, and *Ichabod* (narrated by Bing Crosby), in which the horseman's head, a blazing jack-o'-lantern, is hurled at the frightened, fleeing Crane before exploding across the screen like a Molotov cocktail.

By 1972, the legendary Horseman headed east, riding across Europe where his legend was adapted for the Russian cinema and renamed *The Headless Rider*. Perhaps the most startlingly original retelling of Irving's headless Hessian came from the late singer/song-writer Warren Zevon, who transformed the story into the fabulously macabre "Roland the Headless Thompson Gunner." With the sort of gratuitous violence common to Hollywood films and today's rap art-ists, Zevon wrote "Roland" in 1978, creating a horrifying hero who seemed to embody all the guilt and self-loathing that plagued America in the wake of the Vietnam War and Watergate.

"Restraint has never been one of my virtues," once quipped the songwriter who "smeared the pot roast all over his chest" in his hit song "Excitable Boy." Zevon's lyrics are gloriously gory and sinister, which was rather odd, considering that he was often lumped in with a group of 1970s laidback LA singer/songwriters known as the "Avo-cado Mafia," which included such terminally mellow musicians as James Taylor, Jackson Browne, Joni Mitchell, and the Eagles.

Much like his colonial-era counterpart, Zevon's Roland was an unstoppable supernatural killing machine. After setting out to join the "bloody fray" in Biafra, he arouses the suspicion of the CIA, who become alarmed by his efficiency and enthusiasm on the battlefield.

Deeming him a loose cannon, covert agents coerce Roland's friend Van Owen to assassinate him. Although his skull is blown to bits, the headless mercenary inexplicably comes back to life, avenging his killer by mowing him down with his Tommy gun before wandering off once more into the eternal night.

The song's last verse contains a bizarre twist when Zevon conjures up the image of Patty Hearst, the daughter of the multimillionaire publishing magnate who, after being kidnapped by a group of guerrillas known as the Symbionese Liberation Army, donned the chic uniform of her captors and helped them to hold up a bank (shades of Black Jack Davy's "fair" Eloise?). In Zevon's demented tale, "Tania" as Hearst became known, heard the echo of Roland's Thompson machine gun thundering in her brain, and, like any true American heiress, she "bought it."

Hearst, who will forever remain etched in America's collective memory as the khaki-clad radical chic guerilla girl wielding her M1 carbine with command and poise, is the heroine of the California alternative-rock band Camper Van Beethoven's "Tania," from their 1988 album *Our Beloved Revolutionary Sweetheart* (see Chapter 12, "Street Fighting Man"). One of the band's many spin-off projects included an eclectic group known as the Electric Chairmen, who recorded an album entitled *Toast* in 1996 before they apparently burned out. Over a haunting minor-key melody, they recount the "Ballad of the Headless Skateboarder," which tells of the misadventures of "Poor Icky Crane," who is no longer a schoolmaster or forensic specialist (as portrayed in Tim Burton's film version of the Washington Irving legend) but now a skate punk whose head was severed from his body as the result of an "awful wipeout on Sleepy Hollow Lane."

In this rather silly update, Crane becomes the Horseman himself, an amputated apparition haunting the tree-lined streets of the suburbs every month "when the full moon is silver and bright." Ultimately harmless, this supernatural spirit, we're told, "wouldn't harm a fly." He's simply the grotesque ghost of some kid who gave his all for his favorite sport (which, with or without a head, is still not a crime). It is all very Bart Simpson, whose creators also borrowed Washington Irving's myth, casting Krusty the Klown as the *Headless Horseman* in the 1995 special Halloween episode of *The Simpsons* entitled *Treehouse of Horror VI*.

Over time the archetypal hero (or antihero) of these enduring ballads has been subjected to such extreme makeovers that the original authors would probably fail to recognize their creations. These songs and legends have constantly been changed (not always for the better) to suit new generations; so we see Robin Hood transformed from a free spirit into a married, land-owning member of the gentry and Joaquin Murrieta becoming a superhero in movies and TV.

"It's like the difference between butter and margarine!" Taj Mahal put it. "You know what butter is, while margarine is somethin' they came up with later."

2

POST OFFICE PINUPS

The misadventures of Billy the Kid were soon outdone by twentieth century miscreants like Al Capone and John Dillinger who were front-page news. Their outlawry was far from the high-minded philanthropy allegedly practiced by Robin Hood. These were desperate men who committed violent acts, and yet they continue to be celebrated in song and film to this day. Whether gunfighters or gangsters, these lowlifes also inspired a slew of fictional characters who are, in the public imagination, just as ruthless as their real-life counterparts.

"I'll be with the world till she dies," said William H. Bonney, a.k.a. the legendary "Billy the Kid," talking to the *Texas Star* in March 1881, the year of his death. Bonney, had he lived in another time, might have had a successful career in advertising, with his flair for spinning yarns and manipulating the media. The young gunslinger stoked his legend in the press with genuine panache.

Newspapers were not alone in fueling the myth of "The Boy Bandit King." "Billy the Kid," was originally a ten-verse rhyming poem written by the Reverend Andrew Jenkins. (He also composed "The Death of Floyd Collins," which was popular in the 1920s and revived in 1986 by Phil Alvin of the Blasters on his first solo album *Un "Sung" Stories.*) "Billy the Kid" was first recorded in 1927 by Texas singer/harmonica player Vernon Dalhart (born Marion Try Slaughter in 1883) and later adapted by slide-guitarist/musicologist Ry Cooder. Cooder employed a funky strut on a mandolin, which gave Jenkins's lyric a rustic reading on his 1972 album *Into the Purple Valley*. According to the song, the young, brash William Bonney, who claimed he would live forever in infamy, was apparently still unsatisfied with killing only twenty-one men. Billy would soon meet "his sad end" after foolishly bragging to his pals that "Sheriff Pat Garrett's gonna make twenty-two."

It seems that neither the newspapers nor the history books (let alone songwriters) got much right when it came to the Kid's short life. To begin with, his legal name wasn't William H. Bonney, it was Henry McCarty, and he hailed from New York City, not the Western plains as most folks assumed. Billy wasn't twelve when his legendary killing streak began; he was eighteen. His first victim was a schoolmate whom he claimed to have shot in self-defense after the boy allegedly pulled a knife on him. By the time McCarty turned twenty-one, he had reportedly murdered somewhere between four and twelve men. No one is actually sure; reality has been for the most part useless in deciphering the Kid's myth for well over a century. Two of his victims are said to have been killed in an act of self-defense; another perished in revenge after having killed his boss. The Kid, we are nearly certain, never saw his twenty-first birthday. Most historians estimate his age of death at nineteen.

Ry Cooder chose to omit the final verse to Jenkins's poem, perhaps because he didn't know it (he certainly must have been familiar with Marty Robbins's and Tex Ritter's earlier versions of the song) or felt it was a bit too preachy. Cooder's version ends after the Kid "met his fate" when Pat Garrett drew first. Jenkins had concluded his poem with an I-told-you-so ending, as a moral to warn others inclined to follow the Kid's fast and reckless path:

> *There's many a man with a face fine and fair,*
> *Who starts out in life with a chance to be square,*
> *But just like poor Billy, he wanders away,*
> *And loses his life in the very same way.*

In contrast to Cooder's rendition stands Bob Dylan's updated "Billy," written and performed for the 1974 soundtrack to Sam Peckinpah's bloody western *Pat Garrett and Billy the Kid*, which starred James Coburn and Harry Dean Stanton. Over a loping Tex-Mex rhythm,

Dylan sympathetically recounted the gunslinger's plight, singing to Bonney like a friend in his trademark nasal twang, telling him, "Billy, they don't like you to be so free." Dylan, who appeared in Peckinpah's film in the role of an eccentric ragamuffin named "Alias," reminds his desperate pal that his time isn't long and that the legendary cemetery Boot Hill will soon be his resting place. "Sleep with one eye open," Dylan warned the Kid, as "every little sound just might be thunder," not from the foreboding sky tumbling down around him but from the sudden burst of Pat Garrett's gun.

Two years later Charlie Daniels recorded his own take on "Billy the Kid," an up-tempo country rocker for his 1976 album *High Lonesome*, which features a crunchy riff played on a Les Paul, and a pair of wailing fiddles that drive the song. In Daniels's romanticized version, Sheriff Pat Garrett has the Kid's "name on every bullet in his gun."

With a corny clip-clop introduction and lonesome cowpoke harmonica of the like heard on dog food commercials, Billy Joel's rendition of "Billy the Kid" is not only filled with historical inaccuracy but is transparently derivative of both Elton John's songwriting and his delivery. Joel doesn't stop there: he employs the worst sort of Western musical cliché in a feeble attempt to emulate Aaron Copland, who composed music for his ballet *Billy the Kid* in 1938. There is little doubt that if the outlaw had lived long enough to hear this skewed version of his life story, around the clock protection couldn't have saved Mr. Joel from being hunted down and murdered in cold blood by his subject.

Over the years, Billy the Kid's legend has been borrowed and tried on for size by many performers. The king of the gunslinger balladeers, Marty Robbins, sang it as a minor key Tex-Mex waltz, which loaned the tale a bit more passion and sense of tragedy. Texas singer/songwriter Joe Ely's "Me and the Billy the Kid," is a whole different ballgame. Over a percolating rockabilly beat and searing pedal-steel guitar, Ely slags the legendary outlaw, describing him as a little punk "all hopped up on speed" and claiming that he "wore his gun all wrong." Meanwhile, the German metal band Running Wild scream the Kid's misadventures in a rough and raucous Deutsch over a wall of industrial-strength fuzz-tone.

"I like to dance, but not in the air," the Kid allegedly said. But in the end he "died of lead poisoning," as one Boot Hill tombstone reads. At least he dodged the humiliation of a public hanging (as well as hearing some of the more hackneyed versions of his life story put to song).

Among the dozens of inaccuracies in Billy the Kid's legend, the most common of all, that the Kid had "killed 21 men," one for each year of his life, was a complete fabrication. The truth lay somewhere closer to between four and ten, if you include those shot in self-defense along with the two guards he plugged while breaking out of jail. It's interesting to note that there was never a wanted poster hung nor distributed bearing his name and image. In December of 1880, the Governor of New Mexico announced the generous reward of $500 for one "William Bonny, alias The Kid" (yes, they misspelled his name, which should have read Bonney) in the *Las Vegas Gazette.* Any post office pinup featuring that famous photo of the Kid, cocky in his stove-pipe hat, sneering at the camera, offering a $500 reward (and in some instances $5,000), is purely counterfeit, a souvenir for suckers.

"I invented every gesture and the choreography of every gunfight," author Michael Ondaatje confessed regarding his powerful portrait of the adolescent gunfighter in *The Collected Works of Billy the Kid.* First published by a small press in 1970 when he was still an unknown poet living in Ontario, the book, Ondaatje explained, was "comprised of poems and prose and imaginary interviews and songs and frag-ments [about] a historical figure, who had, by the 1960s, turned into a cartoon." Ondaatje pointed out that he had to "invent Billy from the ground up, because really there was now nothing left of him—no blood or sinew or clue of character behind the known facts."

"It was a very personal book," Ondaatje emphasized. "I impro-vised off the history and geography having never been there when I wrote it."

Just the mention of Al Capone's name evokes the image of a ruthless gangster like none other. Arguably the most famous criminal in Amer-ican history, the notorious Chicago mob boss has been the subject of dozens of TV shows and films, in which he was depicted by the likes of Al Pacino, Rod Steiger, and Ben Gazarra. Yet his legend has inspired very few songs. Most music associated with Capone has either taken the form of an instrumental or a song that briefly name-checks him with the intent of evoking a certain mood or attitude.

An outtake from Michael Jackson's 1987 album *Bad*, "Al Capone" was no more than a shout-out and a bit of chic gangster posturing by Jacko that managed to recount little or nothing of the man's life or character:

> Too bad, forget it,
> 'Cause Al Capone said it.

The crisp gunshot snare and fat booming synth bass line that drive the song seem to conjure Capone's personality more than its superficial lyric or Jackson repeatedly growling "Why did you let him get away?" as the song fades out. The accompanying video, an atmospheric and well-choreographed fantasy that features Jackson done up in a fedora and pinstripe suit, seems to have even less to do with Capone.

Interestingly enough, Al Capone himself was a music lover and something of an amateur musician, proficient on both banjo and mandola, with a passion for opera and jazz. In 1926, Fats Waller was allegedly kidnapped by Capone's goons and forced to play the gangster's birthday party, which lasted for three days.

Once installed behind bars at Alcatraz, Capone (who was surprisingly allowed to have a stringed instrument, as the wires, in his hands, could easily have become a lethal weapon used to strangle a guard or fellow inmate) joined the prison band known as the Rock Islanders. With nothing but time, Capone focused his diabolical mind on melody, eventually presenting a visiting Jesuit priest named Vincent Casey with the sheet music for a song entitled "Madonna Mia." He even signed it, "To my good friend Father Vin Casey with the best in all the world for a Merry Christmas always for you. Alphonse Capone."

> Madonna Mia,
> You're the bloom of the roses,
> You're the charm that reposes,
> In the heart of a song.
> Madonna Mia,
> With your true love to guide me,

Let whatever betide me,
I will never go wrong.
There's only one moon above,
One golden sun,
There's only one that I love,
You are the one.

While the lyrics were laughable (particularly "Let whatever betide me, / I will never go wrong") and trite enough for a Hallmark greeting card, few were about to criticize Public Enemy No. 1's tender offering, whether it had been inspired by his wife, Mae, or the Virgin Mary.

Kicking off with the sounds of screeching tires and a car crashing, ska bandleader Prince Buster's 1967 hit instrumental "Al Capone" was later reworked by the Specials, the 1980s British new wave band, into their first single "Gangsters." The Specials, who pitched the song in a haunted minor key, even borrowed Prince Buster's famous hook, shouting out "Don't call me Scarface!"

Legions of hip hoppers, looking to forge an intimidating image in hopes of capturing the public's imagination, have tried on Capone's XXL legend as well as borrowing his moniker or some variation on it, from Mr. Capone-E, to Al Kapone and simply, Capone, the Queens-based rapper who rose to fame as one half of C-N-N or Capone-N-Noreaga. The notorious crime boss even made a brief cameo in "Al Capone Zone," a 2008 track by the rapper Prodigy. Once more, a macho bass line sets the mood, although the infamous gangster has little to do with the song's "niggas" who are getting wasted "smokin' blocks of shit."

The legend of the Memphis-born gangster George Francis Barnes Jr., better known as Machine Gun Kelly, was revitalized by the "King of Low-Budget Classics," Roger Corman, who directed the 1950s B-movie named after him. *Machine Gun Kelly* starred a little-known actor of Lithuanian descent named Charles Buchinsky, better known as Charles Bronson, in the lead role. Released in 1958, the noir feature remained in obscurity until 1967, when, thanks to the tremendous success of *Bonnie and Clyde*, it was reissued as part of a double feature with 1958's *The Bonnie Parker Story.* In the role of Kelly, Buchinsky, despite his rugged face and macho bluster, became a sniveling coward when stripped of his modern killing machine. Apparently his "tough-talking" wife, called "Flo" in the movie but known as Katherine in real-life, ran the show.

In song, Machine Gun Kelly's myth was revived by James Taylor on his 1971 album *Mud Slide Slim and the Blue Horizon.* Written by Taylor's lead guitarist Danny "Kootch" Kortchmar, "Machine Gun Kelly" recounted the fate of poor George Kelly. According to Kortchmar, he had more reason to fear the ambitious demands of his overbearing, social-climbing wife than the man who tracked him down and sent him up the river for life: J. Edgar Hoover.

Kelly "was a simple man but the woman was as hard as hell," Taylor sang in his trademark mellow voice. Apparently Katherine Kelly henpecked her husband to "kidnap a rich man's son, and make it in the world of crime," as she was "tired of being such small time."

"Watch out Machine Gun, don't let her run you round," Taylor advises. "Don't let the woman put you six feet in the ground." In the end, one can sympathize with Kelly, hoping the poor sap eventually got a little peace and quiet doing time in his Leavenworth cell. Apparently Kortchmar related to George Kelly on a personal level, claiming the song had originally been inspired by his former wife.

All was well in small-town Indiana at the turn of the twentieth century when John Dillinger was born, on June 22, 1903. His father, John Sr., owned a small grocery store, and the family, which consisted of mom, dad, and older sister Audrey, were all good, churchgoing stock. But by the time the boy turned three, little Johnnie's mom, Mollie, had died, and everything went straight to hell. Sister Audrey, who filled in for a while as the lady of the house, soon found a love of her own, settled down, and got married. Then the old man followed suit, leaving the kid feeling cut out of the deal no matter how many toys his pop brought home. In no time, little Johnnie joined a band of juvenile delinquents known as "The Dirty Dozen."

One day, down at the sawmill, to the amusement of his pals, Dillinger and his friend Fred tied a neighborhood kid to a plank of wood, turned on the circular saw, and stood around watching and laughing as the boy screamed in horror. Just inches from his death, they flipped off the switch. Following this little prank, young John and his buddies dragged some hapless girl into an abandoned shack and gang-raped her. By the time he quit school at sixteen, he'd built quite a reputation. After joining the Navy and going AWOL, Dillinger would excel at stealing chickens.

While hardly a traditional narrative, Nashville songwriter David Olney's "Public Enemy Number One" offers a sequence of brief glimpses that illuminate the criminal's desperate, twisted path like a series of exploding flashbulbs. Each verse ends with Dillinger snapping some terse, flippant response to whatever pressing situation is at hand.

"A good friend of mine named Gwil Owen, who I write songs with, found this cheesy paperback on the life of John Dillinger and gave it to me. It was sort of sensational, but I guess you can't write about Dillinger in any other way," Olney said. "But I found some cool little facts in there, like there actually was a guy named Luther in Dillinger's gang, who was wounded, which led to the line, 'Luther's bleeding from a hole in his side.' I'd heard Woody Guthrie's 'Pretty Boy Floyd' and 'Railroad Bill' and tended to think of these people [as being] like Errol Flynn: colorful, interesting people to be around. When I lived in New York in the early seventies, I got mugged, and it sort of changed the way I felt."

Olney laughed: "The guy pulled a knife on me, and I don't remember stopping to think, 'Oh what a colorful guy! I wonder what circumstances could have driven him to this desperate act.' I just thought, 'This really stinks. I don't like this guy.' Read about Bonnie and Clyde, and you'll find it wasn't a very glamorous life. The book described Dillinger as having yellow eyes. So I took it from there, building up an image of the guy that was unpleasant. That song has two points where it takes off from, the life of John Dillinger and bullies in general and the hold they have over people. Dillinger, being the leader of the gang, was the most violent one. All of these people in the song, Ruby and Luther and others, are trying express some sort of human quality, and every time they do, Dillinger tells them to shut up. To Dillinger, farmers losing their farms were nothing but 'suckers.' He repeatedly squelches the best parts of being a human being."

Olney's lyric, delivered with a dry, punchy Raymond Chandler–like economy, successfully captures the desperate, suffocating atmosphere that surrounded the outlaw. The tension in the getaway car is thick enough to cut with a knife, hardly the kind of thrill portrayed in the popular ballads or Hollywood epics that glorify famous criminals.

Inspired by "a kid's tune," the song came to Olney "one night right before going onstage to play a gig in Atlanta. It was goofy, a nursery rhyme kind of song. Then I realized it would be cool if the words were in opposition to the melody, like a modern-day Grimm fairy tale. If you try to make the melody and the emotional quality of the words match up, it doesn't always work, it gets to be overkill. In outlaw songs you've got to go beyond the obvious . . . 'They robbed a bank and shot somebody . . .' You've got to try to get to how they actually felt about it. The quest for realism doesn't go into the emotional quality of things. In movies, you've got special effects. You get to see people's brains explode. In rap lyrics you get very explicit and sometimes quite brilliant descriptions of incredibly violent acts. But my life, thankfully, for the most part doesn't involve gunplay."

It is less common for an ode to be written and sung to the brave lawman who risks his life, doggedly tracking down fugitives, whether as a solemn dirge like Bob Dylan's "Knockin' On Heaven's Door," dedicated to Sheriff Pat Garrett, or Lancelot Pinard's hilarious send-up of the head of the FBI, "G-Man Hoover," as arranged and adapted by Van Dyke Parks, who regarded Pinard as "a hero in my time."

Born in 1903 in Cumuto, Trinidad, Lancelot Pinard made his debut in 1940 at New York's indomitable jazz cellar, the Village Vanguard in Greenwich Village, singing calypso, although he'd been a classically trained musician. Following a West Coast tour, he appeared in over a dozen films, including the Bogart/Bacall classic *To Have and Have Not.* In the 1980s, Pinard returned to performing at small clubs around LA with an all-star band of local luminaries including Van Dyke Parks on piano, Ry Cooder on guitar, and Jim Keltner on drums.

"Lancelot Pinard adopted the nom de guerre 'Sir Lancelot' and found celebrity stateside in the early 1940s with Paramount Pictures' *Murder in Trinidad*, which I believe served as Robert Mitchum's introduction to calypso," Parks pointed out. "When I heard the song ["G-Man Hoover"], which appeared on Smithsonian Folkways *Calypso Songs 1927–1946*, I flipped. As it was not in copyright, I registered the string arrangement that you hear on my [1972] album *Discover America*. I had the joy of Lancelot's friendship when he moved to Los Angeles, which is where he died. He was an admirer of Caruso and bel canto, and impressed by J. Edgar Hoover's bravado."

Beginning with a delicate vamp that seems as if it were designed as a dance number replete with canes and spats, Parks, with tongue in cheek, gently croons "Rat tat tat tat, rat tat tat tat, rat tat tat tat" in imitation of a Tommy gun.

"Criminals come but they have one way to go, / Gangsters are dumb for by now they ought to know . . ." Parks smirks, hinting at the inevitable doom in store for these two-bit punks who are foolish enough to challenge J. Edgar's authority. "Shave off your beard, change the color of your hair, / Step out the door there's Hoover waiting there," he sings, mocking the hapless criminals: "Mud is your name, Hoover always gets his man."

Beginning with *Hopalong Cassidy*, which first aired in June 1949, Westerns began to dominate television programming by 1959, with over twenty-five "Shoot 'Em Ups" ruling the primetime slots. The average American's dedication to the adventures of the unshakable Marshal Matt Dillon of *Gunsmoke* (one of the most popular shows in television history, running from 1955–1975), as well as the hard-boiled but suave "gentleman gunfighter" Paladin of *Have Gun Will Travel*, would inspire a slew of popular country and western songs that helped stoke the public's ongoing love affair with the Wild West.

The enormous success of Marty Robbins's album *Gunfighter Bal-lads and Trail Songs* (which featured Robbins's classic tune "El Paso"), in the fall of 1959, unleashed a wave of outlaw songs that included the top-ten hit "Ringo," recited in a manly baritone by the wavy white-haired Canadian actor and sometime singer Lorne Greene. Best known as "Ben Cartwright" in an immensely popular weekly Western, *Bonanza*, Greene released his first album, *Robin Hood of El Dorado*, in 1961. His perfectly timed gun-fighting ballad "Ringo" shot to No. 1 during the thrall of Beatlemania, three years later in December 1964, despite the fact that the song had absolutely nothing to do with the large-nosed British drummer. Ringo Starr, it turned out, adored country and western music and had briefly played drums for a Liver-pool combo by the name of the Raving Texans in 1959 before joining up with the mop-tops. Although famous for his floppy beat and fond-ness for jewelry, Ringo's nickname was inspired by the legendary gun-fighter, Johnny Ringo (a.k.a. John B. Ringgold and John Peters Ringo) who was tracked down and killed by Wyatt Earp in Turkey Creek Valley, Arizona, in 1882.

Over a steady clip-clopping country rhythm, Lorne Greene recounts the tale of a stranger he discovered lying face down, unconscious in the desert sand. The narrator recalls how he surgically removed a bullet from his back with his knife. Having saved his life, the narrator then nurses the drifter back to health. Meanwhile a chorus of lonesome cowpokes punctuate each verse by ominously chanting the stranger's name . . . "Ringo." Watching in awe as he practices day in and day out with his pistol, the protagonist claims that "No human being could match the draw of Ringo." One day the friends decide to split up at a fork in the road, and go their separate ways. While the narrator soon becomes a deputy sheriff in an attempt to restore order to a lawless land, Ringo, with his blazing six-shooter, begins to spread terror wher-ever he goes. Predictably the two men eventually meet up once again and the gunfighter, not surprisingly, out-draws the lawman, blowing the six-shooter out of his hand in an awesome display of speed and skill. "We're even, friend," Ringo informs his old pal, the deputy, but suddenly the posse, who'd been holed up and waiting quietly in the shadows, let loose with a barrage of weaponry, blasting the outlaw full of holes. Although now a hero wherever he goes, for the rest of his life the melancholy protagonist is forced to live with the nagging truth that he could never outdraw his old friend, the legendary "Ringo."

"You're gonna see my face down at the local post office, babe," sings singer/songwriter/guitarist Paul K, of Lexington, Kentucky, who effortlessly captures the plight of the desperate and dispossessed within the poetic verse of his simple three-chord song, "Post Office Pinup." The artist, known to his mother as Paul Kopasz, has experienced both the ravages of addiction and the view from a jail cell first hand. He knows the pain and desperation of which he sings.

> I couldn't work in no office, man,
> It just doesn't fit into my plans.

"Don't want no job at all," he sneers, "Just wanna punch my banker right in the jaw."

> Dontcha spoil my day,
> I think I found a foolproof way,
> You won't forget my name,
> I'm on the road to dough and fame.

> You're gonna see my face,
> Down at the local post office, babe.

That may be the case, but you get the distinct feeling that this young misfit's joyride is bound to be short-lived. His quest for fortune and notoriety is not only certain to be brief, but most likely forgotten just as quickly as yesterday's news. While "Post Office Pinup" packs a wry, tongue-in-cheek delivery, "Nashville Tennessee," the following tune on Paul K's 1991 album *The Big Nowhere*, is far more disturbing. The lyric recounts the pathetic saga of a musician, living on the edge, hoping to hit the big time as he heads down Highway 65 to Music City in his dilapidated Oldsmobile with "nothing left to lose."

"I wrote my songs and lived them," Paul sings. His song evokes a classic *Twilight Zone* episode (No. 154) entitled *Come Wander with Me*, in which a rock 'n' roll singer named Floyd Burney travels through the backwoods of the American South on a quest for inspiration to write a batch of new songs. A city slicker with a slick pompadour, cut-away guitar, and shiny new Thunderbird, Floyd soon finds himself inexplicably bewitched by the cryptic verse of an old folk ballad that he's discovered.

As Rod Serling cleverly summed up the fate of the wandering "gentleman songster": "He'll find everything he's looking for, although the lyrics may not be all to his liking when the words and music are recorded in *The Twilight Zone.*"

"Never was my life so hard as down there in that sun," Paul K grouses. Things quickly turn from bad to worse. "I bought a box of shotgun shells and loaded up my Colt," he sings, planning to rob a local liquor store. But his scheme quickly goes awry when the clerk refuses to hand over the cash. Rather than go into the gory details of the shooting or his haggard emotional state, the singer calmly, coolly reveals that he "put [the stubborn shopkeeper] in a fresh grave near Nashville Tennessee."

Heading north, on the lam, the song's weary protagonist, who seems oddly detached from the crime he's just committed, takes a moment to reflect on his desperate deed: "There's nothing much I've learned," he shirks. Admitting that his "conscious has been watered down," presumably with copious amounts of booze, in hopes of suppressing whatever guilt is gnawing away at him, he speculates that "If the federal Marshals service ever catches up with me, I hope they'll send me anywhere but Nashville, Tennessee."

3

REBEL MARTYRS AND OUTLAW SAINTS

Quite often the public's perception was more sympathetic towards outlaws than to the fate of their victims or the lawmen who tracked them. At the end of the Civil War, a large segment of disenfranchised Southerners identified with Jesse James and the Cole Younger gang. Pretty Boy Floyd and Earl Durand (as well as the Brazilian brigand Lampião), who fashioned themselves after Jesse, were likewise forgiven by the populace for whatever death and mayhem they left in their wake while battling corrupt and oppressive authority figures. Perhaps this veneration of killers in legend and song is what led Bob Dylan to transform the despicable gunfighter John Wesley Hardin into his heroic protagonist "John Wesley Harding."

A common theme found in old folk ballads, dating back to the days of Robin Hood, was that of the good, honest man who eventually becomes a victim, disillusioned and disenfranchised by an impersonal system to which he could not conform, and who is eventually driven to a life of crime and desperation. While canonized in song for their gallant struggles and occasional selfless deeds, very few outlaws over the course of history were in reality true, tireless champions of the people who, as we are told time and time again, "stole from the rich and gave to the poor."

For well over a century, the legend of America's most notorious outlaw, Jesse James, has continued to flourish through an endless array of songs, TV shows, and movies, to the point where he is now approaching sainthood among the "true believers." The myth of the Missouri train and bank robber has worked its way into the hearts of millions of Americans, whether north or south of the Mason/Dixon line. Like Robin Hood, Jesse has been celebrated for his philanthropic ways, although there is little or no proof of such purported displays of compassion and generosity. Meanwhile, Woody Guthrie's ballad not only praises him for his radical charity but extols James for having "a hand, a heart, and a brain" as well.

With the fall of his beloved Confederacy in 1865, James, his brother Frank, and their friends were pushed to take desperate measures. Jesse soon became a national hero, thanks to the adulatory reportage of John Newman Edwards, a journalist with *The Kansas City Times*, whose glamorized dispatches focused not on the outlaw's desperate, gritty life but on the James Gang's cool criminal style. Edwards' accounts not only sold copies but drew fierce support and sympathy from the populace, spiking Jesse and Frank's fame to that of Wild West rock stars or perhaps a band of swaggering saints.

"Jesse James," a traditional three-chord tune, has been sung and strummed by everyone from Uncle Dave Macon in 1929 to Burl Ives and Woody Guthrie in the 1940s (who'd previously sung his "Ballad of Jesus Christ" to the very same melody and chord changes) to Ramblin' Jack Elliott, Cisco Houston, and the Kingston Trio (whose 1958 hit single "Tom Dooley" set off a brief outlaw/murder song craze) at the height of the folk revival of the late 1950s and early 1960s. Jesse's legend was revived once more by Bob Seger, who loaned his raspy voice to a pot-boiler rock 'n' roll version of the song in 1972.

As fitted their ragged image, Irish punk-rockers the Pogues cut a campy rendition of the tune (slurred by Peter "Spider" Stacy, *not* the band's usual lead singer, Shane McGowan). Complete with clanky banjo, tin whistle, and kitsch pistol shots that ricocheted from speaker to speaker, it appeared on their 1986 breakthrough album *Rum, Sodomy, and the Lash* (produced by Elvis Costello).

Generally considered a traditional cowboy song, "The Ballad of Jesse James" is most often credited to Billy Gashade, who is believed to have written the ode to the beloved outlaw following his death in 1882. Also known as "The Death of Jesse James," the song was first recorded for Columbia Records in 1919 by Bentley Ball who, judging by his eloquent delivery, was clearly not a cowboy. No guitars, fiddles, or banjos are to be heard on the original version. Instead, Ball recited the tragic tale of James's assassination over a frilly parlor piano accompaniment, enunciating each word with precise diction. North Carolina folklorist and banjo picker Bascom Lamar Lunsford claimed he first learned the words of the song from a Tennessee mountain singer called Sam Sumner in 1903. Lunsford's 1924 rendition of the song, with its rustic banjo picking and lyrical twists, is considerably different from the song Bentley Ball recorded five years earlier. A year later in 1925 Vernon Dalhart would croon a more recognizable and popular version of the tune. Over the years "Jesse James" was a staple in the repertoire of everyone from the hot bluegrass fiddler Toby Stroud to Pete Seeger and the Kingston Trio. In 1980 came a "concept album," *The Legend of Jesse James*, featuring Levon Helm singing the role of Jesse James and Johnny Cash as his brother Frank. The cast also included Charlie Daniels as Cole Younger, Emmylou Harris as Zerelda, Jesse's wife, along with Rosanne Cash and Rodney Crowell. Despite some fine songs and vocals, and blazing guitar work from Albert Lee, this ambitious country-rock opera soon fell into obscurity.

Ry Cooder arranged two excellent versions of "The Ballad of Jesse James" in 1980 for the soundtrack to *The Long Riders*. Walter Hill's film depicted the Younger/James gang by teaming up the Keach brothers, Stacy and James, with the Quaid brothers, Dennis and Randy, along with three Carradines, David, Robert, and Keith, as well as Christopher and Nicholas Guest as Charley and Robert Ford (the cowardly assassin of Jesse James). This clever casting, as well as the great music and wardrobe, gave the film a fascinating authenticity.

The vocal version of the song features an amalgam of styles, in which Cooder blended a tin whistle, reminiscent of the cane fife and drum bands led by Othar Turner from the North Mississippi hill country, with a drunk Salvation Army–style burping tuba, tack piano, and a scratchy fiddle. Cooder's chunky electric guitar (although yet to be invented in the 1800s) sounds perfectly at home in this slice of rustic Americana.

In 1998, "the Belfast Cowboy," Van Morrison, would make an unexpected return to his folk roots, when he recorded a live album of rough 'n' ready skiffle tunes in collaboration with the legendary trad jazz bandleader/trombonist Chris Barber and Lonnie Donegan. Donegan, (who inspired a young John Lennon and his first band the Quarrymen to cover "Rock Island Line") rose to fame in the UK by interpreting American folk and blues by Lead Belly and Woody Guthrie, back in the 1950s. This was years before Morrison caught the public's ears with his Ray Charles–inspired vocals and self-penned hits such as the garage rocker "Gloria" and the AM radio perennial "Brown-Eyed Girl." To the crowd's delight, Morrison delivered "The Ballad of Jesse James" in his trademark passionate slur, as Donegan's keening harmonies drifted above the singer's huffing-puffing delivery.

"The Ballad of Jesse James" remains alive and well in the twenty-first century, revived once more by Bruce Springsteen on *The Seeger Sessions*, the Boss's 2006 tribute to the folk legend Pete Seeger. Springsteen's album is particularly unusual as he deliberately opted to steer clear of controversy by choosing not to sing any of Seeger's political songs (for which he is most famous).

A particularly inspired version of "Jesse James" was performed by the South Memphis String Band (featuring Luther Dickinson, best known as the singer and hot lead guitarist with the North Mississippi Allstars, and multi-instrumentalist/singer Alvin Youngblood Hart) on March 18, 2010, at Music in the Hall in Oxford, Mississippi.

Warren Zevon's ballad of "Frank and Jesse James" is an altogether different homage to the James brothers. The lead-off song from Warren's 1976 self-titled debut, produced by Jackson Browne, it featured an Aaron Coplandesque piano interlude that evoked the open plains, along with a catchy chorus compelling the outlaws to "Keep on riding, riding, riding, until you clear your name."

Written and sung by the legendary Cambridge folk/blues singer/painter Eric von Schmidt on his 1973 release *2nd Right, 3rd Row*, "Believer" begins with the story of the gluttonous Diamond Jim Brady, but by the second verse Eric evokes "Two brothers named Jesse and Frank, [who] 'believed in the robbin' of the trains.'"

"Go and dig another hole, while the bells begin to toll, you can hear 'em all over town," von Schmidt growls with the righteous demeanor of a whiskey priest. "There goes two more dead believers in the ground," he sighs wearily.

> Oh the harm that you do will follow after you,
> That's a sermon very well known.
> Still I think that we should try and do a little good,
> Even if it's buried with our bones.

The New Riders of the Purple Sage (a San Francisco spin-off from the Grateful Dead, who took their name from a Zane Grey western) would fashion their own version of Jesse James's legend with a bubbling bluegrass ballad called "Glendale Train." Written by the band's singer/guitarist John Dawson and driven by the Dead's Jerry Garcia on banjo and a slippery pedal-steel guitar, this heavily revised good-time yarn about the actual James Gang bank robbery paints a romantic and highly fictional portrait of the desperate escapade, ending with the heroes thundering off on their horses with "sixteen Gs" stuffed into their saddlebags, after having left "two men lyin' cold." The lyrics also describe the train's faithful porter, Amos Wise, who was found "in fifteen pieces, fifteen miles apart" after having been literally blown to bits by the dynamite that Jesse and his pals allegedly used to open the safe.

While the New Riders' version of the James brothers' legend makes a great song, no one was actually killed during the Glendale (Missouri) train robbery that took place on October 8, 1879. James had a new crew, which included neither brother Frank nor the four Younger brothers, who had joined him after the death of their father and the destruction of their Missouri family farm in the Civil War. The new gang hoisted an enormous boulder onto the railroad tracks, bringing the train to a grinding halt. The passengers, rendered sitting ducks, had very little recourse as the outlaws picked them clean, one by one. It had been three years since the James Gang knocked off the bank in Northfield, Minnesota. In the meantime, they'd been lying low, letting the heat blow over, while living as respectable farmers in Tennessee.

"The second you mention somebody like John Dillinger or Jesse James, everyone's on the same page with you," David Olney pointed out. Of the many songs that recount the famous brigand's legend, Olney's stunning portrait "Robert Ford and Jesse James" manages to get inside the outlaw's head and depict the chaotic, brutal, and desperate lives that he, his brother Frank, and the Youngers led.

The ballad begins as Jesse (now married, with wife and kids) and Bob Ford sit around the table, looking back, laughing over their wild memories. Jesse, not surprisingly, does most of the talking:

> Hey, Bob, do you remember when we robbed that Glendale
>   Train,
> And I shot that engineer and left him lying in the rain?
> You were shaking like a leaf, I thought you'd break and run,
> But hands were never steadier than when I held a gun.
> The horses' hooves a-pounding, bullets flying in the air,
> The bleeding and the dying, hell, I didn't care.
> The chances that I took back then, I must have been insane,
> Hey, Bob, do you remember when we robbed that Glendale
>   train?

Jesse continues into the second verse, recalling the wild night he spent with a "little whore in Kansas City." But since then he's made the surprising transition from outlaw to family man and suggests that Ford, too, should settle down one day if he's hoping to find any real happiness in life. "God has surely blessed me with his mercies from on high," James boasts to Robert, thankful and amazed at his own transformation.

Olney's wry sense of humor illuminates the song's last verse, when "the coward Robert Ford," as history will forever remember him, drew his pistol and shot "poor Jesse" (who was just thirty-four) in the back of the head, on April 3, 1882. The unarmed outlaw had momentarily let his guard down as he stood with his back to Ford, upon a ladder, to adjust a crooked picture frame that hung on the wall.

> Hey, Bob, look at this picture. Does that look straight to
>   you?
> It needs to come up on the right just a touch or two.
> Bob, he never answered for his anger and his shame,
> With steady hand he drew his gun and shot down Jesse
>   James.

*He knew it was too little and he knew it was too late
And it gave but little comfort, but at least that picture's
straight.*

Although he didn't entirely trust young Robert Ford and his brother Charley, James believed it best that the brothers, who'd ridden with him on his most recent escapade, should move in with him and his family and stay out of sight for a while. Although married to his wife, Zerelda, it was rumored that Jesse had maintained an on-going affair with the Fords' sister, Martha Bolton. Whether this was any incentive for Bob Ford's spineless assassination remains questionable at best, as the then governor of Missouri, Thomas T. Crittenden, had secretly met with Ford in hopes of negotiating the elusive outlaw's capture for a $5,000 reward. Interestingly enough, when he found no support from the state, Crittenden would turn to the private railroad companies whom James had pillaged to raise the funds to help insure his arrest.

"Jesse was supposedly straightening a picture on the wall when Robert Ford shot him in the back. Ford has since become a symbol of cowardice while Jesse has become a folk hero. I tried to imagine what they could possibly have been talking about just before the shooting took place," Olney said, explaining his inspiration and songwriting process.

"Jesse was the more powerful personality so I figured he would do most of the talking. He started to emerge as a total narcissist and bully. In his remembrance of the past he is always the dashing hero and Robert is the cowering incompetent. In my mind I pictured Ford sitting there in Jesse's living room, listening to all this boasting and slowly coming to a boil. The incident with the whore in Kansas City is particularly galling. And to top it all off, Jesse has now become a solid citizen with a loving wife and children. It was too much for Robert to take and he draws his gun and shoots the bully who has ruined his life. Jesse is completely unaware of the effect his words are having on Ford. He doesn't really acknowledge Bob as anything other than a bit player in the saga of Jesse James. I didn't have all this in mind when I started the song. It just came out that way, as Jesse tells his version of the past. The more he talked, the more despicable he became. Bob is no prize either but he certainly has cause to hold a grudge against Jesse. Some people have seen a homoerotic angle to the song. I didn't have that in mind but it makes some sense: Jesse as Robert's unrequited love. That adds a little sauce to the line 'at least that picture's straight.'"

Written by Desmond Child and Diane Warren, Cher's 1989 hit "Just like Jesse James" must stand as the ultimate outlaw kitsch anthem. As the music builds to a dramatic crescendo, the lyric, composed of one cliché after the next, portrays a duel between Cher and her outlaw lover, "a small town dude with a big city attitude." Threatening to take him down "dead or alive," Cher taunts her bad beau with a series of tacky innuendos, like "Come on baby show me what that loaded gun is for" and the politically incorrect "My heart is cryin' Indian and I'm beggin' for more." The song's authors don't stop there, shamelessly ripping off the Rolling Stones' classic ballad "Wild Horses," with the familiar line "Now a team of wild horses couldn't drag your heart away."

"You're gonna go down in flames," Cher warns her love-slinger. While the fire of which she sings has nothing to do with the notorious outlaw, it does manage to rhyme with the song's title, "Just like Jesse James."

Accompanying himself on guitar, Edward L. Crain (known as "The Texas Cowboy") recorded "Bandit Cole Younger" for Vocalin Records in 1930. The song was later included in Harry Smith's 1952 quintessential collection of blues, folk ballads, and hillbilly songs, *The Anthology of American Folk Music.* Born in Texas at the turn of the century, Crain was a genuine Lone Star rustler with a reedy voice. Proficient on guitar, fiddle, and mandolin, Crain performed mostly around the Dallas and Fort Worth vicinity, appearing on the radio. While he was on tour with Bing Crosby, Jean Harlow, the blonde bombshell, allegedly advised him to "stick to the cowboy stuff" when Crain wanted to branch out and modernize his sound.

Cole Younger, the hero of Crain's enduring ballad, was raised in Missouri and joined William Clarke Quantrill's notorious band of bushwhackers as a teenager, before enlisting as a Confederate soldier.

Following the War Between the States (as the Civil War is better known below the Mason/Dixon line), Younger and his brothers turned rogue, until eventually joining up with the original James Gang. While robbing a bank in Northfield, Minnesota, Cole was captured and convicted for killing a cashier.

There is very little of the thrill or romance of the outlaw life within Crain's tale of regret:

> *Robbing of the Northfield bank is a thing I'll never deny,*
> *But which I will be sorry of until the day I die. . . .*
> *I had my eye on the Northfield bank when brother Bob did*
>   *say,*
> *"Cole, if you under-to-take the job, you'll always curse the*
>   *day."*

In contrast to Edward L. Crain's gentle reading, the Colorado songwriter Michael Martin Murphy's first person narrative of Cole Younger has a driving backbeat, a bit of Fender twang, and plenty of whiskey growl on his 1993 album *Cowboy Songs III*. While the song's gritty sound evokes the frayed emotional state in which fugitives perpetually live, Murphy's Younger harbors serious misgivings over the "deeds and desperation that brought [his] name to shame." Ultimately Younger's tale is one of lament rather than bravado.

Paroled in 1901, Cole Younger, along with Frank James, would create a popular Wild West Show where the public could witness, firsthand, the riding and shooting skills of the legendary wanted men. In 1903 Cole published his much-awaited autobiography, in which he portrayed himself as a sympathetic figure forced into a criminal's life due to the unjust laws that victimized poor, disenfranchised southerners following the devastation of the Confederacy. Younger died in 1916 in his home town of Lee's Summit, Missouri, after accepting Jesus Christ as his personal savior and fully disavowing his criminal past.

"I was a hunted man," the regretful outlaw confessed in *The Story of Cole Younger, by Himself,* the jailhouse memoir he wrote while serving a twenty-five year sentence. "There is no heroism in outlawry, and the fate of each outlaw in his turn should be an everlasting lesson to the young of the land."

Not surprisingly, outlaws the world over fashioned themselves after the legendary Jesse James. Brazil's notorious "Lampião" was born on June 7, 1897, the third of nine children. As a boy, Virgulino Ferreira da Silva grew up on the family farm, helping his father to herd sheep and cattle. Although Virgulino never went to school, he learned to read and write and proudly wore glasses, which at the time were considered a symbol of intellectualism amongst the impoverished farmers of his village, Serra Talhada.

A general sense of lawlessness permeated the northeastern backlands of Brazil and feuds between families over property were commonplace, which led Virgulino's father José to move the family on two occasions in hopes of peacefully settling disputes. Nonetheless, a violent confrontation with the police or the *macacos* (which translates to "monkeys"), as they were derogatorily called, was inevitable and on May 18, 1921, José was killed.

Distraught over his father's death, Virgulino sought bloody revenge. For the next sixteen years, from the 1920s through the 1930s, "the Brazilian Jesse James," as he became known, led a ruthless band of *cangaceiros*, as they were known, fluctuating in number between ten and one hundred.

Donning hand-tooled leather sombreros and riding chaps, their outlaw chic became nearly as legendary as their violent exploits. The bandits, swathed in custom ammo belts, carried sleek black Lugers, machetes, and *peixeiras*, deadly knives designed for fileting fish as well as slicing up anyone foolish enough to stand in their way.

Lampião's nickname, "The Lantern" or "Lamp," was bestowed upon him in honor of the intense flash from his beloved rapid-fire German-made Mauser rifle, which was said to be as brilliant as the blinding glare of an oil lamp.

As local farmers and ranchers were routinely abused by the police, they often sided and sympathized with the outlaws, in whom they found a better example of justice and morality. Before long, Lampião became the self-proclaimed "governor of the Brazilian backlands" (the Northeast region to be more exact). By 1930 he teamed-up with Maria Déia, a.k.a. "Maria Bonita," who bore him a daughter named Expedita, two years later. Together they forged a romantic image as compelling as that of Bonnie and Clyde in the public's consciousness.

Living constantly on the edge, these renegade desperados turned to the spiritual world for guidance and solace, making regular offerings to local priests and kneeling together every Sunday morning in prayer before a makeshift altar of Christ, in hopes of receiving the Lord's forgiveness and mercy for their wild and violent ways.

Stunning footage of the Lamp and his gang of stylish bandits camped out in the hinterland was shot by Benjamin Abraham throughout 1936 and 1937. Shown for the first time later that year, the film was immediately banned and confiscated, having been deemed too dangerous because of its sympathetic portrayal of the outlaws. Seized by Getúlio Vargas's government, all known copies of the movie were locked away for nearly twenty years until it reemerged once more in 1955 (following President Vargas's shocking suicide). Edited down to ten minutes and given a new narration, the film was soon released as *Lampião—the King of the Highwaymen* to overwhelming public curiosity and critical acclaim. A newly restored version, with four additional minutes of unseen footage, appeared in 2007.

The song most commonly associated with Lampião is "The Woman Lacemaker," also known as "Mulher Rendeira." Over the decades, it has taken on the sanctity of a hymn, as the lyrics were said to have been composed by Lampião himself, based on a letter he'd written to his grandmother, Maria Vieria Lopes, a.k.a. "Aunt Jacosa," on her birthday. "The Woman Lacemaker" was allegedly sung by Lampião's band of sixty men as they galloped into battle at Mossoró in Rio Grande do Norte, in June 1927. Despite their robust vocals, the gang were quickly repelled by the townspeople, who outnumbered them by five-to-one.

The origin of the song's melody seems a bit hazier. Although it is widely assumed that "The Woman Lacemaker" is *folclórica* or in the public domain, it was actually composed by Alfredo Ricardo do Nascimento, better known as Zé do Norte, who was born on December 18, 1908, in Cajazeiras (Brazil) and later moved to Rio de Janeiro in 1926. Written roughly between September 1921 and February 1922, the "The Woman Lacemaker" became internationally famous after it was used as the theme to the popular 1953 film *The Bandit of Brazil*, which not only won "Best Adventure Film" of the year at the Cannes

Film Festival but also received an honorable mention for its haunting soundtrack. The song soon appeared on the 1957 album *Songs of Lantern*, which also included tunes written and sung by Antônio Alves de Souza (also known as Volta Seca, meaning "Dry Gulch") and Antônio dos Santos, both former members of Lampião's gang.

The best-known version of "The Woman Lacemaker" in North America was sung by Joan Baez. She recorded the song as "O Cangaceiro" for her 1964 album *Joan Baez/5*. Overdubbing her transcendent voice on the choruses added a deeper sense of yearning to the lyric. As she sings, she begs the lacemaker to show her how "to make lace." In return she promises to teach her "to flirt." Meanwhile, Lampião returns from the mountains and throws a party for his band of brigands.

While Brazilians tend to glorify Lampião and his gang as national heroes, those who study his life often consider him no more than a lowlife and a murderer, guilty of killing children and struggling farmers while raping their daughters and wives. Hoping to sober those drunk on the romance of Virgulino Ferreira da Silva's myth, one skeptic, discussing the subject online, recently questioned Lampião's character and motives. If the notorious outlaw had "felt wronged by the government," he wondered, "why did he not kill the rulers?" An interesting point, as most of Lampião's skirmishes tended to be with the local populace and against the police.

On July 28, 1938, Lampião, Maria Bonita, and nine other bandits were gunned down in cold blood by a battalion of police who surrounded their camp at dawn after being tipped off to their location by Joca Bernardes, a former gang sympathizer. Their heads were then brutishly severed and sent to forensic specialists in Salvador, Bahia, where, after careful preservation, they became a museum attraction until 1971. Then their respective families, who had jointly demanded their return, were finally satisfied, and the outlaws' remains (and souls) could be laid to rest at last.

The Depression-era bank robber Charles Arthur "Pretty Boy" Floyd, who also modeled himself after Jesse James, turned out to be a remarkably different fellow than the man glorified by Woody Guthrie in the populist ballad that soon found its way into the repertoires of Ramblin' Jack Elliott, Bob Dylan, and the Byrds on their 1968 country-rock opus *Sweetheart of the Rodeo.*

Floyd's criminal career began at the age of eighteen when he was caught pilfering change from his local post office. Three years later, in September 1925, he was nabbed in a payroll robbery and given a five-year sentence; he served only three before being released for good behavior. On that day, Charles solemnly swore he would never, under any circumstances, return to jail again. That pledge, however, did not mean he was determined to follow the straight and narrow path. Quite the contrary: Floyd said he'd rather die than do time and set out on a wild crime spree that lasted for the rest of his short, chaotic life.

Floyd was saddled with the famous nickname he apparently loathed after a local described him as "a pretty boy with apple cheeks" to the detectives who were hot on his trail after a St. Louis bank robbery. Despite his oath, "Pretty Boy" (who also went by the alias "Frank Mitchell") repeatedly wound up behind bars over the next few years, for a variety of violations from vagrancy to suspicion of armed robbery, for which he was freed after a lack of tangible evidence.

Floyd was beloved by the backwoods folks of Oklahoma, who fed him and managed, for a short time, to keep him from the long arm of the law. In reality, he had killed nearly a dozen people. But the blood he spilled was forgiven by the public, who rooted for their "Robin Hood of the Cookson Hills."

According to Woody Guthrie's highly romanticized ballad, one Saturday afternoon, in the town of Shawnee, Oklahoma, "Pretty Boy" Floyd and his wife Ruby, from whom he was later divorced, went riding into town in their wagon when they crossed paths with a foul-mouthed deputy sheriff. According to Woody, Floyd was a gentleman who was offended by such belligerent and brutish behavior and couldn't allow his wife to be subjected to the lawman's offensive language. Defending her honor, Floyd grabbed "a log chain" while the deputy allegedly reached for his six-shooter, and a moment later "Pretty Boy" "laid that deputy down." Fleeing in fear, Floyd vanished into the wilds of Oklahoma. In no time "every crime" in the book was quickly "added to his name."

53

Given shelter by struggling farmers, the outlaw returned their kindness and concern by routinely destroying whatever mortgage receipts he found while robbing the banks of Oklahoma City. Floyd, as Woody sang, not only "saved their little homes" but allegedly provided groceries for the needy one Christmas morning, with a note that even rhymed:

You say that I'm an outlaw,
You say that I'm a thief,
Here's a Christmas dinner
For the families on relief.

Never one to trust appearances, Woody ended the tune with a warning that smiling men who don the cloak of decency and dress in nicely tailored suits, who live seemingly respectable lives in suburban houses circled by white picket fences, all too often get to the top of the heap by bilking the little guy. Guthrie knew it wasn't just the pistol-packing desperado you had to watch out for:

As through your life you travel,
As through your life you roam,
You won't never see an outlaw
Drive a family from their home.

A native of Oklahoma, Guthrie undoubtedly grew up following the exploits of the famous outlaw. His portrait of "Pretty Boy" Floyd seems to have been inspired by John Steinbeck's famous 1939 novel *The Grapes of Wrath*, in which Ma Joad explains that Floyd himself is blameless, a victim driven to a desperate life of crime due to circumstances brought on by the Great Depression.

It's interesting to note that Floyd became the first modern day outlaw to make his getaway not on a horse but in a Ford. He was tracked by highway patrolmen employing the most modern form of technology—the telephone. Floyd (like Jesse James before him) was a brilliant manipulator of the media, giving provocative interviews that fueled the public's imagination. His braggart's swagger undeniably helped plant the seed for the coming gangsta culture.

Not to be confused with John Hardy, the "desperate little man" who is the antihero of Lead Belly's famous folk song of the same name, John Wesley Hardin was the actual Texas outlaw who inspired Bob Dylan's "John Wesley Harding." Dylan's three-chord penny-plain folk ballad (the lead-off track to his 1967 comeback album of the same name) chronicled the adventures of a cool, calm, and collected brigand who, like Robin Hood and Jesse James before him, was also feted as a "friend to the poor." Although notorious for wielding "a gun in every hand," Dylan's Harding was "never known to hurt an honest man." Perhaps even more amazing was that he was "never known to make a foolish move." If that wasn't enough to cement his legend, he was supposedly so tough and quick-witted, that, in the words of his creator, "there was no man around who could track or chain him down." But Dylan's Harding had very little in common with the real-life gambling gunslinger, Hardin, other than his remarkable skill with a pistol, which revealed a "magical precision," as ranger Jim Gillette once observed.

Hardin's autobiography (*The Life of John Wesley Hardin: As Written By Himself*, first published in 1896) was, to put it mildly, a "factually slanted" tome, written while serving seventeen years in prison (from 1878–1894). In it he boasted of having been responsible for the deaths of forty-two men (later discovered by those darn fact-checking journalists to have been a mere twenty-seven). Hardin also claimed to have run away from home to join the Confederate army at age nine. Six years later, after his expulsion from school (for having allegedly stabbed a schoolmate who'd put the finger on him for scrawling a bit of lustful graffiti), Hardin, in the fall of 1868, killed "Mage," a former slave of his Uncle Holshousen. Having humiliated Mage after trouncing him in a wrestling match, Hardin admitted to having fired five rounds into him after Mage allegedly "ambushed" him by shouting and waving a stick at the temperamental fifteen-year-old. A fugitive from justice, Hardin soon found himself scuffling across strange new landscapes, stealing horses, and sleeping rough in haystacks. Although "wounded in the arm," John Wesley claimed to have killed three Union soldiers who'd been trailing him, using a double-barreled shotgun and a six-shooter.

Trouble followed him wherever he rambled. Death and murder were all just in a day's work for John Wesley Hardin, who it is said once shot a man through a wall for the crime of snoring, and blasted another man's eye out to settle an argument over a bottle of rotgut whiskey. Pimps, gamblers, "savages," Mexican cattle rustlers, lawmen, soldiers, and virtually anyone who glanced at him sideways had a way of quickly vanishing from sight, only to turn up again sometime later, in some remote location, riddled with bullet holes.

On the fateful afternoon of August 19, 1895, John Wesley Hardin was rolling dice at the Acme Saloon, standing, uncharacteristically, with his back towards the door. Constable John Henry Selman quietly entered the bar and unceremoniously shot him in the back of the head. As the outlaw fell to the floor, Selman pumped a few more rounds into his chest, just to make sure he was dead. To this day, people still deliberate over why Hardin "allowed" himself to be killed. As author Jesse L. Hardin (no relation to the famed desperado) speculated, "It was something more than alcohol-induced laxness that predetermined his attitude and posture on that fateful day."

In hindsight, one must wonder why socially conscious singer/songwriters from Woody Guthrie to Bob Dylan meticulously crafted heroic odes in honor of such treacherous figures, who continue to be celebrated to this day, despite the details of their tawdry past. Perhaps the best answer can be found within the script to the classic 1962 Western *The Man Who Shot Liberty Valence*, when Maxwell Scott (Carleton Young), the editor of a small town tabloid, tells the idealistic "Pilgrim," Ransom Stoddard (played by Jimmy Stewart), who questions the newsman's integrity, "When the legend becomes fact, print the legend."

With a gentle voice and gingerly strummed autoharp, Charlie Brown (Charles Edward Artman) sang about Walter Earl Durand, the six foot two, 250 pound Wyoming mountain man who was arrested, fined one hundred dollars, and sentenced to six months in jail for the crime of poaching elk out of season.

The in-depth liner notes to Brown's 1967 Folkways album *Teton Tea*

Party described the son of a Methodist minister from northern Iowa as a "mystic, poet, folk singer, baker of bread, and prophet of the New Age of Consciousness." Dropping out of college, Brown hoboed around the West, climbing the glorious Grand Teton Mountains and crashing with friends in the capital of cool—North Beach, San Francisco. A free spirit, "Charlie sets up his teepee when and where he chooses," we are told. He "likes bugging the Establishment, although he does this without malice." While camping in the Grand Tetons, Brown met Jack Langon, who told him the tragic tale of Walter Earl Durand, who only wanted to live freely, hunting and roaming the Wyoming wilderness, just as his father, grandfather, and great-grandfather did before him. But Earl fell victim to the state's newly revised game laws, which required hunting licenses of everyone, whether tourists or full-time residents. Some versions of Durand's legend claim that his pilfering had been a philanthropic deed, in order to help provide his friends and neighbors with meat during the difficult years of the Depression.

Inspired by what he heard, Brown grabbed his autoharp and began to strum a simple three-chord progression, while Langon fashioned a rudimentary verse to fit Brown's melancholy melody. According to the liner notes to the 1967 album, we find that Brown was in the habit of changing the lyrics nearly every time he performed the song. Nonetheless they wound up with "a fantastic and paradoxical tale with a basically realistic message."

As long as he could remember, Earl Durand's family had hunted moose, elk, and stag to feed themselves. Respectful of wildlife, they wasted nothing, stitching animal hides into rustic buckskin clothing, even using animal bones for buttons. But one day the world as Durand understood it suddenly changed, after he and his friends were stopped and interrogated by game wardens. Durand managed to escape, but his friends were arrested after the bodies of two elk were discovered in the trunk of their car. According to Brown's song, Durand was soon arrested and thrown in the local jail. Two days later, he escaped from his cell after conking a deputy named Riley over the head with a milk bottle. Wresting away his pistol, Durand held the lawman hostage and demanded he drive him back to his family home in Powell, Wyoming. Riley obliged, despite suffering an open gash on his forehead and the disorienting effects of a concussion.

Events from this point on quickly spiraled out of control. Deaf to his parents' pleading to turn himself in, Durand then shot both the Marshal and a deputy who'd come to arrest him. About a dozen ranchers in the area were immediately rounded up and sworn in as deputies. Each man was then equipped with a rifle and approximately one hundred rounds of ammunition. The ensuing manhunt lasted for more than a week, during which Durand killed two members of the posse, who, he complained, "were beginning to crowd him." The posse quickly ballooned into a veritable army, including sixty-five FBI agents, sharpshooters, and members of the Wyoming National Guard; they employed a mortar, a Howitzer, and an airplane that tracked the fugitive from above, while dropping tear gas and grenades.

Durand, now known as "Tarzan of the Tetons," thanks to the clever scribblers at *The Denver Post*, who'd been sensationalizing his every exploit, "spent most of his time hiding in the willows by Bitter Creek" as he had told a friend. Then he stole a car and drove into the nearby town of Powell, where he attempted to hold up the First National Bank.

Just a few months earlier, Durand had reportedly spent an entire day at the local theater, binge-watching three screenings in a row of *Jesse James*, starring Tyrone Powers. It doesn't take a degree in psychology to estimate the impact this experience had on an unruly, unschooled backwoodsman who distrusted society and treasured his freedom above all else. Durand, now desperate and on the lam, undoubtedly began seeing the world through his idol's eyes. But his personal drama was hardly as heroic or romantic as the life of Jesse James portrayed in the movies.

Although short on social skills, Durand possessed sharp instincts when it came to survival in the wild. Donning rubber boots, he managed to throw a pack of pursuing bloodhounds off his scent. After meeting a pair of curious "criminal tourists," who'd been combing the countryside, along with their eighty-six-year-old father, in hopes of getting a glimpse of the outlaw, Durand drew his pistol and introduced himself while politely demanding to be chauffeured to the train depot; there he picked up a package of ammunition that was waiting for him. Once more we hear that he was, in the words of his neighbor, "a nice guy" with a reputation for being "polite and considerate." Having generously offered to fill his hostages' gas tank, Durand later informed his captives that he needed their car. He was said to be genuinely relieved after the driver told him he would suffer no personal loss, as he was fully insured for theft.

Earl Durand came sauntering into the bank around 1:30 p.m. on March 24, 1939. Aiming his rifle at the vault, he fired, causing plaster to crack and fall from the ceiling. Hollering orders at both employees and customers to line up against the wall, he began blowing out all of the windows in the building. He then took a few customers hostage, one of whom was accidentally killed by the posse who'd been aiming to kill Durand.

"He had us all terrified," one victim later recalled. After cleaning out the tellers' drawers, Durand demanded they open the safe, but the vault was locked, with its automatic timer set for 3:00 p.m. After he had shot out the rest of the windows in anger, Durand was offered stacks of silver dollars which were too heavy to haul.

One terrified witness claimed Durand was "manic, [like] a cornered animal. His mouth was distorted. He actually bared his teeth, like a mad vicious dog." Wounded while trying to make his escape, Durand slunk back to the bank, put a pistol to his head, closed his eyes, and ended it all. "He'd have been a mountain man instead of shot down in his prime," as Charlie Brown lamented.

Although a strong sense of nostalgia for an idyllic past permeates the song, Charlie Brown, in portraying Durand as an innocent, presents a somewhat misguided, narrow view of the outlaw. No matter how one might sympathize with the free-spirited mountain man whose natural lifestyle was encroached upon by a callous and indifferent government, Durand clearly crossed the line of reason and civility by murdering two lawmen. To be fair, the tragedy that ensued was ultimately of his own making, brought on by his impulsive, uncontrolled response to authority.

Hollywood, not surprisingly, would eventually jump on the story, casting John Wayne as Durand in a B Western called *Wyoming Outlaw*. Later, in 1974, *The Legend of Earl Durand*, starring Peter Haskell, held its world premiere in Powell, Wyoming, not far from Earl's last stand. The local residents were apparently so appalled by the liberties taken in the retelling of their hometown hero's life (including a ludicrous subplot that claimed Durand suffered from some rare disease that forced his parents to lock him away for most of his childhood, making him a social misfit) that the majority of the audience walked out of the theater bewildered, well before the film was over. Proving once again, as the late, great guitarist Snakefinger used to sing, "There's no justice in life."

From the Italian singer/songwriter Massimo Liberatori comes "The Amazing Story of Cinicchia the Bandit." A multi-instrumentalist and composer, Liberatori, best known as a robust ballad singer, also breeds donkeys and tends an olive orchard in the bucolic Monte Subasio region of Umbria, Italy.

Born on January 30, 1830, in Assisi, Nazzareno Guglielmi, later nicknamed "Cinicchia," was, according to Liberatori's lilting ballad, "a saint, but a bandit."

One of eight children, Cinicchia was raised in poverty, helping his father with chores on the family farm. He was described as short, and with a violent temper. All was well at first, as Massimo sings of Cinicchia's marriage to "his great love, Teresa Bucchi":

> *With her and two babies to lull,*
> *He worked as a bricklayer for Earl Fiumi,*
> *Until losing his honor,*
> *After he was accused of stealing a ham.*

To make things worse, it turns out that Cinicchia's arrest and imprisonment were all due to a practical joke "because of a scoundrel fellow." As Liberatori recounts:

> *In his prison cell, alone and innocent,*
> *Cinicchia can't stop thinking,*
> *With blood in his eyes,*
> *And trembling soul.*

Thanks to the help of a sympathetic jailer, who provided him with a hammer and chisel, Cinicchia managed to escape and take revenge on the man responsible for his incarceration. "Earl Fiumi will pay the bill!" Liberatori sings. Once free, Cinicchia formed a ruthless gang who terrorized the wealthy:

> *Sowed a lot of panic,*
> *Rich people were terrified,*
> *But poor the people cried,*
> *"Cinicchia has a big heart!"*

Hoping to capture the fugitive, the authorities arrested Cinicchia's wife, Teresa, and threw her into prison in the hills of Perugia. (Nothing is said regarding the fate of their two children.) One quiet evening, while the citizenry were strolling about the town square, Cinicchia suddenly appeared, brandishing a torch, promising to burn down the city if his wife was not immediately released. But we never learn whether Cinicchia's threat succeeded in liberating his jailed wife. It is not spelled out within the verse. The song only tells us that Cinicchia refused to turn himself in.

"These were times of borders and contraband, times of guns and flags," Liberatori sings of "when Italy was founded" in 1861. It is said that a friar (in some versions of the song it is Saint Francis of Assisi himself, but he had died in 1226) hid "the black robber," Cinicchia, from General Garibaldi, who'd been trailing him in hot pursuit after he allegedly killed Captain Cesare Bellini of the National Guard on October 21, 1863.

Shaving his head and dressing him in a saio (a monk's robe), the brothers offered the notorious bandit sanctuary in their monastery. Later that year, Cinicchia, brandishing a fake passport, fled the country, sailing to Buenos Aries, where, according to a letter dated 1901, he lived incognito for the rest of his life.

Jesse James, Lampião, Earl Durand, and Cinicchia all found themselves victims of changing times and a strange new political landscape in which they no longer belonged. Feeling marginalized and desperate, each of them responded viscerally, taking the law into his own hands. Whether acting alone on impulse, as in the case of Earl Durand and Cinicchia, or leading a gang, like Jesse James and Lampião, these men were lionized in song and legend for their valiant but ultimately futile efforts in battling the law.

4

THE ROMANCE OF THE LAM

Whether they are alone, with a partner, or part of a gang, watching someone take a stand for what they believe in has a way of provoking our deepest sympathy. It inspires us to reexamine the philosophy and values that we hold high. Their drama tugs at our heartstrings; even if they've committed some desperate, dreadful crime, we often find it within ourselves to forgive or at the very least ignore what they've done, if we believe their intentions were honorable. Perhaps it's a criminal couple, passionately in love and running out of time, while they (and we) know they haven't got a snowball's chance. The end is drawing near, quickly, and there's something tragic yet so romantic about it all. It might be a pair of doomed lovers taking a stand against world, like Faye Dunaway and Warren Beatty in Arthur Penn's 1967 ultra-violent *Bonnie and Clyde*, enjoying a brief moment of repose in a sun-drenched field before doing a spasmodic dance to the lightning strobe of the G-men's Tommy guns.

Bored with her life in "Cement City," the poor West Dallas neighborhood where she worked as a waitress while living with her mother, Bonnie Parker composed poetry and kept a diary. The book teemed with her frustrations and regret over an earlier failed marriage, along with mundane details of her trivial existence. Then, one night, fate threw Bonnie together with the charismatic Clyde Barrow, who, after having spent the last few years in jail, had apparently transformed from a likable fellow into what some people described as "a rattlesnake." The sudden change in Barrow's personality allegedly came after he crushed the skull of a fellow con who tried to sexually assault him.

The first movie to depict the misadventures of Bonnie and Clyde was a budget noir called *The Bonnie Parker Story*. Released in 1958, it starred the provocative Dorothy Provine as a cigar-chawing moll who could wield a weapon as well as any man. But nothing fueled Bonnie Parker's legend more than her own rhyming narrative verse, which included "The Story of Suicide Sal" and a sixteen-verse auto-biographical poem, "The Trail's End," which became better known as "The Story of Bonnie and Clyde." The epic poem was first set to music and recorded by Hermes Nye for his 1955 Folkways collection, *Texas Folk Songs*. Over a simple three-chord guitar accompaniment, Nye warbles Parker's lyric, doing his best to sing her slightly lopsided verse, which squeezed in a couple of extra syllables here and there. Parker unflinchingly addressed the fate that she believed inevitably awaited the pair of doomed outlaws:

> They don't think they're too smart or desperate,
> They know that the law always wins.
> They've been shot at before,
> But they do not ignore,
> That death is the wages of sin.

> Someday they'll go down together,
> They'll bury them side by side.
> To few it'll be grief,
> To the law a relief,
> But it's death for Bonnie and Clyde.

Inspired by Arthur Penn's stunning film, the songwriting team of Mitch Murray and Peter Callander quickly knocked off an old-timey ditty entitled "The Ballad of Bonnie and Clyde," which the Brit rocker Georgie Fame sang, topping the UK singles chart for a week in January 1968. The song then soared to No. 7 later that year in America. A slice of nostalgia featuring a strummed banjo and campy brass arrangement, "The Ballad of Bonnie and Clyde" came complete with sound effects of pistol shots and police sirens. Murray and Callander's production was spot on. Strains of trad jazz were a constant in British pop throughout the 1960s, from clarinetist Acker Bilk's corny instrumentals to Herman's Hermits' "Mrs. Brown You've Got a Lovely Daughter" (1965), to the New Vaudeville Band's smash hit "Winchester Cathedral," a year later, to a smattering of Beatles tunes (mostly written and sung by Paul McCartney) such as "When I'm Sixty-Four," "Your Mother Should Know," and "Honey Pie."

Serge Gainsbourg and Brigitte Bardot's smoldering duet of "Bonnie And Clyde" (also the title to their February 1968 album) is the ultimate example of outlaw kitsch chic. Over a Phil Spector–style "Wall of Sound" production, Bardot repeatedly chants the names of the outlaws in a heavy French accent that sounds like she's singing "Bunny and Cla-hiiide." Gorgeous as she was, Brigitte was no chanteuse. She sings in a flat, clipped, husky Marlene Dietrich–like hushed delivery, while a voice that resembles the anguished cry of a mental patient in the throes of a psychotic episode down the hall intermittently whoops and wails throughout the song, adding to Gainsbourg's well-earned reputation for bizarre, extravagant productions.

The song's accompanying video starred a sleek, shapely Bardot clad in a black beret, wielding a tommy gun, with her eyes layered with copious mascara. In just over four minutes the pair nearly manage to steal every ounce of gangster glamour that Beatty and Dunaway had previously brought to the legendary outlaws. Voguing about in their sterile jail cell, Gainsbourg and Bardot create a timeless image, fueling the myth of Barrow and Parker, which still stands today as firm and smooth as a granite gravestone.

In 2011, Serge's son Lulu continued his father's legacy, recording a cover of his dad's arrangement with actress Scarlett Johansson for a tribute album called *From Gainsbourg to Lulu.*

Over a percolating snare drum, clanging banjo, and a pair of wailing fiddles, the hard-boiled troubadour Merle Haggard sings the title track to his 1968 album, "The Legend of Bonnie and Clyde." The song, a straight-ahead ballad that recounts the lives and deaths of the desperate duo, immediately shot to the top of the country music charts, where it holed up for the next two weeks. Known for his stout moralist verse, Haggard solemnly predicted the criminals' fate, singing, "With blood on their hands they were bound to get caught."

Even the "Velvet Fog," a sobriquet bestowed upon pop/jazz singer Mel Tormé for his trademark mellow voice, got into the act, jumping on the bandit bandwagon with his 1968 release *A Day in the Life of Bonnie and Clyde*. Tormé wrote the title song, but otherwise this was a "concept album" of sorts, revitalizing a portfolio of classic pop tunes from the late 1920s and 1930s, including "Brother, Can You Spare a Dime," "Button Up Your Overcoat," and "The Gold Diggers' Song," better known as "We're in the Money."

Over a pulsing bass and groovy backbeat suitable for a gaggle of bell-bottomed teens doing the twist, Tormé's protagonist recalls witnessing a bank robbery through the eyes of a small boy. Clyde Barrow and Bonnie Parker suddenly appear, "happy as kids," toting guns and bags bursting with money. Driving away, they wink and blow kisses at him. The album cover alone was worth the price of admission, featuring a photograph depicting a sneering Tormé brandishing a Tommy gun, while a beguiling blonde in a beret (a dead ringer for Faye Dunaway) lounges in the back seat of his shiny black sedan, with pistols dangling from each hand.

Brooklyn hip hopper Foxy Brown's 1999 release "Bonnie & Clyde (Part 2)" meant serious business as she boasted of all the guns, coke, and the "shitload of cash" that just comes with the glorious gangsta lifestyle. Over a hard, steady snare groove and a brass-knuckle-punching horn section, Jay-Z begs, "Will you die for yo nigga?" She replies, "I'd die for you nigga," like it's nothing more than going to the corner store for a pack of cigarettes and some beer. Deep as their romantic bond appears, an overwhelming sense of hopelessness and impending death permeates the track. "Real life," Brown says coolly as the track fades, and you don't doubt her for a minute.

The real-life adventures of Foxy Brown have included frequent tangles with the law. In January 1997, an altercation at a Raleigh, North Carolina, hotel occurred in which she spat on a maid who couldn't find her an iron when she wanted one. A warrant for her arrest was served, but Brown blew town before the cops came calling. Four months later she returned to face the charges and was handed a one-month suspended sentence but had to complete eighty hours of community service.

Seven years later, in 2004, Brown assaulted a pair of manicurists in Manhattan after refusing to pay a bill for twenty dollars. As part of her probation she agreed to enroll in an anger management class. Service people were not the only target of Brown's raging ego. Miami rapper Jacki-O claimed Brown disrupted her recording session one night, calling her a "new rapper ho" and physically assaulting her after she refused to bow down to the narcissistic star. This outrageous behavior was nothing new to Brown, who was constantly entangled in an ongoing series of feuds with various female R&B and hip hop stars, from her old high school friend Lil' Kim to Queen Latifah.

Three years later, in 2007, she pleaded guilty after attacking a clerk at a beauty shop. She then confronted a neighbor, striking her with her Blackberry, and finally, to add insult to injury, allegedly pulled down her jeans and mooned the poor woman.

Having violated the prior probation decreed after the nail salon brawl, Brown was then sentenced to a year in jail that September. One month later she was locked away in solitary confinement for thirty days following an altercation with a fellow inmate and mouthing off to a guard. By April 2008, Brown was free once again and back out on the street. In 2010, she faced a possible seven-year jail term for criminal contempt arising from the 2007 assault on her neighbor. She pleaded not guilty, and a year later the charges were dropped.

In 2002, Jay-Z revisited the story of the pair of doomed fugitives again, collaborating with Beyoncé on "03 Bonnie & Clyde." This time the song and accompanying video had all the guts and bravado of a Calvin Klein ad, but that didn't keep it from rocketing to No. 4 on the US charts and No. 2 in the UK. "03 Bonnie & Clyde," according to *Billboard* magazine, was "unstoppable from the jump." Written off beats (and lyrics) sampled from Tupac Shakur's "Me and My Girlfriend" by a veritable gang of R&B and rap stars (seven in all, including Prince and Kanye West), the song first appeared on Jay-Z's album *The Blueprint 2: The Gift & The Curse*. The video, not surprisingly, was a stylist's fantasy in which the first couple of hip hop posed as a pair of sleek black Bonnie and Clydes, pulling stickups with gleaming pistols, and making their getaway in a vintage 1960s Pontiac GTO. Bling and piles of cash are everywhere as Jay-Z raps in a flannel shirt, stocking cap, and shades, while the glamorous and curvaceous Beyoncé wields an automatic rifle while wearing a fishnet veil.

A cornerstone of their *On the Run* tour, which they coheadlined in 2014, the video, before all the action begins, reminds you, contrary to Foxy Brown's comment, "This Is Not Real Life."

The legend of the ill-fated outlaw lovers also made for an ill-fated Broadway musical with lyrics by Don Black and a curious score by Frank Wildhorn, which blended rockabilly and blues with gospel. Originally opening in La Jolla, California, followed by a one-month run in Sarasota, Florida, *Bonnie & Clyde—A New Musical* came to New York in December 2011, where it bit the dust in just four weeks. Parker and Barrow's legend then lit out for London, Tokyo, and Seoul, where it was better appreciated from afar.

Whether front-page news from coast to coast, or the protagonist in a crime drama or outlaw ballad, the figure of the fugitive continues to captivate the public imagination. To die together is, for some folks, the one surefire way of attaining eternity, whether we're talking about the vow of a pair of adolescent blood brothers, a young couple embracing on the precipice of the local lovers' leap, or a scene from our favorite buddy movie: Paul Newman and Robert Redford in *Butch Cassidy and the Sundance Kid*, surrounded by a hundred federals with their pistols drawn; or Susan Sarandon and Gina Davis in *Thelma and Louise*, putting the pedal to the medal, as their sky blue Thunderbird takes off for the great beyond.

Maybe it's because, even while staring in the face of inevitable death, we still pile the chips high against all odds. It's that kind of blind faith in the face of doom that makes "1952 Vincent Black Lightning," written and recorded by British singer/songwriter/guitar-slinger Richard Thompson, one of the greatest outlaw songs ever written, if not the most romantic. It's hard to keep from sobbing after "Young

James," the song's hero, is arrested for armed robbery. As he lies with a gaping hole blown in his chest, the result of a shotgun blast, he breathes his last rattling gasp while hallucinating dazzling visions of angels in leather and chrome swirling above him, coming to take him home. At last he gives up the ghost as he hands his sweetheart, "Red Molly" the keys to his "fine motorbike."

"There's a long tradition in British folk music of outlaw songs that goes all the way back to Robin Hood," Thompson explained. "Some of those ballads are very, very long, up to forty to fifty verses and are basically the exploits of an outcast, someone who has been cast out of society and survives on the fringes, in Robin Hood's case, by robbing from the rich and giving to the poor. This is a common theme through the ages. 'Vincent Black Lightning' is a song that's built around an object, the motorcycle, which is the mythological core of the song around which the characters revolve. James is kind of a likeable criminal, as most criminals in songs are unless they are outright murderers like Tom Dooley. They are championed. They are characters with which one sympathizes. James is desperate, but in spite of that he still winds up as a sympathetic character. You don't get a detailed description of everyone's character in a song. You don't get to interview the families of the people he killed!" Thompson said with a chuckle.

"The idea of the motorcycle was the beginning of the song. I was trying to find something British that was both romantic and mythological. In American popular music it's much easier to find mythology. In a lot of cases all you need is a place name. There's a whole romance attached to names. Like 'Do You Know What It Means to Miss New Orleans?' or 'Memphis in June.' In Britain you don't have that, not in the recorded music era. If you mention place names in a song in England, it's often thought of as a novelty, or even laughable. But singing about London, of course, will have more resonance than say Scranton [Pennsylvania] perhaps.

"[In America] just saying 'the West' or 'the South,' is pretty cool and gives you half a song right there. Just mention Cadillac and you have half a title of a song—'Cadillac Dream.' With 'Vincent Black Lightning,' I was looking for an object that had the same resonance for a UK audience, and the Vincent is a rare motorcycle. When I was a kid it was a much-desired object, very beautiful, very black, and sexy looking. I thought it would be an interesting theme to build a song around."

"1952 Vincent Black Lightning" is very much like an old English folk song about a hero and his horse, but in this case Thompson has replaced the glorious steed with a "fine motorbike." The song packs a deep emotional punch. Young James's death is very moving and romantic. The song ends with glorious Blakean visions of angels in "leather and chrome" swooping down from heaven to carry him off as he hands the keys to his love, Red Molly, literally giving her her freedom, just as he leaves his body, the ultimate release.

"I was just writing the song," Richard said. "I wasn't thinking of any of that stuff. When you write, it's a semiconscious exercise. I usually have kind of an idea of what I want to do at the start. Songwriting can surprise you. It's usually good not to think about the theory behind a song. You're basically trying to just pull the stuff out. Then you edit it a little bit. The whole process is instinctive, at least it is for me. If I like a song I don't always go into the reasons why. My instincts just tell me whether I should persevere with it."

In "Living on Borrowed Time" (from Richard and Linda Thompson's 1979 album *Sunnyvista*), Thompson evokes the experience of being hunted down and cornered like a wild animal. The drums pound heavily like the beating of the hooves of a bounty hunter's horse "riding like a hurricane." Time is running out. The good life he'd once known is no more than a fleeting memory. "We've been too many nights sleeping in a feather bed," Thompson sighs. "You can't close both your eyes with a price on your head," he sings, punctuated by the haunting chorus, "Living on borrowed . . . Living on borrowed . . . Living on borrowed time."

Although Thompson never states the exact nature of his narrator's crime, he is certain he'll soon be swinging from the hangman's rope if he hesitates and fails to make his escape. "You got to stand and fight for what you believe. You got to face death with your heart on your sleeve," he sings. In the following verse the protagonist claims that all he did was to "dare to tell the truth." Whatever he said, it was clearly offensive, whether politically or morally. "A man ain't safe these days under his own roof," Richard sings wearily. Karma—action and the consequences that spring from that act—comes into play in the last couplet, as Thompson, resigned to his fate, spells out what is in store for his oppressors: "They'll all pay double for what they've done. / Our day's coming but their day's come."

One of Thompson's favorite themes (often found in Alfred Hitchcock's films) is of the innocent man who is just going about his life when he suddenly finds himself thrust into a nightmarish scenario, not of his own making and completely beyond his control. In "Living on Borrowed Time," we are never told what crime the protagonist has committed. All we know is that time is running out fast. There's a price on his head, and he's being systematically tracked down.

"It was deliberately vague in its setting," Thompson pointed out. "You can't say where it is. It's more metaphorical than my other songs. It's more about a situation in which you feel you're being pursued like a criminal. It's a brooding kind of song, full of paranoia."

Written by Gregg Allman and Kim Payne, "Midnight Rider" first appeared on the Allman Brothers' second studio album *Idlewild South* (Capricorn Records 1970). Photographs of the early Allman Brothers Band reveal a clutch of young Southern rebels who appear to be desperate yet romantic figures. Unlike most groups of the late 1960s and early 1970s who donned old fashioned duds when posing for promo shots and album covers, these guys actually look like they might have holed up back in the woods after robbing a bank or a train when they posed for the camera. With their thick sideburns, droopy mustaches, slouched hats, buckskin jackets, and muddy boots they resemble a pack of bedraggled confederates who, much like the James and Younger Brothers before them, have been driven to extreme measures.

Blurring the line between fantasy and reality, their devoted manager Twiggs Lyndon Jr. took things too far one night when he stabbed and killed a club owner with a ten-inch blade after he stiffed the Allman Brothers for showing up late to a gig. When encouraged to make his getaway before the law arrived, Twiggs could only stand and mutter, "I ain't runnin'. I ain't goin' nowhere."

Over the steady clip-clop of Jaimoe Johanson's conga drums, Gregg Allman delivers his weary first-person saga of a lone desperado. The singer's crime once again is never revealed, and we have no clue as to why he's riding alone through the darkness. "The road," he groans, "goes on forever." Like Levon Helm in the Band's classic "The Weight," Allman's protagonist is just searching for a place where he can temporarily lay his head for some much-needed rest.

When Allman sings of sharing "someone's bed," is he boasting of the sexual prowess that just comes with being an outlaw on the run? Perhaps that last "silver dollar" in his jeans will buy him some comfort at the nearest bordello? Or maybe, as in Hollywood's portrayal of *Butch Cassidy and the Sundance Kid*, the local schoolmarm will coyly remove her spectacles and let down her hair down once more to comfort her lost outlaw.

Pseudo-outlaw or not, Allman's raspy drawl remains convincing. Like Twiggs, Allman also sounds weary, to the point where he's "beyond the point of caring." The song's title, "Midnight Rider," would soon take on a more profound if somewhat eerie meaning after a pair of motorcycle accidents in Macon, Georgia, claimed the lives of two of the Allman Brothers; slide guitarist Duane Allman (October 29, 1971) and bassist Berry Oakley (November 11, 1972) just over a year later.

Written by Jerry Garcia, John Dawson, and Robert Hunter, "Friend of the Devil" is a lighthearted bluegrass romp that first appeared on the Grateful Dead's 1970 benchmark release, *American Beauty*.

Exactly what the singer's crime is, is hard to say. But from the jump he is running from Reno, with twenty hound dogs on his trail. By the second verse we discover he's a polygamist, with a wife in Chino and another stashed away in Cherokee. Although he's a rather likeable fellow (most likely due to Jerry Garcia's sniffling vocal delivery), he's clearly a deadbeat dad. Yet at the same time, this sad sack appeals to our sense of sympathy. We'd like to lend him a hand and wouldn't think twice about hiding him up in the attic for a few nights until the heat blows over. But it's hard to take this guy's deal with the devil seriously. Although he bemoans his fate of having to sleep in cold, lonely caves while missing his darling Ann Marie, along with the threat of having to spend the rest of his life behind bars, he is far from the haunted, tortured fugitive of Robert Johnson's "Hell-Hound on My Trail," who sold his soul to Old Scratch one full moon night at a Mississippi crossroads in order to become the greatest guitarist of his day, while living with the nagging feeling that his days were numbered.

The Dead song's gentle acoustic arrangement on the original studio version featured David Grisman's dancing mandolin. "I was just tryin' to get the part right," David offered, recalling the *American Beauty* session. "I played it a lot of times with Jerry but oddly enough I never paid too much attention to the words," he confessed.

By the mid-1970s, the Dead had reinterpreted this lighthearted ramble, transforming it into a spooky dirge, which loaned some much-needed credibility to the protagonist, making his impending doom all the more real.

"'Friend of the Devil' is one of the Grateful Dead's most cherished chestnuts," explained Oliver Trager, author of *The American Book of the Dead: The Definitive Grateful Dead Encyclopedia*. "Its loose narrative was cribbed from similarly titled tunes from the Mississippi Delta, perhaps most pointedly Robert Johnson's 'Me and the Devil Blues,' a song that deals with Faustian bargains struck with ol' Beelzebub himself, usually at the crossroads 'round midnight. The theme is an ancient one, but one that, metaphorically at least, promises to haunt us wherever we roam.

"The Dead, or, more specifically, Jerry Garcia and lyricist Robert Hunter, made a studied practice of reinventing choice selections of Americana lore. 'Friend of the Devil' was easily the best known and most performed of these and rather uncharacteristic of the Dead, who presented it in two distinct, wildly dissimilar arrangements. There was the spritely, near grinning affair, familiar to those for whom *American Beauty* provided the soundtrack to their youth; and then, commencing in the late 1970s, it became a lush ballad that resonated with Garcia's increasingly world-weary persona. The earlier versions may have left some hope that the narrator, who's got nine lives and nine miles of rough road, jilted lovers, and maybe a kid or two behind him, might escape his fiery fate unscathed. But the latter versions provide no such hint at redemption."

"Long before Kate and I entertained a career in music, our cousin Anne Marie Miller Fauteux-Namaro wrote a poem in 1965 called 'The Ballad of Bordeaux Jail,' which we first heard recited by a Montreal disc jockey," recalled Canadian singer Anna McGarrigle. "The deejay made a 45 rpm of it, and it became a big hit in Canada at the time. It's a poem more than a song, [although Alan Mills would later set the verse to music] about a prison escape by one of Canada's leading criminals, Lucien Rivard, [a.k.a. "The Gallic Pimpernel"].

"Lucien Rivard, it turns out, wasn't merely a small-time local crook," McGarrigle pointed out. "He had ties to the French Connection, the New Orleans mob, and owned a club in Havana. Jack Ruby had once allegedly bailed him out of a Cuban jail!"

Written in the style of the popular narrative poet William Henry Drummond, Fauteux-Namaro's campy ballad begins with the warden of Bordeaux Jail ensconced behind his big old oak desk, smoking "a fat cigar," trading barbs with his notorious prisoner. Rivard complains that the skating rink has turned "soft like slop" (well, it was July after all) and offers to hose it down to create a nice, smooth surface. The warden begrudgingly obliges and then lies down for a brief nap. Upon awakening he discovers "Rivard, like the quick brown fox, / Who must outwit the hound," has made his escape, employing the hose to scale the prison wall. The judge is furious.

> *He grind his teeth, he pull his hairs,*
> *He'll never smile again,*
> *As he implore, encore, encore,*
> *"WHERE ARE YOU LUCIEN!!!"*
>
> *The search goes on relentless,*
> *Through valley, hill and dell.*
> *They seek him here, they seek him there,*
> *That Gallic Pimpernel.*
>
> *For years to come in Crooksville,*
> *They'll tell the epic tale,*
> *How Rivard left his footprints,*
> *On the walls of Bordeaux Jail.*

Lucien Rivard was hardly an anomaly in Canadian lore. Although Canada has a reputation as a peaceable land, they've had plenty of famous criminals of their own, including a French-born hold-up man by the name of Jacques Mesrine, who was incarcerated in a Quebec maximum security prison before escaping and returning to France, where he was eventually killed by the cops.

An international fugitive of legendary proportion, Jacques Mesrine was wanted in both France and Canada for everything from theft to kidnapping, bank robbery, and murder. Mesrine, a master of disguise and a legendary ladies' man, foiled and humiliated authorities by escaping from prison four times, including from a new maximum security facility that was built specifically to contain him, in La Santé, France.

Born in 1936, and raised in the northern suburbs of Paris, Mesrine survived the degradation and brutality of German occupation when he was sent to a prestigious private Catholic school, from which he was soon expelled for his flagrant disregard for authority. Following a failed marriage that lasted barely a year, Jacques was drafted and shipped off to Algeria, where he participated in a massacre allegedly sanctioned by the French army; for that he was awarded the Cross of Military Valor by the country's most famous general, Charles de Gaulle. This baptism in blood and chaos, along with being lavishly rewarded for such heinous behavior, helped forge Jacques Mesrine into the fearless criminal he soon became. With a new wife and three kids to support, Mesrine turned to armed robbery but was quickly arrested and served a year-and-a-half sentence. Upon his release, he briefly attempted to walk the straight and narrow path by working in an architectural firm and then managing a restaurant, but it wasn't long before he began to plan his next heist.

With an appetite for fine wine, good food, and beautiful women, Mesrine was said to have held up banks while dressed in the latest fashions. He rapidly gained the sobriquet "the Robin Hood of the Paris streets" not only for repeatedly outwitting the gendarmes, as well as kidnapping and robbing the rich, but for generously donating a percentage of his bounty to the homeless. Brutal as he could be, Jacques apparently possessed a conscience and a big heart, which stirred the sympathy of the public, who followed his every exploit in the daily tabloids.

Incarcerated for bank robbery in Montreal, Mesrine escaped from the Saint-Vincent-de-Paul prison on August 21, 1972, and began robbing banks again, stashing away the loot with the intent of freeing the fifty-six fellow prisoners that he'd left behind, languishing in their maximum security cells. Two weeks later, Jacques returned to the jail again with a stockpile of guns and wire cutters that he and an accomplice planned to toss over the prison yard walls. He was also said to have left a small fleet of cars, with keys in their ignitions, parked, ready and waiting in the woods for the fleeing fugitives to make their getaways. Not only that but he'd allegedly rented various apartments throughout Montreal, where his fellow jailbirds could comfortably hole up until the heat blew over. But the whole operation was quickly aborted when Mesrine arrived and discovered an army of armed guards stationed around the prison, following his astounding escape.

The first film to glamorize the notorious criminal's life was *Mesrine,* starring Nicolas Silberg, which debuted in 1984, while two additional movies were made in 2008—*Mesrine Part 1: Killer Instinct* and *Mesrine Part 2: Public Enemy No. 1*—based on his highly embellished jailhouse autobiography *L'Instinct de mort* (*The Killing Instinct*), which had been published in February 1977. Not surprisingly, Mesrine's exploits also inspired a number of songs. For their 1980 LP *Repression*, the French metal band Trust recorded two tunes in the outlaw's honor, "Le Mitard" and "Instinct de Mort," which featured a loping beat, crunchy guitars, and Bernie Bonvoisin's raspy vocals. Three years later, an obscure band of anarchist Brit punk-rockers called the Blood, whose songs usually slagged society and religion, feted "Mesrine" on their curiously titled album *False Gestures for a Devious Public*, with a Clash-like anthem that featured a wall of snarling guitars and rumbling tom-toms. "Mesrine, law is obscene!" screamed the Blood's front man/guitarist J. J. Bedsore. Within his curt and concise rhymes, Bedsore (better known to his first grade teacher as Jamie Cantwell) made a few clever observations, claiming that the Gallic Robin Hood was "the best thing to come out of France." The notorious French outlaw would also inspire a hardcore band from Quebec to adopt his name as their handle.

Born on February 25, 1939, Monique Proietti, better known as "Machine Gun Monica," was raised in the rough and tumble east-end neighborhood of Montreal. Growing up in a large, poor family comprised of eight siblings, she soon turned to petty crime. She was tutored by, of all people, her grandmother, who was described by one police detective as "a Fagin . . . who taught kids how to steal and gave them a cut of the take." Taking in various wayward children, Monique's felonious grandma formed a small gang of local kids who "roamed the streets begging and stealing."

Having dropped out of school by the fifth grade, Monique is said to have turned to prostitution to help keep her large family afloat. By seventeen she'd married Anthony Smith, a Scottish gangster nearly twice her age. Together they raised two children, named Ginette and Anthony, and for a brief time enjoyed a somewhat normal domestic life, until 1962, when they were both arrested after robbing a local café. Smith was immediately deported back to Scotland, while Monique was faced with the prospect of raising their children on her own. With no education and little work experience, Proietti was unable to find regular employment. She soon met Viateur Tessier, with whom she had a child, named Gilles. Tessier, it turned out, was a veteran bank robber who taught his trade to Monique, while she had an innate gift for planning well-coordinated heists. Together they worked as a team until 1966, when Viateur was nabbed for armed robbery and sent to jail for the next fifteen years. Once more Monique found herself a single mother. But within a year she dumped her three kids off at her sister's house, formed a new gang with her new beau Gérard Lelièvre and his brother Robert, and returned to robbing banks. Between the twenty credit unions and banks they held up over the following two-year spree, Monique and the boys allegedly cleared nearly $100,000.

Known for donning wigs and men's clothing as a disguise, Monique would stroll into a bank and announce her arrival by blasting a round of bullets into the ceiling, unnerving both employees and patrons alike while making everyone more instantly cooperative. Proietti, it is said, never harmed or killed anyone during a holdup.

The newspapers soon dubbed Proietti "Machine Gun Molly," or, in French, "Monica la Mitraille," meaning "Grapeshot Monica," elevating the female bank robber to the status of folk hero amongst the people of Montreal. "If Al Capone had had a daughter, he would have wanted her to be Monique Proietti," wrote *Le Petit Journal*, stoking Monique's legend, while the *Montreal Star Reporter*'s Tim Burke brought a more sobering view of the female outlaw's desperate life to the public: "In her first few jobs, she was just the driver of the getaway car. But when the boys saw how she could handle a machine gun and what icy nerve she had, they promoted her.

"Unlike a lot of her male cohorts, she didn't need goofballs or booze before going out on a job," Burke reported. Monique apparently had no need of drugs or alcohol to steady her already steely nerves. In contrast to her fellow brigands, she preferred sobriety, which kept her focused on the job at hand.

On the morning of September 19, 1967, Proietti, along with Gérard and Robert Lelièvre, robbed the Caisse Populaire bank of a paltry $3,000. Although the heist went off without a hitch, the getaway was fraught with disaster. Careening through the city streets with the police in hot pursuit, Proietti eventually lost control of the stolen Plymouth and crashed into a city bus. A moment later the scene was crawling with cops, whom she managed to hold off long enough for Gerard and Robert to make their escape unscathed.

Despite her larger-than-life nickname, "Machine Gun Molly" never once fired a machine gun. Instead she preferred a semi-automatic M-1 rifle, rumored to have been gold-plated and given to her as a gift from Gérard. But whatever firepower she wielded that fateful day wasn't enough to make the squadron of cops stand down. The ensuing shootout lasted just a few minutes before a rain of bullets penetrated her chest, killing her instantly.

Having masterminded twenty bank heists throughout the 1960s, Caisse Populaire was supposedly going to be Monique's last stickup. She had hoped to take her kids to Florida, where she planned to change her name and lead a quiet life from that day forth. With her death, the legend of Montreal's most famous female gangster only continued to grow over time, in the shape of magazine articles, made-for-TV documentaries, and a film. *Machine Gun Molly*, released in 2004, starred Celine Bonnier and featured the song "Le Blues de Monica," sung by Lorraine Richard and written by Michel Cusson and Pierre Houle. A musical based on Monica's misadventures is said to be currently in the works.

Townes Van Zandt's outlaw opus "Pancho and Lefty," from his sixth album *The Late Great Townes Van Zandt*, released in 1972, is considered by many to be the benchmark of the outlaw song genre. Covered by Willie Nelson and Merle Haggard, "Pancho and Lefty" quickly shot to No. 1 on the country charts in 1983. Ten years later, in April 1993, it was performed on prime-time television for millions of viewers by Nelson and Bob Dylan at Nelson's "Red-Headed Stranger's Sixtieth Birthday Bash."

As with much of Van Zandt's songwriting, "Pancho and Lefty" teems with metaphor and mystery throughout its enigmatic verses. Van Zandt's signature song is a perfect sonic Rorschach test to everyone who hears it, as it allows each person to draw a different conclusion about what took place between the two outlaws on the desert plains of Mexico. Beyond Van Zandt's spellbinding poetic verse, betrayal lays at the heart of this enduring tale. Some believe that Lefty turns Pancho in for the "bread" that pays for his bleak journey back to Ohio, where he winds up living out his last days in a cheap, run-down Cleveland hotel.

"Pancho and Lefty" even remained a mystery to Van Zandt himself, who claimed to have never "figured it out." One thing we do know is that the song's inspiration had nothing to do with Mexico's most famous outlaw, Pancho Villa. "I've heard that a grad student at Harvard or Yale is doing his doctorate on the song, so the answer may be forthcoming," joked Van Zandt (who was as famous for his dark, depressing ballads as he was for his quirky sense of humor).

> *Living on the road my friend,*
> *Was gonna keep you free and clean.*
> *Now you wear your skin like iron,*
> *Your breath's as hard as kerosene.*
> *You weren't your mama's only boy,*
> *But her favorite one it seems.*
> *She began to cry when you said goodbye,*
> *And sank into your dreams.*

For Steve Earle, a friend and acolyte of Van Zandt's, "Pancho and Lefty" went against every standard for success set by the music industry, openly defying the unspoken rule that a song must be short and concise with a good beat, and not too literate or arty; otherwise the public (whose attention span seems to be growing shorter every day) are certain to ignore it. "You won't find a song that's better written, that says more or impresses songwriters more," Earle declared.

"Even now when I'm driving to a gig and getting sleepy, I'll go over every word of 'Pancho and Lefty.' There are so many amazing things about that song. Every word really counts," David Olney marveled. "The first verse is delivered in the voice of the second person," he points out. "From there it's all in the third person, which is really striking. You can imagine a Greek chorus singing it. And with each repeating of the chorus, a subtle change takes place. Townes connotes the passing of time when he sings 'a few gray federales say . . .'"

Olney then pointed out how Van Zandt suddenly breaks character, employing hip slang when he sings the lines, "Lefty split for Ohio" and "Where he got the bread to go" in a tale that clearly took place back in the days of the old West. "I think it makes it somehow more universal," Olney reckoned.

"You get the feeling from 'Pancho and Lefty' that someone close to you is telling you a very intense story. There's no words or music that can really convey that kind of intensity. It's beyond explanation."

"The lyrics say that Lefty was an old poet and Pancho was the hero of the story he told. The song really shows the way that poets pass stories down from one generation to the next," Townes' widow Jeanene Van Zandt explained. "And once and for all, let's set the record straight. It's 'Pancho and Lefty' not Poncho! One is south-of-the-border for Frank. The other is a goddamn raincoat," she laughed.

"Pancho and Lefty" was one of the few songs to eventually generate any real revenue for Van Zandt. But writing the song paid off in a strange and unexpected way, years before he received his first royalty check. Van Zandt, who was something of an outlaw himself, was driving from Houston to Austin one day when he was pulled over for doing seventy-five through the little town of Berkshire. He wasn't sure what sort of illegal contraband he was carrying at the time. He just always considered himself "felonious while movin'." Surprisingly his driver's license was up to date, although it still showed an old address. But his inspection sticker had expired. Townes knew his bedraggled appearance wasn't going to win any points with the law and in no time he found himself in the back seat of the cruiser, in the custody of a pair of mixed-matched highway patrolmen straight out of that old TV show *Chips*. The driver was a blue-eyed Aryan type with a blonde crew cut, while his partner was a bronze, dark-eyed Mexican. They began grilling Townes with a slew of questions, asking where he was from and what he did for a living. "Well, I'm a traveling folk singer and song-writer," Townes replied, as they rolled their eyes and groaned.

Then Van Zandt played his trump card. "Have you ever heard that song 'Pancho and Lefty'?" he asked. "Well, I wrote it." The pair of cops scoffed. "No you didn't!" "Oh, sure I did," replied Van Zandt. "I gave it to Willie." Then he sang the opening line: "Livin' on the road my friend was gonna keep you free and clean." The cops looked at each other and grinned. A moment later they huddled in the front seat. Meanwhile, Townes just sat there, "tryin' to be as nice as possible. Not sayin' a word and tryin' not to even smell bad." Finally the Aryan-looking cop turned and said, "Well, Townes, we're gonna drop the speeding ticket. Just remember when you get back to Austin to file for a change of address on the driver's license. But we're gonna have to get you for the inspection sticker, 'cause we already wrote it down. But that will only be about five bucks."

"Well, thank you officer," Van Zandt replied appreciatively. He understood the code of the road, that once a cop lets you off, you don't utter another word other than "Thank you, officer." You make no eye contact and be on your merry way as quickly as possible. But curiosity got the best of him, and before he could stop himself he turned around, walked back to the squad car, and asked, "Hey, what prompted y'all to drop the speeding ticket?" The cops told him their police radio code names were Pancho and Lefty.

"Well, that sure is nice," Van Zandt grinned. "Thanks again," he said, and began to walk off. But just as he reached his car, he spun around on his boot heels and sauntered back again. "Uh, which one of y'all is Pancho?" The Mexican pointed at the Aryan and said, "He is!"

Texas singer/songwriter Robert Earl Keen's "The Road Goes on For-ever" weaves a wild tale of a mismatched couple who are suddenly thrown together by fate in the wake of unexpected, uncontrollable events.

"I was living in Bandera, Texas, when I first got the idea for that song," Keen recalled. "Bandera is a real outlaw town. They've dis-banded the police force 'cause there was just no point in having one. It's a small town but it's crazy wild, with fistfights outside the honky-tonks every night. At the time my wife was working at a nursing home, and there was a woman there who was pretty tatted-up and she had this bad guy friend. In a town full of outlaws, they were famous! And one day they just drove off. No one knows exactly where they went or what happened to them. So that gave me a pretty good start, and I wrote the first few verses of the tune inspired by them."

"The Sonny and Sherry characters are based on a couple real char-acters who just couldn't stay out of trouble," Keen had previously told Chris Parton of Country Music Television. "And they just, no matter what happened, no matter what fortune fell on them, they would screw that up. That's where it started from."

The song's hero Sonny, a small-time pot dealer/loner, gallantly defends Sherry's honor one night after she, "a waitress at the only joint in town," was defiled by "some drunken outta towner" who reck-lessly put his hand up her dress. After clubbing the clod with a pool cue, Sonny "stuffs a dollar in her tip-jar" and swaggers out the door into the night and his uncertain future. But just as he's about to climb into his pick-up truck, she runs up alongside him and grabs his hand, as Keen dryly chants the famous refrain that bookends each verse: "The road goes on forever and the party never ends."

Love struck by Sonny's spontaneous (and brutal) display of chiv-alry, Sherry, who, Keen explains, has "a reputation as a girl who'd been around," apparently has no second thought of taking it on the lam with her noble defender at the wheel. Wasting no time, they head straight for a Miami Beach motel, where they promptly polish off a bottle of Bombay gin. With a pistol in his boot, Sonny then convenes with a bunch of Cuban refugees to sell them some unspecified "con-traband." But as the deal is going down, the cops burst through the door and tackle Sonny, who fails to escape after ducking down the alley. In return for Sonny's previous act of gallantry, Sherry responds immediately, coming to her man's rescue by pumping the pursuing lawman full of lead "with a single-shot 410." A true mensch, Sonny doesn't want Sherry to take the rap for saving his hide. Although we can only assume it breaks his heart, he gives her a quick kiss, hands over all the money, and tells her, "If they ask you how this happened, say I forced you into this." A moment later she stands in the doorway of the motel hideaway watching "his taillights" as they "disappeared around the bend."

Two years later, Sherry is picking up a six-pack of beer at the local market when she happens to catch a glimpse of a newspaper headline about her old pal Sonny, who is "going to the chair" for killing the cop. She climbs into her "new Mercedes Benz" and drives off into the night as Keen once more delivers his classic punchline: "The road goes on forever and the party never ends."

"I'm a huge fan of Marty Robbins's album *Gunfighter Ballads*. I love the outlaw genre," Keen explained. "In a four-minute song there's so much action. On every one of my albums there's an outlaw song of one kind or another."

Released on his third album, *West Textures*, in 1989, the song has been covered by Joe Ely as well as the Highwaymen. "It kind of became my anthem," Keen confessed. "If I ended up in Branson, Missouri [where over-the-hill country musicians are put out to pasture], I'd play it five times a day."

5

GANGSTERS OF LOVE

Love, as needlepoint pillows gently remind us, "makes everything worthwhile." Like death, it often arrives without warning. Love changes everything. It makes us intoxicated, ecstatic. As Dolly Parton sang, "When love is new, it's magic." Without it, we feel worthless. Life is grim, pointless. We become desperate, hopeless. We court tragedy. While love drives some to drink, others will steal or kill for it, whether in a jealous rage or in the throes of deep depression, turning the weapon on themselves to end their pain and sorrow. Pick up a deck of cards, and you'll see the King of Hearts, driven mad by love until he thrusts a sword into his own skull to free himself from its all-encompassing spell.

Metaphors about hiding one's heart away or breaking into another's are as old as the romantic ballad itself. "If I had known before I had started, that love was such a killing thing," sings the lovesick loser in the wistful "Come All Ye Fair and Tender Ladies," "I'd lock my heart in a box of golden and fasten it up with a silver pin." A traditional ballad from Southern Appalachia, the song has been solemnly recited by everyone from Pernell Roberts (the black-clad "Adam Cartwright" in *Bonanza*) to Mother Maybelle Carter, whose high-lonesome lilt hangs over a jangling autoharp. "Fair and Tender Ladies" (a.k.a. "Fair and Tender Maidens," "Tiny Sparrow," or even "Little Swallow") continues to haunt despondent romantics everywhere who were first beguiled and then betrayed by their "false true lover."

As sung in a husky whisper by Eric von Schmidt, who accompanied himself on a gently fingerpicked acoustic guitar, with Garth Hudson (of the Band) playing a shimmering concertina, the song became a navel-gazer of the first order.

While odes to pilfering love and hearts are rather commonplace and usually filled with trite lyrics (perhaps best typified by the lusty bump and grind of "The Stealer" by Free), von Schmidt's "Envy the Thief" manages to employ the metaphor in a clever and meaningful way. This is a different kind of love, unlike the warm, enduring variety he longed for in "Fair and Tender Ladies." Vexed by desire and frustrated by "the high cost of loving," Eric's protagonist is on the prowl, teeming with the raw lust of Willie Dixon's "Back Door Man." Having been "holed up in these woods" he now desperately tries to "find some relief." "If I was a thief and a robber, here's how I'd make my start," he bellows in a bluesy growl, "I'd steal away on some midnight hour and break right into your heart."

When lust flares out of control, it can quickly lead to violence. The prime motivation for murder, as sung in everything from old English folk ballads and bluegrass tunes to contemporary "New Country" hits, has most often been love, or some strange variation on it.

Written and sung to the tune of "Where Is My Love?" also known as "The Bloody Miller," the seventeenth-century broadside "William Grismond's Downfall," a.k.a. "William Grismond at Lainterdine," is the tale of a guilt-ridden young man who cuts the throat of his neighbor's daughter after reneging on his promise to marry her. Based on the actual "Lamentable Murther" (as it was known) committed at Lainterdine, in the county of Hereford, on March 12, 1650, the song is a well-worn tale of inner conflict and fear that drives Grismond to commit such a grisly act.

> *I had my pleasure on her, I had my lewd desire,*
> *The using of her body was that I did require,*
> *I was o'ercome and snared by him that is a liar,*
> *And for my offence I shall die.*

She claimed of me marriage and said she was with child,
Saying, "Marry me sweet William now you have me defiled,
If you do now forsake me, I utterly am spoiled,"
And for my offence I shall die.

In flattering sort I brought her into the field of broom,
And when we both together into the field were come,
I had my pleasure with her and then I was her doom,
And for my offence I shall die.

Then in the broom I killed her with my accursed knife,
There hatefully I killed her who loved me as her life,
I cut her throat, I killed her, who should have been my wife,
And for my offence I shall die.

"Rose Connally," also known as "Down in the Willow Gardens," is a similar tale that recounts the murder of "a pretty little miss" by one Patsy O'Reilly, who is also known by the names of Morrison and Pattimaredo. The song is a particularly disturbing tale, as the protagonist, whose love quickly sours, first tries to poison his unsuspecting girlfriend with a bottle of tainted burgundy (oddly referred to as "burglar's wine"). Unsatisfied with the results, he stabs her repeatedly with a "bloody knife" (sometimes described as a "skeever," "saber," or "dagger") and then throws her cadaver into the river, which he admits is "a dreadful sight."

We never learn the motivation for this dreadful murder, but can only assume that Rose (like "Pretty Polly," "The Knoxville Girl," the young victim of "The Banks of the Ohio," and so many others) is probably pregnant and pressuring her unaccountable beau to marry her. The key line, "My father always taught me that money would set me free," provokes the question of whether the killer didn't try to pay off Rose to drop the entire affair and leave town. The father, once full of what he thought was helpful advice, now sits, regretfully "a-wiping his weeping eyes," watching "his own dear son," who is about to hang by the neck "upon the scaffold high" for the murder of the girl he claimed he once loved. "My race is run," the killer sobs. "Hell's now waiting for me."

"Not every outlaw is heroic," Samantha Parton of the Canadian folk group the Be Good Tanyas reminds us. "Murdering a pregnant woman can hardly be considered an act of bravery."

There is little doubt that folk songs about killing pregnant girl-friends were, to some degree, written and sung as lessons to young ladies tempted by the idea of premarital sex. While the songs frequently portray the murderer as remorseful, the girl remains a voiceless anonymous entity. She winds up dead for trusting her boyfriend enough to follow him into the woods to most likely engage in "an immoral act." In a time when a girl who wasn't a virgin was considered "spoiled," these songs served as a moral lesson to young women. While that may be the case, it doesn't explain the appeal these songs continue have today.

The nineteenth-century ballad "The Banks of the Ohio" is a mournful tale of murder and betrayal sung by everyone from Johnny Cash and the Carter Family to Bill Monroe, Doc Watson, Dolly Parton, Alison Krauss, and many others. Once again, some young stinker by the name of "Willie" walks his betrothed out in the woods, where he drowns her "where the waters flow." Joan Baez's version, uniquely sung from the man's perspective, tells essentially the same story, although this time, as in "Pretty Polly" and "Knoxville Girl," the woman is stabbed by that no-good "Willie" instead of being pushed into the river and swept away by its swift current. Olivia Newton John's 1971 recording of "The Banks of the Ohio" (which went to No. 1 in her homeland of Australia) is particularly unusual, as it is sung by a woman about a woman who takes her groom-to-be for a little walk in the woods, only to murder him by plunging a knife deep into his chest after she discovers he has reneged on their plans for marriage.

The enduring murder ballad of the 1960s, "Hey Joe," whether it is a traditional song, as some claim, or written in the mid-1950s by Scottish folk singer Billy Roberts, has been recorded by everyone from Jimi Hendrix and the Byrds (whose groovy rock 'n' roll version was sung by David Crosby) to Arthur Lee's band, Love. In the 1970s, punk rocker/poet Patti Smith gave "Hey Joe" a new edge, before the song migrated into the repertoires of Willy DeVille and Nick Cave. Whoever sang it, "Hey Joe" clearly drew its inspiration from a long line of traditional murder ballads from "Pretty Polly," "Little Sadie," and "Delia" to the Louvin Brothers' haunting "Knoxville Girl."

All these songs are built upon the moral that justice, severe as it may be, is certain to follow any act of infidelity. In "Hey Joe," the protagonist's promiscuous partner is justifiably murdered, at least in Joe's disturbed mind, "for messin' round with another man." "Shoot her one more time, baby," Jimi Hendrix exclaimed, before breaking into an astounding guitar solo, as if killing your girlfriend was a hip thing to do.

Although we have come a long way in terms of women's rights, as well as the condemnation of violence against women and domestic violence, there remains a lingering misogyny in our society, particularly within rock and rap lyrics. While in real life it is unacceptable to kill one's unfaithful girlfriend, it is, at least, to some degree, okay to fantasize about it.

Disturbing portrayals of misogynist murders, in which the victim is typically a young girl who faithfully follows her boyfriend into the deep dark woods, where she is then brutally slain for whatever twisted whim her deranged beau deems fit (most often an unwanted or unexpected pregnancy), continue to remain popular to this day.

Ira and Charlie Louvin's "Knoxville Girl" has its origins in an early nineteenth-century Irish murder ballad known as "The Wexford Girl," which is said to have originated in Oxford, England. "The Knoxville Girl" was "maybe almost the first song we ever sang," Charlie Louvin wrote in his memoir *Satan Is Real*. "If it wasn't the first, it was the most requested . . . audience-wise."

What is it about these songs that appeals to us? Why do we still need to hear these dreadful tales, handed down from one generation to the next? They have remained basically the same, with just a few minor changes to names and towns, since the Elizabethan era that gave us one of the original murder ballads, called "The Cruel Miller."

"The reason is simple," Peter Rowan explained. "Murder has always sold newspapers. It's titillating. People vicariously enjoy reading and hearing about other people's dramas. And then there's also the feeling of relief: 'Oh, I'm glad it wasn't me! I'm happy that my throat wasn't slit!'"

The death of "The Knoxville Girl" (like those in Oxford and Wexford before her) also takes place deep in the primordial woods where "Willie dear" lures and then kills his loving and trusting (and most certainly pregnant) girlfriend, beating her with the branch of a tree until the ground below his feet is stained red with her blood. Horrible as the act of murder is, things get even creepier when Willie confesses to grabbing her "by her golden curls," dragging her down to the edge of the river and throwing her into the rushing water "that flows through Knoxville town."

The image of the Knoxville girl's "dark and roving eyes" can only imply that Willie's bride-to-be was flirtatious and had a reputation for being loose with other men. The harsh judgment that "Willie dear" passes, "You can never be my bride," seems meant to somehow justify the act of murder, at least in his twisted, jealous mind.

In "Pretty Polly" we find a similar case of pre-meditated murder. This "Willie," we learn, has been digging his girlfriend's grave for the best part of last night. Once the heinous deed has been done, Willie hurries back home, where he tells his doting mother that his blood-stained clothes are all due to a sudden nosebleed. Willie then proceeds to roll and tumble all night, wracked with guilt as visions of hell fire consume his bed. By morning, the forensic team has figured out that Pretty Polly's murder was the handiwork of "Willie dear" and the sheriff and his posse arrive to drag the little monster off in chains to the county jail, where he will rot in a cell for the rest of his life after committing terrible violence against the girl he "loved so well."

"There's a real disconnect in those old ballads that you can hear now with the passage of time," Peter Rowan pointed out. "There was something about the vocal delivery that was quite unemotional. The singers often sang in a monotone, although the songs were about a guy who murdered his girlfriend because he got her pregnant. Whenever I sang 'Pretty Polly,' it was more emotional. But hey, we're in show business," Rowan said. "The music business was a creation of RCA Victor. They put Waylon [Jennings], Willie [Nelson], and Tompall [Glaser] all together on a wanted poster and created a new style of music that became known as 'Outlaw Country.'"

Guitarist/author Lenny Kaye, coauthor of Waylon Jennings's autobiography (*Waylon: An Autobiography,* published in 1996), saw the Outlaw phenomenon in a somewhat different light, not as a fabricated genre but as a natural expression of musicians who felt that commercial country music had lost its soul. Kaye believed Waylon was the real deal: "His image grew out of the person he was, an honorable idealist who played the music with integrity, the way it was intended to be played. Waylon was at the core of the Outlaw movement, which in many ways mirrored both punk rock and hip hop, in that the musicians had integrity, took risks, and stood for something that deeply mattered, not just to themselves but to society as a whole. Waylon was forthright. He was like, don't fuck with me! He'd draw a line in the sand and if you crossed it . . . well, you found yourself out, standing on the other side. He believed in what he did and he won. Along with the Highwaymen—Johnny Cash, Willie Nelson, and Kris [Kristofferson]—they were the Mount Rushmore of country music . . . and Jessi Colter too, the true six-gun cowgirl of country music, and perhaps the toughest of them all. The music they made was real. It came from the heart and soul."

Since the early twentieth century, the tragic ballad of "Little Sadie" has been sung under a variety of titles from "Bad Lee Brown" (the name of Sadie's accused killer) to "East St. Louis Blues" (where the murder allegedly occurred) to "Late One Night" (which designates what time the crime took place). Although it originated as a folk ballad, the song's lyrics, as is common in the blues tradition, have been continually changed and retitled as "Cocaine Blues," "Transfusion Blues," and "Penitentiary Blues." Although "Little Sadie" appears to have been written in 1922, it wasn't published for another twenty-four years, when it first appeared in the massive collection *Ozark Folksongs Vol. II*, under the title of "Bad Lee Brown," who confessed to the murder within its rhyming verse:

> *Last night I was a-makin' my rounds,*
> *Met my old woman an' I blowed her down,*
> *I went on home to go to bed,*
> *Put my old cannon right under my head.*

Jury says murder in the first degree,
I says "Oh Lord, have mercy on me!"
Old Judge White picks up his pen,
Says you'll never kill no woman ag'in.

The lyric soon morphed into the more commonly known version of the song, in which "my old woman" is identified as the hapless victim, "Little Sadie." Although the details of Lee Brown's arrest and sentencing are made quite clear, the killer never explains his motive for what otherwise appears to be a rather casual act, as if, while on his "little round," he could have been going out to buy some cigarettes or a newspaper just as easily as committing murder.

Went out last night to take a little round,
I met my little Sadie and I blowed her down,
I ran right home and I went to bed,
With a forty-four smokeless under my head.

I began to think what a deed I'd done,
I grabbed my hat and I began to run,
I made a good run but I ran too slow,
They overtook me down in Jericho.

Here the lyric most likely refers to Jericho, South Carolina, while other versions occasionally swap the location of his capture to Mexico. Brown continues his regretful tale:

Standing on a corner a ringin' my bell,
Up stepped the sheriff from Thomasville.

(Thomasville is located across state lines in North Carolina.) The line portraying Brown "a 'ringin' [his] bell," makes little or no sense, considering he is a fugitive, desperately running for his life, who would not want, under any circumstances, to draw attention to himself. Some suggest the original line may have been "reading a bill," as in reading a handbill or wanted poster that prominently displayed both his name and image. The conversation the murderer then has with the sheriff seems flippant, as if murdering his girlfriend was no big deal:

> He said, "Young man is you name Brown?
> Remember you blowed Sadie down."
> "Oh yes sir, my name is Lee,
> I murdered little Sadie in the first degree,
> First degree and second degree,
> If you've got any papers will you serve them to me?"

Brown then continues, recounting the details of his sorry fate:

> They took me down town and they dressed me in black,
> They put me on a train and they sent me back,
> I had no one to go my bail,
> They crammed me back into the county jail.

> The judge and the jury they took their stand,
> The judge had the papers in his right hand.
> Forty-one days, forty-one nights,
> Forty-one years to wear the ball and the stripes.

This is where most versions of "Little Sadie" end, with a man who has thrown away his life for what seems like the casual murder of his "old woman." What the dynamic of their relationship was we'll never know, whether they were married (as the slang term "old woman" or "old lady" usually infers) or whether she was yet another slain pregnant girl, which doesn't seem to be the case here. Either way, "Little Sadie" is unusual for the protagonist's dispassionate recounting of what otherwise would be a crime of passion. Lee Brown's motivation remains a mystery, and perhaps that enigma has kept the song alive and thriving under various titles for more than 100 years.

The definitive version of "Little Sadie" was recorded under the title "Cocaine Blues" in 1947 by singer T. J. "Red" Arnall with W. A. Nichol's Western Aces, becoming the template for everyone from Johnny Cash and Doc Watson to George Thorogood. "Cocaine Blues" has made the rounds through many a singer's repertoire, from Luke Jordan, who recorded the first song by that title in 1927, to Mississippi John Hurt, to Johnny Cash (who sang it with a country twang to the cheering inmates of Folsom Prison). Then there was the man who perhaps knew the effect of the drug better than anyone who ever uttered the lyrics, Keith Richards. He cut a Reverend Gary Davis–inspired version of the song in 1993 for the Rolling Stones' download-only album *Voodoo Brew*.

Although the song's lyric has gone through drastic changes over the decades, the protagonist remains remorseful over his coke habit, whether bemoaning that "cocaine is for horses, not for men," or being sentenced to "ninety-nine years" in jail for killing his lover in a jealous rage while under its wicked influence. Both of Bob Dylan's renditions of "Little Sadie" were based on Clarence Ashley's performance of the song. (They appeared on Dylan's disastrous 1970 double album *Self Portrait* as "Little Sadie" and "In Search of Little Sadie." The latter took a number of bizarre musical twists, modulating with each line of the song to create a nightmarish tension as the fugitive tries in vain to flee from the police.)

We discover an additional verse in Wayne Erbsen's folksy chapbook, *Outlaw: Ballads, Legends and Lore*, a compilation of bad man ballads found in the public domain, which also includes such humorous asides as "Frontier Etiquette and Wisdom" and "Desperado Gossip."

"Popular in 1885, [the song] has been collected in North Carolina, Tennessee, and Missouri," Erbsen wrote, adding that the musicologist John Lomax originally collected "Little Sadie" under the name of "Bad Man Ballad" from "a tongue-tied Negro convict at Parchman [Farm]," the notorious Mississippi penitentiary.

Dylan, who ends one version of the tune with a resounding "Oh no!" may have found the last verse superfluous, with its trite morality.

> *Now all young men take my advice,*
> *Never take another young girl's life.*
> *It'll cause you to weep, cause you to mourn,*
> *It'll cause you to leave your home sweet home.*

A pair of songs portraying romance gone bad, with the female partner meeting a violent end, were recorded in 1969 by California-based songwriters Warren Zevon and Neil Young. It's surprising how many people sang along with these tunes without acknowledging their misogynistic lyrics.

On his obscure first album, *Wanted Dead or Alive* (1969), Zevon, famous for his erratic behavior and glorification of violence in his lyrics, wrote and sang the twisted country-rock ballad "A Bullet for Ramona," about a woman he tracks down and shoots after obsessing over her for the previous two years. The protagonist rationalizes his harsh deed as retaliation for her cheating ways. The album's title track, "Wanted Dead or Alive," portrays a desperate, "violent man . . . trying to do [his] best," who is ultimately incapable of finding peace in this world due to having been born with an "outlaw face."

While the hapless victim of Neil Young's broody opus "Down By the River" remains faceless and forgotten, listeners oddly find themselves sympathizing not with "the lady" who has been shot but with the singer, a cold-blooded murderer. Oddly, we root for him and his new love (and most likely his next victim) to safely make their getaway to a more perfect world "over the rainbow," which Judy Garland once dreamed of and Young desperately yearned for.

Rivers have always been a convenient place to dispose of things, from shopping carts and tires to bodies. Amazingly, it seems that these brutes who murder their girlfriends routinely lack the foresight that the bodies they dispose of may soon come floating up to the water's surface as a grim reminder of their dastardly deeds. In the Southern murder ballad "Omie Wise," we find a familiar narrative of a man, John Lewis in this instance, who leads a seemingly naïve lass into the deep dark woods with ill intent, until she suddenly begins to suspect her beau's behavior:

> *"John Lewis, John Lewis, will you tell me your mind?*
> *Do you intend to marry me or leave me behind?"*

"Little Omie, little Omie, I'll tell you my mind,
My mind is to drown you and leave you behind."

"Have mercy on my baby and spare me my life,
I'll go home as a beggar and never be your wife."

The nature of folk ballads is to condense a story into short, economical rhyme, but all too often many details are lost in the process. This is particularly true in the tragic tale of Omie Wise and John Lewis. While there is no justification for violence against women, the real Omie, it turns out, may not have been as innocent as she is portrayed in the song. It is said that Ms. Wise routinely had affairs with various men, usually of a higher social standing, and gave birth to a number of their children. It is also rumored that she extorted money for the children's care as well as for her own well-being. John Lewis turned out to be the last stop on that train. As he leads her to her doom, Lewis appears emotionally conflicted, still caring for and attracted to Omie, as the song recounts: "He kissed her and he hugged her" before he "turned her around . . ."

And pushed her in deep waters where he knew that she
would drown.
He jumped on his pony and away he did ride.

Ignoring Little Omie's pathetic cries as she goes under for the last time, John Lewis hops on his horse and hightails it back home. But it's not long before the specter of Little Omie reappears once more:

'Twas on one Thursday morning, the rain came pouring
down,
When the people searched for Omie but she could not be
found.
Two boys went to fishin' one fine summer day,
And they saw Little Omie's body go floating away.

Then they threw their net around her and drew her to the
bank,

Her clothes all wet and muddy, they laid her on a plank.
They sent for John Lewis to come to that place,
And they brought her out before him so that he might see
   her face.

Though he made no confession, they carried him to jail,
No friends nor relations would go on his bail.

It turns out that "Omie Wise" (also spelled "Ommie") was based on true events that took place in 1807, when an eighteen-year-old orphan girl named Naomi Wise from Franklinville, North Carolina, became romantically involved with Jonathan Lewis (traditionally sung as "John" in the ballad), a ne'er-do-well from a wealthy family, who was apparently already engaged. Lewis allegedly led Wise to believe that they would soon run away together to nearby Asheboro, where they would be secretly married. But there was an unforeseen detour along the way to their bright, happy future together, and he wound up drowning her in the Deep River, which runs through the town of Randleman.

Arrested on April 8, Lewis was incarcerated in Randolph County Jail, where he was formerly charged with the murder of Naomi Wise on October 5, to which he pleaded not guilty. Four days later, Lewis broke out of prison, apparently aided by the sheriff, Isaac Lane, and five other men; all were deemed suspects in the jailbreak. (Lewis, it is said, may have paid off Lane, as he came from a wealthy family). Following Jonathan Lewis's capture, four years later in 1811, the sheriff was cleared of any wrong-doing, having ensnared the fugitive.

Lewis then spent two years in jail before standing trial, not for the murder of Naomi Wise but for having escaped from prison. As far as the drowning of "Little Omie" was concerned, the case was eventually dropped due to lack of evidence. Not only was the hapless Omie a poor mother, she had no family or anyone willing or able to fight her case. Years later, on his deathbed, John Lewis allegedly confessed to the murder.

Included in Harry Smith's epic *Anthology of American Folk Music* (Folkways Records 1952), "Ommie Wise" was recorded in 1927 by G. B. (George Bauman) Grayson, a blind fiddler and street singer from New River Valley, North Carolina. In the album's accompanying booklet, Smith, an eccentric song collector and filmmaker, summed up the plot of each of the songs with one or two brief, clever sentences that sounded as if they'd been written as a fortune cookie or tabloid headline. "Ommie Wise" is described thus: "Greedy girl goes to Adams Spring with liar, lives just long enough to regret it." Smith also made a comment on the music: "The combination of [Grayson's] voice and violin (played by the singer) is quite archaic."

Occasionally we find the shoe on the other foot, with the man becoming the victim for a change, as in the case of "Young Hunting," an eighteenth-century Scottish ballad, better known in England as "Earl Richard" or "The Proud Girl," but commonly sung in America as "Love Henry" or "Henry Lee." Whether passed down over the centuries as "Lady Margot and Love Henry," "Song of a Lost Hunter," or "My Love Heneree," the tragic tale of "Love Henry," like "Pretty Polly," "Omie Wise," and "Knoxville Girl," describes a young woman (most likely pregnant) faced with harsh rejection and brutal punishment meted out by her alleged lover. But "Love Henry" reveals an unexpected plot twist.

First recorded in 1929 for Brunswick Records by Dick Justice, a coal miner from Logan County, West Virginia, "Henry Lee" would later appear as the opening track to Harry Smith's *Anthology of American Folk Music*. It is gently strummed on the guitar as a lilting waltz, and sung in a high, lonesome nasal twang by Justice, who allegedly played with African American musicians and learned the rudiments of the blues directly from them.

The Wisconsin-born folk singer Judy Henske recorded "Love Henry" live at the Unicorn on Sunset Strip in 1963. Elektra Records soon released it as the B-side to her version of "I Know You Rider," a song first heard and collected by John and Alan Lomax that found its way into countless musicians' repertoires from Joan Baez and James Taylor to the Grateful Dead and Hot Tuna.

Although it seems incongruous to introduce a tragic tune in such a light-hearted manner, Henske (once known as "The Queen of the Beatniks") pulls it off with panache. In a routine on par with the Smothers Brothers, she cracks up her audience with a zany update of "a special murder ballad, which will cheer us all in our hour of need," referring to it facetiously as "Henry in the Well." Amongst the giggles and guffaws, Henske describes "a fair lady who lived in a castle," who slashes her reluctant lover's throat with straight razor. "He lay on the floor dead and all," she jokes. The lady then calls to a bird, singing outside her window, to come sit upon her knee; but the bird, who saw it all, flatly refuses, replying "In a pig's eye!" Henske laughs, "What we can glean from this, is that the lady had the wrong attitude about a lot of things." A moment later, Henske shifts gears, breaking into a heart-felt rendition of the tune as she sings the fate of poor Henry.

"You know that song from *Mary Poppins*, 'A spoonful of sugar makes the medicine go down'?" Henske asked. "I like singing murder ballads but I don't want people to be bummed. It's hard enough to be mortal with death always hanging around, so I bring humor into it. I love stand-up comics. I want people to laugh. But Henry wasn't too smart, was he? Who tells their lover he's leaving her to spend the night with someone younger and better looking? That was no way to talk to an armed woman!"

Judy first heard "Love Henry" from a folk singer in Oklahoma City named Bob Grossman. "I think anyone who played the song either learned it from me or Bob. He had a great voice. He taught me 'Love Henry' and one thing led to another! It was very warm that day and we were very young," she giggled. "I saw him forty years later in LA and we just laughed. I think he'd become a cantor."

Two years after Judy's version of the song first appeared, Peggy Seeger would join her brothers Pete and Mike to recount the tale of "Love Henry," in a mellifluous voice over a trundling banjo rhythm, on the 1965 double album *Folk Songs with the Seegers*.

In 1993, Bob Dylan released *World Gone Wrong*, the second of two solo albums in which he recorded a series of bare-bones traditional ballads with voice, acoustic guitar, and harmonica. Bob, who had turned his back on folk music when he "went electric" at the Newport Folk Festival on July 25, 1965, was picking and singing with renewed passion.

"Folk music is the only music where it isn't simple," Dylan once told Greil Marcus. "In that music is the only true, valid death you can feel today off a record player." Amongst the arcane collection was the macabre "Love Henry," who, in this version, is offered "gold chains" and various love tokens (in previous accounts his lover/murderer lures Henry with "both candle and coal [and her] fire burning bright," if he "will only stay all night"). Henry, who was clearly unfamiliar with the old adage, "Hell hath no fury like a woman scorned," makes the fatal mistake of answering his "lover" honestly, explaining that he "can't stay all night" as there is "some pretty little girl in Cornersville (also referred to as "a lady" from "Lord Barnet's Hall") I love far better than thee." What happens next varies slightly from version to version. Henry most often climbs down from his horse, or bends over to kiss her goodbye three times; but it is also said that he gets drunk and lays "his head on a pillow of down," when suddenly his jilted lover reaches for "a penny knife that she held in her hand, [and] murdered mortal he." Having sliced up Henry in cold blood, she is suddenly overcome by an assortment of powerful emotions, from regret for her wrong-doing, to the fear of getting caught, to vindictiveness towards that "pretty little girl" from Cornersville. But most curious of all is the jealous rage that led her to commit such a ghastly act in the first place.

> "Get well, get well, Love Henry," she cried
> "Get well, get well," said she.

To which the mortally wounded Henry answers:

> "Oh don't you see my own heart's blood
> Come flowin' down so free?"

No matter how she implores the dying Henry to "Get well," it is clear he's finished. And so the murderous nightmare continues, growing more bizarre by the minute:

> She took him by his long yellow hair,
> And also by his feet.
> She plunged him into well water,
> Where it runs both cold and deep.

> *"Lie there, lie there, Love Henry," she cried,*
> *Till the flesh rots off your bones.*
> *Some pretty little girl in Cornersville*
>   *Will mourn for your return."*

Things take a surreal turn when his cold-hearted lady seeks comfort from her pet parrot, which also fears for its life, having witnessed her cruelty:

> *"Hush up, hush up, my parrot," she cried,*
> *"And light on my right knee.*
> *The doors to your cage shall be decked with gold,*
> *And hung on a willow tree."*

Skeptical and frightened, the bird replies:

> *"I won't fly down, I can't fly down,*
> *And light on your right knee.*
> *A girl who would murder her own true love*
>   *Would kill a little bird like me."*

Judy Henske's version of "Love Henry" contains a few additional verses at the end, in which the murderess threatens the little bird who is able to see into her dark heart:

> *"If I had my arrow in my hand,*
> *Bow on a tuneful string,*
> *I'd shoot a dart straight through your heart,*
> *And you'd no longer sing!*

Logan English was a Woody Guthrie acolyte and an inspiration to the young Bob Dylan. He worked as MC at New York's legendary folk club, Gerde's Folk City. On his 1957 Folkways album, *Kentucky Folk Songs and Ballads,* he delivers, in a pure, wholesome, almost theatrical voice, a rather upbeat rendition of "Love Henry," over a lively plucked guitar. As in every version of the song, Henry's lover offers her warm "bed and fireside too" and, once rejected, stabs him repeatedly. But this time the knife that plunges into his neck and chest has a different effect on Henry, making him change his tune instantly. Whether out of self-preservation or the delirium brought on by an abrupt loss of blood (which in some versions goes "a tricklin' down her knee"), Henry immediately changes his mind, deciding that he can "get down" with her. He even offers an apology, claiming "For there's no little girl in the old River Clyde that I love any better but thee. (Note: the location, whether Cornersville, the Clyde River, or simply the "city wall," constantly changes at the whim of the singer.)

Suddenly regretting her rash actions, his murderous lover mounts her trusty steed in a panic and "rides to the west and rides to the east, anywhere under the sun, to find a good and clever doctor who can cure this wounded man." But it's all to no avail. Henry is in serious shape and "only God's own hand" can possibly help him now. As there is no one able to patch up her handiwork, she decides to dispose of Henry's lacerated body, so it's "into the well, 60 fathoms deep goes he." The coast seems to be clear when suddenly she "heard a little bird sing, 'Go home, go home you cruel little girl, lament and mourn for him.'" Attempting to bribe her winged witness, she offers the taunting bird the comfort of her lap and a swell life in a gilded cage, which shall hang from a willow tree. But the creature has more sense than to trust a cold-blooded killer, who is left wishing she'd had her bow to shoot an arrow "straight through [its] heart," so it could "no longer sing" of her heinous crime to the world.

As one perceptive commentator wrote of the original Scottish song, "*Young Hunting*," "Talking birds are not uncommon in traditional ballads but this one is unusually moral and immune to bribery, a stark contrast to the behavior of the human characters."

"I've often found it amusing and distressing the way the great ballads metamorphosed when they crossed the water," said British folk-singer June Tabor. "Something as disturbing as 'Young Hunting,' with its supernatural references, with the corpse bleeding when the murderer approaches, and the real weight of horror that is in that tale of murder and the attempted concealment by the former true love, turns into a kind of Disneyfied version that becomes 'Love Henry.' And yet it still has so much strength. Now I appreciate much more the power of the Appalachian versions, whereas I might once have said, 'Yes, but it's not as good as the original.' This one sneaked through because it's got so many good lines in it," she pointed out. "The bird flies away into the sunset to star in the sequel, while everybody else dies unhappily ever after."

In 1996, Nick Cave, the undisputed "King of Unhappy Endings," gave "Henry Lee" a goth makeover when he sang it as a duet with PJ Harvey. Their chemistry was nothing short of smoldering as they circled each other like a pair of hungry/horny jaguars. Gazing into Cave's eyes with a mixture of desire and repulsion, Harvey tells him flatly, "You won't find a girl in this damn world that will compare with me."

The story line remains essentially the same as in Dick Justice's earlier version, but this time each verse ends with a haunting refrain, typical of old English folk ballads: "And the wind did howl and the wind did blow, la la la la la, la la la la lee." There are a few other curious changes in Cave's rendition of song. Lee's body is dragged to the well by his "lily-white hands"; the image either describes his pale corpse or might be interpreted as the dead man's innocence. In the final verse the little bird will not be coerced down to bring the murderess comfort but instead "lit down on Henry Lee," this time, perhaps, in sympathy for the murdered man.

Embroidered by her unearthly whistling and breathy harmonies, Jolie Holland's delicate reading of "Love Henry" (from her 2008 release *The Living and the Dead*) is nothing short of mesmerizing. Performing on a harp guitar (now in the collection of the Metropolitan Museum of Art), Holland sings with an eeriness that befits the supernatural aspects of the song.

"I always felt that the song was about entitlement," Holland stressed. "She (the murderess) thinks she can buy everyone, including Henry. In some versions she even bribes other women to help throw Henry's body down the well. Her soul is doomed but she just doesn't seem to know it yet."

In October 2016, "Love Henry" made its debut (first in LA and then in New York) in a ballet by the modern dance troupe Body Traffic, whose *Death Defying Dances* were inspired by songs from the 1966 album *The Death Defying Judy Henske*.

Mississippi John Hurt's rendition of "Frankie" (a.k.a. "Frankie and Albert," also sung as "Frankie and Johnny") portrays a betrayed woman who kills her boyfriend in a jealous rage, in retribution for his no-good philandering ways. The enduring murder ballad (which has been recorded by more than 250 artists, including Charley Patton, Lead Belly, Jimmie Rodgers, Charlie Poole, Fats Waller, Lena Horne, Johnny Cash, Jerry Lee Lewis, Elvis Presley, Bob Dylan, Taj Mahal, Van Morrison, Stevie Wonder, and many others) is based on the real life story of a twenty-two-year-old "ebony-hued cakewalker," named Frankie Baker, who shot Albert (a.k.a. Al or Allen) Britt (who was just seventeen at the time) at two in the morning in St. Louis, Missouri, upon "the culmination of a quarrel." According to an article that appeared in the *St. Louis Globe-Democrat* the following day, October 16, 1899, "The bullet entered Britt's abdomen, penetrating the intestines." Albert lingered for four days longer before dying at the City Hospital. According to the final line of the news item, "The woman [Frankie Baker] escaped after the shooting."

Eventually arrested and put on trial, Baker was acquitted after successfully pleading that she killed Albert in self-defense, claiming he pulled a knife on her after she discovered him dancing with Alice Pryor (a.k.a. Nelly Bly). Frankie Baker would die decades later, in 1952, after having been committed to an Oregon mental hospital. One has to wonder if Frankie wasn't driven mad by hearing the details of Albert's murder repeatedly sung over the course of her lifetime in every sort of musical setting.

Allegedly composed in 1899 by the St. Louis balladeer Bill Dooley, "Frankie Killed Allen" became a popular topical song during the Baker/Britt murder trial. A similar tune, entitled "He Done Me Wrong," appeared in 1904, credited to Hugo "Hughie" Cannon, who was best known for his 1902 ragtime hit "Won't You Come Home Bill Bailey" (which he allegedly wrote at age sixteen). Four years later the song reappeared as "Bill, You Done Me Wrong," with the copyright attributed to Frank and Bert Leighton. When the Leighton Brothers recorded the tune in 1912, they retitled it "Frankie and Johnny." They also changed the name of the home-wrecking hussy from Alice Frye to "Nellie Bly." It was this version (in which "Albert" was replaced with "Johnny" for whatever reason . . . perhaps it was easier to sing) that was first published in Dorothy Scarborough's 1925 anthology *On the Trail of Negro Folk-Songs.*

The previous year, the blind street-corner singer Ernest Thompson had recorded a country blues number entitled "Frankie Baker" for Columbia Records. Then Mississippi John Hurt cut what is considered to be the definitive version of "Frankie" during his first recording session, on Valentines' Day, 1928, in Memphis. Hurt seems to have gotten the story of the star-crossed lovers secondhand as he referred to Frankie's teenage lover as "ol' Albert."

By 1930, the infamous murder had not only inspired a handful of popular songs but become the impetus for Tay Garnett's full-length feature film, *Her Man*, in which the murder was taken out of the black American South and relocated in Paris. The leading lady, Helen Twelvetrees, plays a barroom girl by the name of "Frankie Keefe," who lusts for a young sailor, despite her volatile relationship with a tough, jealous gent not surprisingly named "Johnnie" (Ricardo Cortez). The role defined Ms. Twelvetrees's acting career, typecasting her as the kind of woman who is hopelessly attracted to tragically flawed men.

While both songs and movies have drawn inspiration from the notorious Baker/Britt murder, poet Carl Sandburg, who published the ballad under the title of "Frankie and Johnny" in his 1927 compendium *The American Songbag*, believed the song had been popular before 1888, while Leonard Feather's *The Biographical Encyclopedia of Jazz* claims it (whether titled "Frankie and Albert" or simply "Frankie,") originated before the Civil War and was sung by Confederate troops as early as the Siege of Vicksburg in 1863. To further complicate matters, the eccentric balladeer/song collector/transcriber John Jacob Niles contradicts both theories, dating the song as early as 1830, before the Civil War.

"Frankie was a good girl, everybody knows," the tune begins innocently. "She paid a hundred dollars for Albert's one suit of clothes." Each verse then ends with the telling refrain, "He was her man and he done her wrong."

"Frankie and Charlie" tells the tale of an altogether different pair of doomed lovers. Once more jealousy is the motive for a gruesome murder, on the night of December 22, 1831, when eighteen-year-old Frankie Silver butchered her husband Charlie with an axe while he was fast asleep in bed in their North Carolina mountain cabin home. Guilty of first-degree murder, Frankie Silver was hanged by the neck until dead on July 12, 1883. Silver, it turns out, passed her time behind bars composing jailhouse rhymes. Her poem entitled "The Ballad of Frankie Silver" didn't see the light of day, for whatever reason, until nearly three years after her execution. It was first published, in March 1886. It has been suggested that Silver was not the sole author, if she in fact wrote it at all.

In 1996, 110 years later, director Tom Davenport made a low-budget film about the shocking homicide, entitled *The Ballad of Frankie Silver*, which began with folk singer Bobby McMillon delivering Frankie's poem in a wistful a cappella as the camera scans the peaceful mist-covered landscape:

> *This dreadful, dark and dismal day*
> *Has swept my glories all away,*
> *My sun goes down, my days are past,*
> *And I must leave this world at last.*

In the next verse, Silver evokes the "frightful ghosts" she foresees gnawing upon their own flesh in a Hieronymus Bosch–like vision of hell. But most of all, Frankie dreads meeting her husband again in the afterlife, which she is certain will soon happen:

> *There shall I meet that mournful face,*
> *Whose blood I spilled upon this place.*
> *With flaming eyes to me he'll say,*
> *"Why did you take my life away?"*

Guilty of premeditated murder, Frankie confesses how:

> *For months and days I spent my time,*
> *Thinking how to commit the crime.*

At this point in time it was unusual for a murderer, particularly a murderess, as in this case, to make an insanity plea. That makes Bessie Smith's bawdy "Send Me to the 'lectric Chair" all the more outrageous, considering it was recorded in 1927. Smith sings in the guise of a gal who has either gone crazy or is hoping that her shocking, sordid tale will help her beat a murder rap. In a most scandalous manner, she recalls the gory details of her lover's slaying, describing how she stood laughing as he died, after fatally slicing him up with her Barlow knife. "I don't wanna spend no ninety-nine years in jail," the "Empress of the Blues" tells the judge, "So send me to the electric chair."

Recorded in 1930 by Willie Walker, "Dupree's Blues" is based on actual events that took place eight years previously, in 1922. It recounts the pitiful story of one Frank Dupree who, unable to afford a diamond ring for his beloved Betty, grabbed a pistol and robbed the local jewelry story. But the stick-up was fraught with "bad luck" and Frank lost his cool, shooting the jeweler, along with a number of policemen (anywhere from one to five, depending on which version of the song you hear).

Walker was a legendary guitarist who played in the Piedmont fingerpicking style of Blind Blake. His "Dupree's Blues" curiously includes the well-worn verse, "Standin' here wonderin' would a matchbox hold my clothes." It is a lyric most commonly attributed to Blind Lemon Jefferson, which inspired rockabilly guitarist Carl Perkins to compose his 1956 hit song "Matchbox," popularized by the Beatles in 1964.

Wasting away in prison, Dupree sends a desperate letter to Betty reading "come home to your daddy, I'm almost dead." As the song concludes, with a cascading guitar riff played by Walker, a despondent Betty arrives at the jailhouse, crying, "Let me see my used to be." It's interesting to watch the details of the song continuously change over the years. Walker's "Dupree's Blues" tells how Frank hires a taxi to drive him all the way to Maine before he's ensnared by the long arm of the law; in Sonny Terry and Brownie McGhee's version, the police catch poor Dupree and carry him all the way "back to the Atlanta jail," where Betty, overcome with shame for having pushed Frank to a life of crime, leaves a note for her man, confessing, "I could not see your face.

Although I love you, I just can't take your place." Over Sonny Terry's wailing harmonica, we hear the judge sentence the doomed Dupree to hang.

Chuck Willis, famous for his 1957 No. 1 arrangement of "C.C. Rider," originally known as "See See Rider" and recorded by the sassy blues belter Gertrude "Ma" Rainey in 1925, would also fashion "Betty and Dupree" into a chart-topping R&B hit. In his version, "The King of Stroll," as Willis was known, presents a tale of love and devotion between two lovers that continues to endure no matter what challenges they face. "Will you be my wife?" Dupree begs his paramour, as Betty replies without hesitation, "I'm yours the rest of my life."

With its lazy beat, seamless sax section, and rolling piano, the Louisiana swamp pop group Cookie and the Cupcakes' take on "Betty and Dupree" strongly resembles the Chuck Willis version until the last line of the song, when singer/tenor saxophonist Huey "Cookie" Thierry changes the tale to one of bitter, unrequited love as Betty suddenly drops the bomb on Dupree, telling him, "I'm in love with someone else. I'm sorry, you're not my man."

For his 2006 performance of the song on German television, the tragic romantic balladeer Willy DeVille leaned heavily on Chuck Willis for inspiration. Accompanied by Darren Brown's New Orleans–style rolling piano, he growls and roars about Dupree's infatuation with Betty to a sleazy bump and grind. DeVille doesn't bother with the superfluous particulars of the crime, its cause, or even its tragic outcome. For him the song is all about passion and seduction—Betty's ruby red lips and swaying hips.

"Willy performed the song on the last couple of tours, between 2007 and 2008, before his illness took its fatal toll," DeVille's percussionist Boris Kinberg recalled. "I was fortunate to have been on stage when he sang the tune. Considering how ill he was, it is amazing that he could still summon his voice and soul to deliver yet another great moment on stage."

"Lie down Betty, see what tomorrow brings," sang Peter, Paul, and Mary in their groovy rendition of this traditional song. Strange how the lyric, taken out of context and illustrated with a windblown portrait of the famous folk trio snapped during a breezy day at the beach, became the perfect title of their 1965 album, which seemed to evoke the prevailing mood of youthful optimism of the time. With a rockin' rhythm, briskly played on a pair of nylon-string folk guitars, this was folk music that was ideal for doing the Twist, as Dupree, desperate to satisfy his lover's every desire, wields a .44 and kills two policemen. (Years later, Josh White Jr.'s strutting blues version of the song would claim three, along with four or five additional people that allegedly Dupree wounded.) Making his getaway, Dupree grabs a cab and heads for Baltimore this time, for no apparent reason other than that it rhymes rather easily with the gauge of his weapon, a .44.

"Grateful Dead songsmiths Robert Hunter and Jerry Garcia made a veritable cottage industry out of reinterpreting some of the most venerable songs in the American folk canon, including new versions of 'Candyman' and 'Stagger Lee,'" Grateful Dead scholar Oliver Trager wrote. Another song in that canon was "Dupree's Diamond Blues," which appeared on the Dead's third album *Aoxomoxoa*.

"Hunter claimed that both 'Dupree' and 'Stagger Lee' were studied efforts to continue the oral tradition," Oliver explained. "He claimed that 'Dupree' was the only song he ever wrote while drunk. 'Dupree' was one of Garcia's favorite tunes. He said it was like 'a little cartoon strip. . . . It has a banjo in it, a little 12-string, and stuff like that. Texturally, it's really successful to my ears. It does what it's supposed to. It has a little sort of calliope sound where T.C. [Tom Constanten] is playing a perfect organ part for it.'"

"'Dupree' was based on an actual event," Trager stressed, pointing to the legendary theft on December 15, 1921. "Frank Dupree shot and killed a Pinkerton detective and gravely wounded B. Graham West, Atlanta's comptroller, during a robbery that took place in broad daylight, in which he absconded with the legendary bauble. But before the dashing twenty-one-year-old South Carolina native met his fate on the gallows the following September, he'd already become a celebrity in the region, a veritable O. J. Simpson of his time. Dupree's crime spree began to spring up in folk songs, even as he was in jail, waiting to meet his Maker.

"In Hunter's embellished version of the legend of Betty and Dupree, Betty is never actually mentioned by name in the song's lyric," Trager emphasized. "His account focuses more on the robbery itself and his comical portrayal of courtroom drama. It hints that the judge threw the book extra hard at Dupree because he too had some-thing going with Betty!"

Dupree, as the Dead sang, had been driven "stone mad," by Betty's "sweet jellyroll." No matter who tells the story, or how they might embroider the tale, poor Frank, under Betty's sexy spell, always winds up taking the fall for her in the end.

In "Betty's Ball Blues," from his 1972 collection *Conjure,* poet/novelist/satirist Ishmael Reed evokes the night that "Betty dressed in scarlet and threw her man a ball."

> *Betty touched his organ, made his cathedral rock.*
> *His worshippers moaned and shouted,*
> *His stained glass windows cracked.*

The raw lust and magnetism that were only hinted at in earlier versions of their fateful romance are suddenly front and center in Reed's rendition. As with nearly everything Reed has written, a mys-tical quality of hoodoo permeates these verses. Beyond Betty's sexual hold over Frank, there seem to be some supernatural underpinnings that drive Dupree beyond reason, to freely commit murder and rob for her. As Reed tells:

> *Dupree he shot the jeweler,*
> *She had him under a spell.*
> *The calmest man in Sing-Sing*
> *Is happy in his cell.*

Originally written in a blues cadence, Reed's lyric was later recorded as a slinky shuffle by Taj Mahal for the 1983 album, *Conjure,* the first of three albums produced by Kip Hanrahan that celebrated Ishmael Reed's poetry. The session featured a stellar band led by Allen Toussaint.

"My friendship with Ishmael Reed goes back almost four decades," Hanrahan explained. "His contrarian posture, and prowess, and clear enjoyment of verbal boxing has put him at uncomfortable odds with enough fashionably established voices in the media and the cultural scene to have blocked him from the center stage. As far as the *Conjure* project goes, it was almost too easy to set up. More than any other writer I know of, Ish and his American Magic Realist Griot genius—and I'm using that word with care here—has had a hold on musicians from a cascade of musical and cultural angles, including musicians who weren't famous for being the type to 'read.' From the beginning, almost any musician I approached said 'Yes!' with the first phone call. Allen Toussaint, Steve Swallow, Taj Mahal, David Murray, Don Cherry, Carla Bley, Lester Bowie, and Olu Dara all jumped in at the mention of Ish's name. Some, like Steve Swallow, Gil Evans, and Taj, knew his work intimately."

Recalling the 1983 session for "Betty's Ball Blues," Hanrahan marveled at "Taj's presence and joy of music, and enthusiasm and his love of Ish's work," and how he masterfully "brought the band down to a slow mid-tempo easy ride," to create the right groove to deliver Reed's fateful saga of Betty and Dupree.

"Peg and Pete and Me," from Stan Ridgway's 1989 album *Mosquitos*, recounts the sordid tale of a pair of star-crossed lovers, evoking the plot to the classic 1946 film noir *The Postman Always Rings Twice,* starring Lana Turner and John Garfield.

"Like a lot of my songs, I wrote the music first to 'Peg and Pete and Me,'" Ridgway recalled. "It was urgent music and racing towards some kind of climax. Sometime later I went to a swap meet out in Newhall, [California]. It was about 100 degrees that day. I'd walked by a couple arguing over the stuff they were selling there. Then another man approached them, dressed in oil stained bib overalls, and said 'Hey you can't sell that stuff! It's mine!' I kept walking as they started to argue over boxes of old clothes and books, and who owned what and who didn't. When I got home I started to write about a drifter kind of guy who worked at a gas station for a couple whose marriage was on the rocks. I could see where it was going and from there it took off."

The song's protagonist, "Me," works for Pete, fixing cars, until his boss passes out one night after drinking himself into a stupor. Bored and unfulfilled, Peg then pulls their bewildered employee down on the floor for a good time.

"Forbidden fruit, but what the hell, I bit," "Me" shrugs. Casual about their sleazy liaison at first, he begins to worry as their fling quickly flares out of control. "Tonight Peg, we gotta stop this thing," he pleads, to no avail. Peg, it turns out, has got "a certain plan" of her own. "Everything is in my name," she coos in his ear. And after the magic words "I love you so very much," "Me" is immediately convinced to do her bidding and kills Pete while unconscious.

> He'll never feel a thing,
> Just like he never woke up,
> And after that it will be just us.

Having murdered his boss, "Me" wakes up the following morning to discover Peg long gone and a detective standing over him. The jury, not surprisingly, finds him guilty and sends the poor sap up the river "for ninety-nine to life" where he's got nothing but time to ruminate over the whole wretched affair. "If there's any advice I can give from this cell," Ridgway sings, his reedy voice rife with irony, "Never trust a rich dead man's wife."

As evil as the act of murder between lovers, the heinous act of matricide is portrayed in Townes Van Zandt's "Dollar Bill Blues," in which the protagonist slits his mother's throat just "to get her pearls" before casting himself, "into a whirl before a bunch of swine" down at the local saloon. Built on minor chords, the song reveals strains of traditional Appalachian fiddle tunes that give its deeply disturbed lyric a haunted, timeless quality, while the images in Van Zandt's lyric conjure the surreal carnival atmosphere of peasant taverns portrayed by the Flemish Renaissance painter Pieter Bruegel the Elder.

Perhaps the most disturbing of all love-gone-wrong songs comes from Violent Femmes' Gordon Gano, who sings of a man who commits the atrocious act of throwing his "darling daughter" down a well. Gano seems to teem with self-loathing as he delivers the stark lyrics of his child-murder ballad "Country Death Song."

Like the poor, alienated, struggling South Dakota farmer "Hollis

Brown," from Bob Dylan's chilling tale of the same name, Gano's protagonist, who confesses he "never knew still waters," also follows a mad path of twisted logic to a tragic conclusion, which ultimately leads him to "making plans to kill his own kind."

In a calculated act of murder that follows in the tradition of "Pretty Polly" and "Little Sadie," the deranged father lures his helpless child to her doom by promising her an unforgettable adventure:

> *"Come, little daughter," I said to the youngest one,*
> *"Put your coat on, we'll have some fun.*
> *We'll go to the mountains, the one to explore."*
> *Her face then lit up, I was standing by the door.*
>
> *"Come, little daughter, I will carry the lantern,*
> *We'll go out tonight, we'll go to the caverns,*
> *We'll go out tonight, we'll go to the caves,*
> *Kiss your mother goodnight, and remember that God*
> *saves."*

"Where do you draw the line between an outlaw and a murderer?" Gano mused. "I don't know. . . . I don't think I ever wrote a traditional outlaw song per se, of a guy who pulled a stickup and then got away on his horse or in a Buick."

Gano makes a good point, one that I and many others have wrestled with. Murder *is* a crime and a criminal *is* an outlaw, so where does one draw the line exactly? Must there be a chase involved for the perpetrator to be an outlaw? Does the term imply that the offender must become a fugitive preceding arrest? Unfortunately the definition offered by *Webster's Dictionary* will not end the debate. On one hand it describes an outlaw as: "a person who has broken the law and who is hiding or running away to avoid punishment," while a little further down we read: "one that is unconventional or rebellious," which throws the door wide open to ne'er-do-wells of every shape and stripe.

"'Country Death Song' was actually written back when I was in my junior year of high school," Gano continued. "I started writing a verse per class, throughout the day, in no particular order. It began with the idea of the man pushing his daughter into the well."

While alienated high school students have a knack of composing poetry of an unnerving nature, Gano's two-chord Appalachian-style ballad conjured the desolation of the human soul in words worthy of a Truman Capote story.

"Country Death Song" is a particularly diabolical portrait of the cold-blooded slaughter of a complete innocent. With utter detachment, the cajoling father reassures his little girl every step of the way until he finally fulfills his nagging goal of premeditated murder.

> *I led her to a hole, a deep black well.*
> *I said, "Make a wish, make sure not to tell,*
> *And close your eyes, dear, and count to seven.*
> *You know your papa loves you, good children go to heaven."*
> *I gave her a push, I gave her a shove,*
> *I pushed with all my might.*

And this is where things turn seriously bizarre.

> *I pushed with all my love.*
> *I threw my child into a bottomless pit,*
> *She was screaming as she fell, but I never heard her hit.*

"I can't recall the first time I heard the Carter Family or Johnny Cash records," Gano said. "I was pretty young. My father used to play guitar and their music was always around the house. So a line like 'Gather round boys to the tale that I tell' wasn't that unusual for me to hear and pick up and sing."

The Violent Femmes' best known songs from their 1983 self-titled debut album were for the most part autobiographical, stark personal confessions that focused on the foibles of teenage life, from sexual frustration and contempt for authority to back-stabbing friends and contemplations on suicide.

"Country Death Song," which kicked off the trio's second release, 1984's *Hallowed Ground*, was a radical departure for Gano and the band. "This song was the least un-me thing I'd ever written. It's complete fiction. I'm just a narrator telling a story," Gano explained. "It was just a way of telling the news or a story, an old tradition that goes way back before cowboy songs, to ancient Greece and Egypt. My sister who, has kids of her own [Gano became a father himself in late 2015], forbids the song to be played around her house! But for me, oddly enough, it connects with good, warm family feelings. It's an enjoyable song to do."

Every time Violent Femmes perform "Country Death Song" live, the song inevitably elicits a strong reaction from their audience, not of shock or horror over the murder of a helpless child, but oddly of cheers, as if they are rooting for the pitiful lunatic confessing to have lost his mind.

"I must be oblivious or ignorant," Gordon ruminated. "I never thought they were cheering because the narrator threw his daughter down the well! There's a pause in the song and then we go into some improvised music. I always figured that maybe they loved our wild solos."

6

BAD TO THE BONE

Outlaw songs are a celebration of human potential or energy, even in the extreme negative," Jolie Holland ruminated. "They're a statement of possibility, an acknowledgement that people can be violent or choose to love. The songs are reminders that gentleness and law-abiding are not essential givens of humanity. We also can't forget that outlaw songs evolved in the absence of movies or theater in general, so that outlaw songs were the Westerns, which my Grandpa called 'shoot 'em ups,' the gangster movies or the crime dramas of their day."

Following in the tradition of Wild West gunslingers and Prohibition-era gangsters, bluesmen from the Mississippi Delta and the Texas Piney Woods to the South Side of Chicago, intending to create a larger-than-life image by fueling the public's imagination, inevitably adopted evocative nicknames such as Lightnin' (Hopkins), Muddy Waters, Howlin' Wolf, and Skip (as in "skipping town") James. Perhaps the greatest handle of the time belonged to Peetie Wheatstraw, better known as "The Devil's Son-in-Law" or "The High Sheriff of Hell," whose slick style, razor-sharp pressed suits, and blinding smile ultimately eclipsed his forgettable music.

The most legendary of this bunch of musical toughs went by the innocuous handle of Robert Johnson. Johnson would put every future Madison Avenue adman to shame by concocting one of the great myths of the twentieth century, when he claimed to have sold his soul to the Devil, one moonlit night at a Mississippi crossroads, in return for a few brief years as one of the most brilliant songwriters and guitarists of his (or any) day. While most musicians and their outlaw counterparts led bands, Johnson, the poet laureate of the Delta blues, was a loner who traveled and played solo for most of his brief career. According to Son House, the backsliding preacher who allegedly taught young Robert to play guitar, the mysterious explanation that Johnson gave for his supernatural virtuosity was "a joke" that now, even in the twenty-first century, continues to elude most folks.

These days, hip hoppers are rarely seen without their posse, much like Jesse James, who relied on his gang (and was, in the end, killed by one of its members). The road is a lonesome and dangerous place and desperados need somebody they can trust to watch their backs and handle the driving while they shut their eyes for a couple hours to catch up on some much-needed rest. But as Muddy Waters used to sing, "Who can you trust?"

The origins of gangsta style can be traced back to the fabled lives and evocative lyrics of Robert Johnson and Chicago songwriter Willie Dixon. Dixon, originally a prize-fighting boxer who turned house bassist for Chess Records, was known for his gold-tooth grin, rakish derby, and fine suits. His economic, imagist poetry captured the true "flava" and hustle of Chicago's South Side, telling of colorful characters like "Automatic Slim" and "Butcher Knife Totin' Annie," from his tune "Wang Dang Doodle." Willie wrote dozens of hits for Muddy Waters and Howlin' Wolf, including "Little Red Rooster," "Spoonful," and "Back Door Man." Over the decades, these songs became standards of the blues genre, recorded and performed worldwide by a younger generation of longhair rockers, from American bands like the Doors, the Grateful Dead, and the Allman Brothers to the Rolling Stones, Cream, and Led Zeppelin on the other side of the pond.

Dixon's greatest interpreter Muddy Waters was the epitome of solid cool as he sang "I'm drinkin' TNT, I'm smokin' dynamite" in Willie's gangsta anthem "I'm Ready." From his carefully coiffed pompadour and meticulous mustache down to his alligator shoes, it was clear that Muddy Waters meant business, and nobody, not even his old, unpredictable rival, the blustery Howlin' Wolf, could manage to wrest his legacy as the King of the Chicago Blues away from him.

Originally a folk song sung by African American workers around Memphis levee camps, the ballad of "Stagger Lee" is also known as "Stack O'Lee" (as sung by Woody Guthrie) and even "Skeeg O'Lee" (recorded by the little-known Chicago-based duo Ford & Ford, who had the good fortune to be accompanied by the great clarinetist Johnny Dodds). It was passed down orally from the mid-nineteenth century until it was first recorded by the "Mother of the Blues," Gertrude "Ma" Rainey, in the 1920s. Numerous recorded versions soon followed, most notably from Furry Lewis and Mississippi John Hurt. "Stagger Lee" would become a standard in the repertoires of many New Orleans piano players, from the legendary Archibald to Professor Longhair and Dr. John. Malcolm Rebbenack (better known as Dr. John) cut the tune for his 1972 roots rock album *Gumbo*. He recalled in the record's liner notes that Leon T. Gross (a.k.a. Archibald), a Crescent City ragtime piano professor who played a Bourbon Street saloon called the Pink Poodle for more than twenty years, had a hit with the song on the Imperial label back in 1950.

"I don't think Archibald made a dime for this song," Rebbenack wrote in his memoir *Under a Voodoo Moon*. "'Stack-A-Lee' had already been in the public domain for years, and no matter how singular or popular Gross's arrangement was, no music publisher would cut him a check for it. After that he would never make a record again," Rebbenack said.

Over the years, Stagger Lee, the man, as well as the lyric recounting the fatal night that he shot Billy Lyons, continued to go through constant transformation. Woody Guthrie turned the song into a cowboy ballad, singing of Stack's outrageous exploits in his thick Okie accent. Whether sung as a folk song or a funky R&B number, hollered over a row of horns, the lyric relates the story of a famous murder (committed in either Memphis or St. Louis) perpetrated by one Lee Sheldon upon Billy De Lyon, or Billy Lyons, or even in some instances Billy the Lion (who is occasionally described as a friend of the "bad man, cruel ol' Stagger Lee"). In the song, Billy impulsively snatches Sheldon's beloved Stetson hat from his head while in the heat of a gambling dispute. Starting out so cocky, he winds up begging for his life, pleading down on his knees that he has, in some versions of the tune, up to five children and a very sickly (sometimes "shapely") wife dependent upon him back home. None of which means much to Mr. Lee, who draws his pistol and plugs Billy full of holes, making a Swiss cheese of him, until, as we're told, the "bullets went through Billy and broke the bartender's looking glass." Apparently, Mr. Lee wanted it well understood that no one was going to mess with his beloved Stetson and live to tell about it.

"The story of Stagger Lee is all about materialism," Jolie Holland pointed out. "Like so many other criminals, he was driven to commit murder over an act as trivial as Billy snatching his Stetson hat!"

It seems that nearly everyone who ever has sung the tune has claimed authorship of it. One of the most popular versions of the tune was "written" by Lloyd Price and Harold Logan. Price, who grew up in New Orleans, singing gospel music, would transform "Stagger Lee" into a catchy R&B hit that shot straight to No. 1 for four weeks at the beginning of February 1959. In Lloyd's rocking rendition, Lyons winds up face down on the barroom floor, dead in a pool of his own blood, while the backup singers gleefully chant "Go Stagger Lee! Go Stagger Lee!"

The "Wicked" Wilson Pickett would also break into the Top 30 with a hard funk version of the song in 1967. "Stagger Lee" returned once more in 1971, ascending the charts to No. 25, thanks to a clean-cut bubble-gummer by the name of Tommy Roe, who undoubtedly would be more at home on the set of Dick Clark's *Where the Action Is* than cruisin' the mean streets of Stack's 'hood, be it Memphis, East St. Louis, or Compton.

"Stackalee" was originally submitted to the song collector/record producer John Lomax in 1910 by Ella Scott Fischer. Said to be based on an actual shooting in Memphis, some time around 1900, the tune was already popular amongst black longshoremen. But Lomax couldn't find any evidence of the famous murder when he later researched it in a 1933 city survey, which causes one to wonder if it didn't indeed take place in St. Louis (the setting for a slew of outlaw and murder ballads, from "Pretty Boy Floyd" and "Brady and Duncan" to "Little Sadie").

There have been hundreds of versions of Stagger Lee's legend, most of them recorded since the 1960s, by Bob Dylan, the Grateful Dead, Taj Mahal, and even the California hippie/feelgood band, the Youngbloods. Nick Cave and the Bad Seeds' take on "Stagger Lee" (from his 1996 album *Murder Ballads*) is absolutely harrowing. Growling over a bone-crunching beat, Cave virtually spits the story, sparing no detail, while punctuating his chilling verse with a smattering of "motherfuckers" that fly as fast and furious as hot lead from his brutal mouth.

"The personification of Stagger Lee goes on anywhere there's people who emigrated out of the South, particularly in African American society," Taj Mahal explained.

The ritual of toasting a young man was akin to a tribal bar mitzvah. "When you're around fourteen or fifteen your uncles toast you into the life of being a man," Taj said. "Stagger Lee was also a toast. It was a big boasting thing that Stagger Lee fell into, to show everybody how bad of a motherfucker he really was. People just ran with it in every possible direction and the song has worked its way into the American songbook. The first time I heard it was from Lloyd Price. It was so good the way he laid it down that I knew there had to be a backstory to it. It obviously wasn't just something somebody'd thought up and just wrote down. It had too much critical mass and density to it. It was a true story, something that actually went down. Then I started hearing other versions of it from Mississippi John Hurt, Mance Lipscomb, and Jesse Fuller."

Stagger Lee, the every-pimp, smolders with style and bravura, like Robert Johnson, whose "Stop Breakin' Down" warns ladies everywhere, "the stuff I got'll bust your brains out, baby."

Oliver Trager points out that "the [Grateful] Dead's version of 'Stagger Lee' [written by Jerry Garcia and Robert Hunter] brings the tale full circle by having Delia De Lyons, the widow of the song's victim, Billy, who was killed over the talismanic Stetson he lost in a crap game, wreak revenge by taking matters into her own hands and felling the notorious, some say demon-like, Stagger Lee with a revolver. After concluding her necessary dirty work, Delia leaves the bucket-of-blood bar and strolls down Singapore Street, passing a three-piece band standing on the corner playing 'Nearer My God to Thee.' Delia, however, whistles a different tune, identified by the song's narrator as 'Look Out Stagger Lee,' the very song being sung, which coyly implies that the song and by extension the legend, and even the outlaw song tradition, shall continue to live on."

"Stagger Lee," like Willie Dixon's "Hoochie Coochie Man" and Curtis Mayfield's "Super Fly," has remained a definitive portrait of the inner city thug, pimp, and pusher who brazenly boasts of the power of his guns and money, along with his unquenchable sexual desire and ultimately his supernatural power: a mojo he claims to possess and can call on any time, at a moment's notice, to psych out his many enemies. Stagger Lee does as he damn well pleases and takes whatever he wants as he passes by, flaunting his outrageous style in the face of an uptight (and predominantly white) society.

Yet something always seems to be gnawing at him. He's a rather touchy fellow and is known to impulsively dust any fool for just looking at him the wrong way. For in the back of his mind Stagger Lee knows he owes a debt to the devil, and his time, he is certain, won't be long. But Stagger Lee's spirit can never die. He is eternal. Even hell can't hold him. A number of versions of the song claim that when Stagger Lee makes the journey down below, he quickly winds up taking over the joint. Satan, loath to do battle with Stack, immediately tries to coerce him to return to earth, with the lavish promise that he can have his run of the place on the condition that he stays out of Satan's neck of the woods.

Going to hell for Stack is akin to taking a trip to the spa, where he stops by to rest a spell and bathe his weary soul in the bubbling sulfur pits of Hades before returning to the earthly plane once more. There he takes the form once more of the latest badass, whether a musician like Miles Davis, Jimi Hendrix, or Prince, a sports figure like Jack Johnson, Muhammad Ali, or Dennis Rodman, or even perhaps a radical militant like Huey Newton or Eldridge Cleaver. Wanted dead or alive by the self-appointed sheriff of the free world, George W. Bush, Osama Bin Laden, while on the lam in the mountains of Pakistan, was clearly one man's devil and another man's hero.

"There's just so many variations of the song, it's nearly impossible to keep track of all of them," explained Greenwich Village guitarist/actor Erik Frandsen. "Once, years ago, Dave Van Ronk and I had what you might call a 'Stagger Lee–off.' We both sat down with our guitars and shared about a dozen of the same versions until Dave eventually won. He knew two or three others that I'd never heard before."

While Frandsen's tale intrigues, Greil Marcus, author of *Mystery*

Train, claims that Dr. John is capable of singing "Stagger Lee" "for half an hour without ever repeating a lyric."

Amongst a million rumors and half-baked hypotheses, Mike Wilhelm's explanation of Stagger Lee, and the man behind the myth, remains one of the most durable. While providing names, dates, and even an old newspaper article to back up his theory, Wilhelm (lead guitarist and singer with the legendary 1960s San Francisco psychedelic band the Charlatans) never loses the mystery of the man: "Most of us of a certain age remember the hit song from the 1950s, sung by Lloyd Price, but most are not aware that Stagger Lee was a real person. The real Stagger Lee was a St. Louis resident named Lee Shelton, born March 16, 1865, and known on the street as 'Stag Lee.' Shelton was a taxi carriage driver and pimp of sorts, known as a 'mack.' Macks were known for their flamboyant dress and manner, the prototypes of the modern 'gangsta.' He shot his friend William 'Billy' Lyons following a drunken argument on December 27, 1895. Lyons subsequently died from his injuries, and Shelton was tried, convicted, and sentenced to prison for the murder and died in prison of tuberculosis on March 11, 1912, just five days shy of his forty-seventh birthday."

A news article appeared the day after the shooting in the *St. Louis Daily Globe-Democrat* on December 28, 1895, under the headline, "Shot in Curtis's Place." "Shelton's name," Wilhelm pointed out, "is misspelled in the article as 'Sheldon.'"

"William Lyons, 25, colored, a levee hand, living at 1410 Morgan Street, was shot in the abdomen yesterday evening at 10 o'clock in the saloon of Bill Curtis, at Eleventh and Morgan Streets, by Lee Sheldon, also colored. Both parties, it seems, had been drinking and were feeling in exuberant spirits. Lyons and Sheldon were friends and were talking together. The discussion drifted to politics and an argument was started, the conclusion of which was that Lyons snatched Sheldon's hat from his head. The latter indignantly demanded its return. Lyons refused, and Sheldon drew his revolver and shot Lyons in the abdomen. Lyons was taken to the Dispensary, where his wounds were pronounced serious. He was removed to the city hospital. At the time of the shooting, the saloon was crowded with Negroes. Sheldon is a carriage driver and lives at North Twelfth Street. When his victim fell to the floor Sheldon took his hat from the hand of the wounded man and coolly walked away. He was subsequently arrested and locked up at the Chestnut Street Station. Sheldon is also known as 'Stag' Lee."

"If there is a lesson to be learned from this tale it is this," said Wilhelm, drolly. "Never bring up politics on social occasions."

According to the eccentric song collector/film animator Harry Smith, who chose Frank Hutchinson's 1927 recording of "Stackalee" as the opening track to his epic compilation *Anthology of American Folk Music Vol. 1, Ballads*, the murder "probably took place in Memphis in 1900." Greil Marcus has pointed out that at the time Memphis was not just the murder capital of America, but of the entire world. "The daily carnage between blacks was unbelievable," he wrote. Under such circumstances, Marcus thought it "odd" that "a single incident would be considered that memorable" and speculates that Stacker Lee may actually have been a white man as he was "never even charged [with Billy Lyon's murder], let alone hung." Beyond the curious question of Stack's racial heritage lies the sad truth that black-on-black violence would have mattered little at that time to the notoriously corrupt judicial system of the American South.

To further complicate matters historically, there seem to have been two Stacker Lees: one white, the other African American. Samuel Stacker Lee was the brother (Greil Marcus firmly believes that he was probably the son, based on birth and death dates) of James Lee Sr., the magnate of the Lee Steamship Line, and a friend of Jefferson Davis. At age sixteen, Samuel "Stacker Lee" had joined the Confederacy to fight alongside the notoriously brutal General Nathan Bedford Forrest, who later became the first Grand Wizard of the Ku Klux Klan. Tainted by the moral degradation that came with the devastation of his beloved South, "Stacker Lee" became a ne'er-do-well gambler and philanderer who sired a bi-racial son, also known as Stacker Lee (further adding to the confusion of Stagger Lee's identity), who quickly garnered a reputation that surpassed that of his wayward father. Author Shields McIlwaine described the younger Lee, an employee of the Anchor Steamship Line, as "a small dark man with a bad eye," while others portrayed him as "tall, good looking, and mean."

Once more, Harry Smith summed up the song with a few choice words that pop with wit and economy: "Theft of Stetson hat causes deadly dispute. Victim identifies self as family man." Frank Hutchinson's rustic reading of the tune featured a twangy voice and a driving guitar, accompanied by a harmonica played in a rack, which influenced future interpretations by both Doc Watson and Bob Dylan. Judging by Frank's strident rendition of the tune, it seems nearly impossible to imagine all the funky versions of "Stagger Lee" to come, particularly the Isley Brothers' 1963 romping rendition, which featured a young Jimi Hendrix drilling the groove with Chuck Berry–style riffs, while the Brothers whoop in falsetto like the sons of Little Richard.

In the twenty-first century, the myth of "Stagger Lee" is still very much alive and thriving, thanks to Beck, who recorded the song with a clean, sparse, fingerpicking style and steady tapping toe in the tradition of Mississippi John Hurt, and the tattooed, writhing Amy Winehouse, who performed the tune live, bringing to Lloyd Price's arrangement all the sleaze of a self-conscious housewife auditioning at a seedy neon-lit strip club on the outskirts of town.

A silver-haired, gold-cap-toothed Samuel L. Jackson talked more than his fair share of trash when performing "Stack O Lee" with the help of a sizzling backup band in the 2006 film *Black Snake Moan*. In the role of Lazarus Redd (who, much like Son House, is a conflicted bluesman who turns to god and farming in penance for his sinful ways), Jackson pays homage to the Mississippi barrelhouse bluesman R. L. Burnside, who regularly performed "Stack-O-Lee" as a driving John Lee Hooker–style blues, dropping whatever melodic nuances had become associated with the tune over the years.

With its rumbling drums and funky, grungy guitar riff (played on a searing slide and wah-wah) the Black Keys' "Stack Shot Billy" evokes the lonesome cry of Jimi Hendrix's "Hear My Train A'Comin'." The garage rock duo of Dan Auerbach and Patrick Carney helped usher the legend of Stacker Lee into mainstream America by way of *The David Letterman Show* on January 5, 2005, inspiring their host (arguably the ultimate Caucasian) to declare "Nice job," before breaking for a commercial.

"Super Fly" is the title song to the 1972 Blaxploitation film of the same name and the moniker of its coke dealer hero. Written and sung by Curtis Mayfield, it was a breakaway from the typical girl-boy love song that dominated the soul charts at the time, thanks to Berry Gordy and his stable of hit-makers at Motown Records. By the early 1970s, a handful of black artists, inspired by the populist anthems of Sly and the Family Stone (who'd been inspired by Bob Dylan's early protest songs to speak his mind on matters of race and war), began to make a new, grittier "message music" that finally addressed the real problems of inner city life that most African Americans faced on a daily basis.

Mayfield had begun his career singing in gospel groups before joining the Impressions in the late 1950s. Among his chart-topping R&B hits was the sultry "Gypsy Woman," which featured his trademark brandy-smooth falsetto vocals and his slinky Stratocaster style. Mayfield's standard "People Get Ready" sounded like a hundred-year-old gospel number that revealed a soul-deep spirituality. At the same time, Mayfield could also write irresistible chart-topping dance hits like "Monkey Time."

"Super Fly" soared straight to No. 8 on the pop charts and No. 5 on R&B charts, while the album sold over two million copies. With "Freddie's Dead" (which shot to No. 4 on the pop charts, No. 2 on R&B) and "Pusherman," Curtis was one of the few black artists of his day to speak directly to the excess of sex and drugs as well as the obsession with materialism in ghetto culture. A reincarnation of "Stagger Lee," "Super Fly" was just another sparkling link in the fourteen-carat gold chain of black audacity. Along with *Shaft* and its accompanying funky soul/jazz soundtrack, composed and arranged by Isaac Hayes, *Super Fly* and the Blaxploitation movies of the early 1970s helped elevate the black antihero to prominence, while serving as a harbinger of the gangsta rap culture to come.

Written by harmonica wailer Noah Lewis, "Minglewood Blues" was first recorded in 1928, as a clanky twelve-bar progression, by banjo-player Gus Cannon's Jug Stompers, which featured Lewis in its original line up. Two years later, Lewis recorded the song again under his own name, this time as the "New Minglewood Blues." Over the years, the tune has captured the mythic imagination of everyone from the blind guitarist extraordinaire Doc Watson to the eccentric Jim Kweskin, whose Jug Band recorded it simply as "Minglewood" on their 1967 release *Garden of Joy*. The song's infamous lyric, "I was born in a desert and raised in a lion's den," seemed almost believable when roared by Geoff Muldaur.

"If ya go by Memphis, please stop in Minglewood," Muldaur moans, "'cause the women in a cave don't mean no man no good." Located about an hour north of Memphis, near Ashport, Tennessee, or within its city limits, the legendary town of Minglewood (actually known to the locals as Menglewood) housed a thriving sawmill and box factory in the 1920s, which was demolished sometime in the 1940s. Known for showing "a good time" to the proletariat looking for a place to drink and gamble, Minglewood had quite a reputation, thanks to Noah Lewis's song, that spread near and far. Geoff Muldaur's old pal and sometime collaborator, painter/folk singer Eric von Schmidt, not only sang the song in his alternately gruff and tender voice, but christened his Sarasota, Florida, art studio "Minglewood" in honor of the mythical town. There was even a Canadian roots rock group who went by the name of the Minglewood Band, formed in 1974 by Matt Minglewood (better known to his mother as Roy Alexander Batherson).

The Grateful Dead first recorded a bouncy psychedelic dance version of "New Minglewood Blues" (featuring Ron "Pig Pen" McKernan pumping a Vox Continental organ) for their 1967 self-titled debut album. Sung by rhythm guitarist Bob Weir, it was an excellent vehicle for Jerry Garcia's sinewy lead-guitar riffs. Nearly a decade later, the Dead reprised the song with a swampy blues groove, renaming it the "All New Minglewood Blues" for their 1978 release *Shakedown Street*.

Whether titled "New," "New New," or even "All New," "Minglewood Blues" has continued to change stylistically over the years, taking the shape of everything from a zany jug band rave-up or somber folk-blues tune to a groovy dance number or sultry funk groove. Despite its rather chauvinistic advice—"Don't you never let one woman rule your mind, She keep you worried and troubled all the time"—the song continues to appeal to one generation after the next, as witnessed by the Old Crow Medicine Show's high-octane rendition, recorded in 2006. While hardly PC, the hard lovin' protagonist's crime of "stealing pretty women from their men" remains a misdemeanor at best.

Teeming with supernatural bravado, Willie Dixon's "Hoochie Coochie Man" seems to magically expand the aura of anyone who delivers its lyric, from Muddy Waters to Mose Allison to the Allman Brothers. Whether wielding a black cat bone, a John the Conqueror root, or a silver-plated pistol, Muddy Waters was not a man to be trifled with.

The same can be said for Bo Diddley, whose romping "Who Do You Love?" boasts of the singer's extraordinary mystical powers. Not only does he live in a house whose chimney is "made from a human skull" but also, like the Hindu god Shiva, he wears a "cobra snake for a necktie."

Inspired by such hoodoo poetics, the Rolling Stones' Mick Jagger would fashion the lyrics to their hard-rocking 1968 hit, "Jumpin' Jack Flash," inspired by Keith Richards's gardener, a character so thick-skinned and crusty they imagined he was "born in a cross-fire hurricane." Having survived a torturous childhood, being reared by a "bearded hag" who administered the occasional Dickens-like parochial-school whipping, the indomitable Jack manages to come to terms with all life has handed him; for better or worse, everything in the end is "all right now, in fact it's a gas," as Jagger yowled.

Donning the bad boy persona came naturally to Mick, who'd begun to flirt with the dark forces at the time of the release of the Stones' psychedelic disasterpiece *Their Satanic Majesties Request*, in December 1967. Inspired by Kenneth Anger's films and Mikhail Bulgakov's gothic novel *The Master and Margarita*, Mick and Keith would transform the three-minute pop song into a terrifying voodoo ceremony, melding pulsing conga drums and savage grunts and cries into their 1969 ode to the Prince of Darkness, "Sympathy for the Devil." But Jagger's Mephistopheles posturing would soon spank him and the band, on December 6, 1969, at the doomed Altamont Speedway free concert. Bullied and beaten by the Hells Angels who'd been hired to handle security, the stoned crowd surged towards the stage in fear and panic as the band slogged through their fragmented set. Suddenly, a black eighteen-year-old man, pistol-toting Meredith Hunter (who, some claim, intended to kill Jagger) was fatally stabbed by the Angels. The infamously brutal "Wild West" suddenly achieved a new level of weird. Not even Keith Richards, the degenerate king of outlaw rockers, had any influence over the situation as Jagger begged the bewildered throng of fans, gathered just months after Woodstock, to be "cool."

Released just one day before the Altamont tragedy, the Stones' *Let It Bleed* featured some of their gloomiest songs to date. With the opening track "Gimme Shelter," Jagger and Richards paint an apocalyptic vision of the future, a world besieged by sweeping fires, foreboding storms, and imminent war (which was just "a shot away"). The haunting lyric conjures a scene from Shakespeare's *Macbeth*, where the transgressions of mankind have triggered an imbalance in nature. Horses, once gentle and tame, bust free of their stalls and begin to devour each other.

The down and dirty "Midnight Rambler" leads off the second side of the album, portrayed as a knife-toting nocturnal predator ("wrapped up in a black cat cloak") who evokes Bertolt Brecht's "Mack the Knife." But Jagger's "hit and run raper" is far more menacing than the charming murderer of *The Threepenny Opera*. The Stones' perverse protagonist wrestles to control his "cold-fanged anger" before sticking his "knife right down your throat."

The cocky protagonist of George Thorogood's "Bad to the Bone" clearly suffers from an incurable case of narcissism as he unabashedly pulls every trick in the book, trying to psych out his competition with a preposterous display of bluster and bravado. Over a raw, driving John Lee Hooker–style boogie, courtesy of his band the Destroyers, Thorogood repeatedly growls his mantra of "Buh-buh-bad! Buh-buh-bad to the Bone," while his grungy guitar slips and slides and a raspy sax howls the blues. Thorogood's vocal stuttering and spluttering is second only to that of the Who's Roger Daltrey when he stammered his way up the charts with their 1965 anthem of disaffected youth, "My Generation." Both Thorogood and Daltery apparently shared the same inspiration for their jumbled deliveries: John Lee Hooker's classic "Stuttering Blues," in which the singer nervously begs a gorgeous girl for her phone number.

"I'm So Bad, Baby I Don't Care" by Motörhead, from their 1999 album *Everything Louder Than Everyone Else*, cleverly incorporates every imaginable cliché from the blues canon, brazenly borrowing lyrics from Gus Cannon's "Minglewood Blues" and Jimi Hendrix's "Voodoo Chile," while freely tossing in classic phrases from Willie Dixon and the Rolling Stones' lascivious "Stray Cat Blues." Over a bone-crunching beat and grinding buzz-saw guitar, Motörhead's legendary lead singer/bassist Lemmy Kilmister claims his bed is crawling with rattle-snakes. Thankfully, he never takes himself too seriously as he boasts of making love to mountain lions. Evoking Willie Dixon's "Eyesight to the Blind," Lemmy brags of his supernatural healing powers, claiming he can make the lame walk. Kilmister's famously droll sense of humor glimmers through the song's hilarious lyrics as he claims to be "Black-hearted to the bone" and "Older than the Rolling Stones."

Lemmy and company would once more revisit the perils and pit-falls of the fugitive's fleeting life, with their hard-driving song "Outlaw," from their 2010 album *The World Is Yours.*

Jimi Hendrix's "Voodoo Chile" paints the sultry portrait of an other-worldly blues shaman who is not to be trifled with (after all, he can chop down a mountain with the edge of his hand!), but the image of the psychedelic R&B sorcerer doing psychic battle "with a satchel of gris-gris in his hand" was perhaps best personified by Dr. John during his flamboyant "Night Tripper" phase, when, adorned in an array of paint and feathers like a medicine man, he coolly informed his fans that walking on "Gilded Splinters" was no sweat.

Back in the 1960s, young rock singers, looking to prove themselves, regularly adopted the XXL personae of respected older bluesmen like Muddy Waters, Howlin' Wolf, and Willie Dixon, who wrote the Rolling Stones' 1964 hit "Little Red Rooster." With the British blues explosion of the early 1960s, every "beat" group of the day seemed to adopt its own American bluesman for its muse. Performing and recording their songs loaned these young neophytes a bit of "cool" and "cred," but it also helped revitalize the aging artists' careers by introducing them to a younger "mod" audience. Van Morrison wholeheartedly idolized

Lead Belly, while the pint-sized punk from Newcastle, Eric Burdon of the Animals, flaunted John Lee Hooker's smoldering "Gangster of Love" image as he growled a righteous rendition of "Boom, Boom, Boom." When Howlin' Wolf croaked "I eats mo' chicken [than] any man seen," you never doubted him for a minute. The Wolf unabashedly celebrated himself as "three hundred pounds of joy" in the Willie Dixon–penned song of that name. He apparently had a voracious appetite, whether hungering for drumsticks or wings or "the little girls" who, as he groaned and growled in Dixon's "Back Door Man," innately seemed to "understand" everything that "the men don't know."

Although the Wolf put his personal stamp on everything he sang of Willie's, the Doors managed to own a piece of Dixon's tune as well, bringing its gritty street poetry to a new generation of rock fans. Side Two of the Doors' 1967 self-titled debut album opened with one of Jim Morrison's most blistering screams. Morrison sounded (and was) volatile, dangerous, and unpredictable, like a wild animal suddenly freed from its cage and on the loose, making his "midnight creep." Meanwhile, Robby Kreiger's guitar, fat with fuzz-tone, soared and swooped around his every word like a maniacal bumblebee.

But what exactly is the dreaded Back Door Man's crime? What law, if any, has he broken? His offence is ultimately the trespassing of an unspoken code of ethics; he skulks from door to door, "picking someone else's patch" (as Neil Young put it in his song "Country Home"), making passionate love to one woman after the next. Married or not, they all find him terribly irresistible. Even after he's put on trial "for murder in the first degree," the judge's wife, unable to control herself, causes a public spectacle. Embarrassing her husband, who's deliberating on the bench, she pleads from the courtroom gallery, "Let the man go free!"

Countless songs have glorified mythic figures, from "Stagger Lee" and "Superfly" to "Back Door Man" and Ice-T's "Cop Killer." All celebrate the irrepressible ego and attitude that fuels the outlaws' motives, no matter what form their crime ultimately takes, from devious to brilliant, even if in the end it remains a nagging impulse, ultimately unacted upon. As the Four Lads remind us in their 1956 hit "Standing On the Corner," "You can't go to jail for what you're thinking, / Or for that woo look in your eye."

The American gangster, Al Capone (1899–1947). Mugshot taken June 17, 1931. *(Wikimedia Commons)*

A monument of the ace archer and freewheeling philanthropist Robin Hood, beneath Nottingham Castle. *(Wikimedia Commons)*

Machine Gun Kelly, a.k.a. George Kelly Barnes (1895–1954), bootlegger, bank robber, and kidnapper. *(Wikimedia Commons)*

Bonnie Elizabeth Parker and Clyde Chestnut Barrow, March 1933. This photo was discovered at their hideout in Joplin, Missouri. *(Wikimedia Commons)*

FBI Wanted poster for Patty
Campbell Hearst, a.k.a "Tania,"
urban guerilla, 1974.
(Wikimedia Commons)

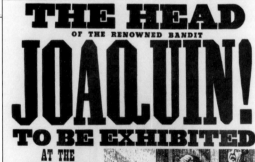

Poster advertising the
decapitated head of Joaquin
Murrieta, "the Mexican
Robin Hood," (1829–1853).
(Wikimedia Commons)

I DID TIME WITH
DAVID ALLAN COE

This bumper sticker proves it! Sharing the glory with David Allan Coe.
(Author's collection)

Butch Cassidy and the Sundance Kid poster. Film released September 23, 1969.
(Author's collection)

The Harder They Come poster. Starring Jimmy Cliff, the 1972 film helped spread reggae worldwide.
(Author's collection)

Outlaw chic. The South rises
again with the release of
the Allman Brothers Band's
debut, November 4, 1969.
(Author's collection)

Arlo Guthrie's dope anthem
"Coming into Los Angeles,"
from his 1969 album
Running Down the Road.
(Author's collection)

Dylan's hit song from the soundtrack to Sam Peckinpah's bloody western *Pat Garrett and Billy the Kid*, released 1973. *(Author's collection)*

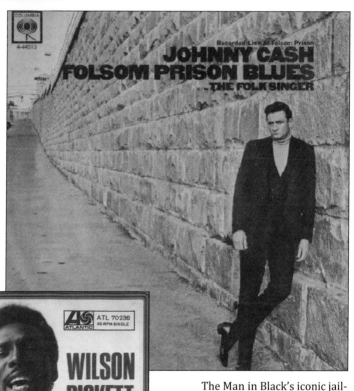

The Man in Black's iconic jail-house ballad, "Folsom Prison Blues." Originally released December 15, 1955, and re-recorded April 1968. *(Author's collection)*

It just don't get any badder than Wilson Pickett singing "Stagger Lee." This funky, jumpin' version of the gangster ballad peaked at No. 13 on *Billboard*'s R&B Singles chart in November 1967. *(Author's collection)*

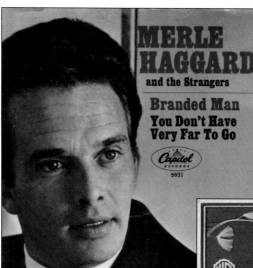

Released July 8, 1967, Merle Haggard and the Strangers' dark and brooding "Branded Man" shot to No. 1 on the Country Charts. *(Author's collection)*

"Little Criminals," from Randy Newman's 1977 album of the same name, in which the cynical pianist paints a musical mugshot of a small-time crook. *(Author's collection)*

With its sepia-toned album jacket and raw honky-tonk sound, *Wanted! The Outlaws*, featuring Waylon Jennings, Willie Nelson, Jessi Colter, and Tompall Glaser, razed commercial country music and forged the new "Outlaw" genre. Released January 12, 1976. *(Author's collection)*

Promo poster for Jay Z and Beyoncé's On the Run tour of 2003, which featured the single "'03 Bonnie & Clyde," released on October 10, 2002. *(Author's collection)*

Released on December 6, 1993, KRS-One's "Sound of da Police" is still as relevant as ever. *(Author's collection)*

Gil Scott-Heron, the Godfather of Hip Hop, said it loud and clear with "The Revolution Will Not Be Televised," all the way back in 1971. *(Author's collection)*

Joan Baez, backstage at Boston Symphony Hall, 1984. *(Photo by John Kruth)*

Townes Van Zandt, Franklin, Tennessee, mid-1970s. *(Photo by William Dibble)*

Richie Havens, New York City, early 1980s. *(Photo by John Kruth)*

Pete Seeger, backstage at the Lone Star Café, New York City, mid-1980s. *(Photo by John Kruth)*

New York antifolk singer/
songwriter Paleface.
(Photo by Gigi Sharp)

Peter Rowan. From
"Panama Red" to "Joaquin
Murrieta," Rowan has kept
alive the tradition of outlaw
balladry like few others.
Marblehead, Massachusetts,
September 1984.
(Photo by John Kruth)

Taj Mahal. Whether taking "Black Jack Davey" to Jamaica, or delivering bluesy renditions of "Betty and Dupree" and "Frankie and Albert," Taj is a great repository of American song. Backstage at the Bottom Line, New York City, June 1984. *(Photo by John Kruth)*

Gordon Gano, the Violent Femmes' frontman has fearlessly tracked our darkest fears. New York City, mid-1980s. *(Photo by John Kruth)*

John Prine. Just trying to have himself some fun. Nashville, Tennessee, 1986.
(Photo by John Kruth)

Aaron Neville, New Orleans' very own Frank Sinatra. Newark, New Jersey, mid-1990s.
(Photo by John Kruth)

7

AN ILLEGAL SMILE

As with the era of Prohibition in the 1920s, the United States government managed to alienate a sizable percentage of its populace by making them into criminals when Richard Nixon first declared the war on drugs, in June 1971. Nelson Rockefeller, the governor of New York at the time, followed in the crooked president's straight and narrow footsteps when he passed the toughest drug laws the country had ever known. A conviction for possession or sale of narcotics in the Empire State brought with it a minimum jail term of fifteen years, while a maximum sentence guaranteed somewhere between twenty-five years to life. Suddenly recreational marijuana smoking carried the same severity of punishment as committing murder.

The state of Michigan also harbored some very stringent laws as well (later deemed unconstitutional) and would sentence John Sinclair, the poet/manager of the Detroit rock band MC5, to ten years in prison for giving two marijuana joints to an undercover policewoman. Overnight Sinclair would become the Dope Christ of the Counterculture, immortalized in song by John Lennon on his 1972 double album *Some Time in New York City*. Sinclair was soon released from prison, three days after a rally in Ann Arbor, Michigan, that featured performances by Lennon, Stevie Wonder, protest singer Phil Ochs, and Heartland rocker Bob Seger, as well as a plethora of speeches, rants, and poems by Allen Ginsberg, Yippie activists Abbie Hoffman and Jerry Rubin, and Black Panther Bobby Seale. Although the "people" had spoken, the die had already been cast. Sinclair was freed, but the United States government's (unpopular and highly ineffective) War on Drugs has continued to this day, incarcerating everyone from kids to kingpins ever since.

"Nixon and his criminal brain-trust—Haldeman, Ehrlichman, Mitchell, and Dean—they were out of their wigs!" John Sinclair declared. "The whole thing grew out of their hatred of black people and hippies, as both were known to use drugs. In the long run it was really about nothing more than keeping people from getting high and to create a big prison industry, of which I was at the vanguard!" he laughed. "There weren't too many people in prison on marijuana charges at the time. So what was the big deal? It was all right for Thomas Jefferson to grow marijuana in Virginia! Sadly dope is a product. When they realized how popular it was, it turned into this big fight over who was going to control the sales. They will either put you in jail for it, or they will make you buy it!"

"Some good things came out that terrible mess," Sinclair allowed, referring to his arrest and imprisonment. "They held that big rally and John Lennon got me out of prison. I had liked the Beatles a lot before I got to know him, but I mean, that was like heaven-sent!"

Growing up with the looming threat of nuclear annihilation, compounded by the fear of being drafted into an unpopular and unjust war in Vietnam, the 1950s "Rebel Without a Cause" suddenly had something very real to protest beyond the prospect of a dead-end nine-to-five job and potentially soul-numbing life in the suburbs.

By the mid-1960s, a new breed of insubordinate American youth had sprung up in the wake of the "beatniks" who had heeded the warning of the raging Welsh bard Dylan Thomas, not to "go gentle into that good night." The rambling verse of beat writers Jack Kerouac, William S. Burroughs, and Gregory Corso stood in stark contrast to the mundane middle-class values of Eisenhower's America, as seen on TV. Meanwhile, Allen Ginsberg condemned the absolute madness of "Moloch," the rampant materialism and fear that controlled most of our lives then (as it still does today).

An Us versus Them mentality began to polarize the country, as the hippie counterculture lifestyle proliferated among America's youth, inspired by the Beatles' carefree attitude towards pot and LSD. Young people now began to openly experiment with drugs while becoming increasingly disenfranchised and estranged from their parents' code of morals and goals for their future.

Disillusioned with President Johnson's "Great Society," the election of Richard Nixon, and the escalation of the Vietnamese war, the hippies, heads, and freaks (or whatever you chose to call them) sought to create their own new peaceable kingdom by dropping out of what they deemed an increasingly violent and dysfunctional system. Instead they focused on communal living and sought spiritual alternatives to the Judeo/Christian traditions they'd been raised in, by investigating exotic Eastern mystical religions, techniques of meditation and yoga, alternatives to the meat and potato diet, and broader parameters of physical gratification through sexual freedom and rampant psychedelic drug use.

The short-lived flower-power movement of the 1960s (originally triggered by beat poet Allen Ginsberg) ultimately stood as a fragile symbol of peace in the face of the seven million tons of bombs dropped on Vietnam by the United States. Written in 1955, Pete Seeger's earnest anthem "Where Have All the Flowers Gone?" planted the seeds of dissent in thousands of young people's minds. "When they will they ever learn?" Seeger wearily begged, in his nagging rhetorical question. Eight years later, in 1963, Bob Dylan provided a resounding reply as he sang, "The answer my friend is blowin' in the wind."

In May 1967, John Phillips of the Mamas and the Papas turned his pal Scott McKenzie into the overnight "High Guru of Flower Power" by writing the hit single "San Francisco (Be Sure to Wear Some Flowers in Your Hair)" and giving it to him to record. Within weeks the song poured out of radios from coast to coast, beckoning the "beautiful people" to flock to the Monterey International Pop Festival for "a gathering of the tribes." But flower power quickly withered and died on the vine. Naïve to the treacherous hazards of speed, the hordes of starry-eyed vagabonds, cranked on crystal meth and camped on the streets of Haight-Ashbury, soon began to find themselves in dire straits.

"Frank Zappa recorded a public service message at the time

saying that if you take speed you'll be dead in five years," said Peter Stampfel, the high-octane fiddler and banjo picker from the 1960s anarchist string band the Holy Modal Rounders. Stampfel and fellow Rounder Steve Weber would briefly join the Fugs, bringing their old-timey guitar, banjo, and fiddle to a trio of bedraggled Lower East Side anarchist poets whose songs of social satire sized up the human condition with lyrics that were at once abhorrently profane, insidiously refreshing, and antiestablishment to the core. Although neither of the Fug's frontmen, Ed Sanders and Tuli Kupferberg, could actually play an instrument, that didn't stop them from forming a rock band. Inspired by the maelstrom the British Invasion bands were causing at the time, they joined forces with Ken Weaver, who had formerly pounded drums in his high school marching band, and in no time the trio penned more than fifty songs, concocting a funky musical stew from such diverse strains as Yiddish folk songs, Christian hymns, and Leftist union anthems, with a dash of Chuck Berry and a bit of C&W tossed in for good measure.

"We were sort of a punk band. Our idea was that anybody could do this," Tuli Kupferberg said in a late 1990s interview. "I'm not a musician. The only thing I know how to play is the radio. I sing and write and compose songs."

The Fugs were true sonic outlaws, recognizing absolutely no protocol whatsoever and breaking down barriers of every shape, size, and designation. They hated war, extolled dope, and loved sex—lots of it. Kupferberg admitted years later that even he was "shocked by Ed Sanders's freedom of sexual expression."

The folk song collector and filmmaker Harry Smith soon corralled the Fugs into the recording studio, where, with Weber and Stampfel on board, they cut a whopping twenty-three songs in one three-hour session. Nineteen sixty-five saw the release of *The Village Fugs Sing Ballads of Contemporary Protest, Point of Views, and General Dissatisfaction*, the first and largely uncelebrated underground rock album. Two years later (after Stampfel had left the band) an album titled *Virgin Fugs* was released, featuring a batch of outtakes from their earlier marathon recording session. This was truly radical stuff. The Fugs had no interest at all in the typical girl/boy songs that flooded the airwaves and record store shelves at the time (unless they could somehow manage to slip in a titillating graphic sexual description), and although songs with drug references were nothing new, Kupferberg's "Hallucination Horrors" and Stampfel's "New Amphetamine Shriek" were either a new high or low, depending on your perspective on the genre.

It's hard to call what the Fugs did "singing," exactly. Their vocals were more a slobbery sing-along of cheers and chants, scat, mad cackle, and incantation. Stampfel's trademark "amphetamine shriek," was a cross between Little Richard's falsetto yowl, Uncle Dave Macon's rustic yodel, and the nerve-wracking yelp of a Chihuahua.

"The song's lyric, 'If you don't like sleeping and don't want to screw, then you should take lots of amphetamine too,' is a little misleading," Peter Stampfel pointed out. "Speed actually makes people super horny and less careful about what they do and who they do it with. It's a dangerous combination. Otherwise I think it's an accurate portrayal of the amphetamine scene of the early 1960s, which was full of people called 'meth monsters,' who were into black magic and put spells on each other all the time." (The song's chorus, a nonsensical jabber that goes: "Gabba, gabba, gabba gabba" foreshadowed the Ramones' "Pinhead," with its chant of "Gabba, gabba, hey," by little over a decade.)

Chester William Powers Jr. was a fountain of aliases. "Chet" as he was known to his friends in his hometown of Danbury, Connecticut, first changed his name to Jackie Powers, before morphing into Jesse Oris Farrow when he began performing in the coffee houses of Greenwich Village in the late 1950s. The author of "Get Together" (the all-pervasive peace and brotherhood hippie anthem made famous by the Youngbloods), Farrow would become known to the world as Dino Valenti. Busted repeatedly for marijuana and amphetamine possession, Valenti had his cabaret card revoked by the police, a practice that had left Thelonious Monk and many other musicians unable to make a living from playing New York clubs. By 1965, Valenti headed out west, but soon found himself in trouble with the law again and wound up doing a stretch in Folsom State Prison. Upon his release (thankfully he didn't serve his entire ten-year sentence), Valenti formed a short-lived band known as the Outlaws with Quicksilver Messenger Service's guitarist Gary Duncan. As Quicksilver already had a devoted following, Dino joined them as their new front man and main songwriter. In 1970, they released their fifth album *What About Me?* Although he went by the handle Dino Valenti while in the guise of the band's lead singer, many of the album's songs, including the title tune, "What About Me?", were credited to Jesse Farrow. "I smoke marijuana," Valenti brazenly sang, taunting the Establishment who'd already wreaked havoc with his life over whatever gratification he found in getting high.

Valenti was an inspiration to Richie Havens, whose early repertoire included his "Get Together." The Village folk singer remembered Valenti fondly as the true embodiment of the bohemian troubadour of his day: "Like Freddie Neil, Dino was below the radar and really shaped the scene," Havens explained. "He'd spend a month or two here [New York] and then go to San Francisco. This was back in '58, '59, when the beatniks were still around, when Ginsberg used to read his poetry at the Gaslight. He was so passionate. He could put music together like nobody else. There was a little bit of Jimi [Hendrix] in what Dino was doing, long before Jimi appeared on the scene."

Recorded in 1974, Havens' mellow version of Valenti's "What About Me?" contained no trace of its original bitterness. Within his weary delivery, there is a profound sense of forgiveness in his smoky voice as he sings Dino's ode to disenfranchisement shared by the disillusioned counterculture:

> *And I feel like a stranger*
> *   in the land where I was born,*
> *And I live like an outlaw*
> *   and I'm always on the run.*

Valenti knew what he was writing about, first-hand, while Havens drove his old friend's point home with his incredible rhythmic guitar strumming and a grooving conga drum.

In 1967, Woody Guthrie's son Arlo made a name for himself with the hilarious "Alice's Restaurant Massacree," a rambling, eighteen-minute talking-blues number in which Guthrie, the "every-hippie," recounted his run-ins with the law, an absurd list of misdemeanors ranging from littering to dodging the draft by staging a psychotic episode.

When Arlo slyly sang of "bringin' in a couple of keys" to the great unwashed camped out in Max Yasgur's cow pasture, the citizenry of "Woodstock Nation," as Abbie Hoffman dubbed the enormous crowd, immediately caught his drift. "Keys" was slang for kilos, whether hashish or grass. In his folk-rock fantasy "Comin' Into Los Angeles," Arlo, a happy-go-lucky smuggler, approaches the customs agent with a bag full of contraband, and asks him kindly "Don't touch my bags," as if a friendly grin and wave of the hand would stop the authorities dead in their tracks.

A living repository of American folk music, singer/songwriter Michael Hurley picks guitar and banjo and saws a scratchy fiddle in an idiosyncratic style that sounds as timeless and natural as the swamps, "wildegeese," and werewolves that inhabit his songs and comic strips. (He is also a painter, whose album covers often portray the adventures of a pair of half-humans/half-wolves, named Boone and Jocko, who lust after booze and loose women.)

Hurley's "National Weed Grower's Assoc."—"a good old dope song," in the words of its enigmatic creator, sometimes known as "Snock"—recounts the pitfalls of growing one's own private patch of Mother Nature. The singer, a self-admitted "slave to the weed," finds himself in a tight squeeze between the law, determined to lock him up, and a bunch of "young drunk punks" out to steal his prized stash.

No song really summed up the "Back to Nature" movement better than Neil Young's "Homegrown." "First I thought it was a drug song," Neil told his audience at the London Hammersmith in 2008. "Then I thought no, no, no, it's about growing your own food, organic . . . It's good for you. Everybody should have that kinda food, no chemicals . . ." Young rambled on for another minute, seeming to lose his train of thought (no doubt due to the effects of some powerful homegrown) before picking up a banjo guitar and strumming it with a doo-wacka-doo rhythm. Originally a crunchy fuzz tone–drenched shitkicker from Young's 1977 *American Stars and Bars* album, the acoustic version of "Homegrown," took on an old timey quality.

For many, getting high has always been an act of freedom and rebellion. Looking back, the rampant and random drug abuse in the 1960s seems out of control. By the end of the decade, rock stars were dropping like flies. To keep it all in perspective, we should remember that the average American in 1830 drank nearly two bottles of hard alcohol each week, triple the amount consumed in 2012.

John Prine, was a Maywood, Illinois, mailman before becoming a folk singer. His uncanny lyrics, rustic voice, and simple guitar-picking earned him the dubious title of the "New Dylan." He released his debut album in 1971 after being discovered by Kris Kristofferson. *John Prine* contained a number of first-rate songs. Along with the Band's Robbie Robertson and Robert Hunter (lyricist for the Grateful Dead), Prine helped define the new genre of music dubbed "Americana" with songs like "Paradise," which describes how his Kentucky childhood home was lost to the callous greed of the coal industry. With tongue in cheek, Prine addressed issues of narrow-minded patriotism in "Your Flag Decal Won't Get You Into Heaven Anymore," and fashioned visions of a vanished America with "Angel from Montgomery," which resonated with a new generation as deeply as the covers Norman Rockwell once painted for *The Saturday Evening Post*.

Prine, like Johnny Cash before him, was sympathetic towards America's many social outcasts. With "Hello in There" he addressed the loneliness of aging, stopping to peer into the lonely eyes of an old forgotten soul, while in "Sam Stone" he portrayed a vet returned from Vietnam, still battling the memory of war while dealing with the added nightmare of addiction.

While hardly an acolyte of LSD guru Dr. Timothy Leary, who advised an entire generation to "Turn on, tune in, drop out," Prine gently encouraged his listeners to rethink their place in the rat race and consider finding peace in a simpler way of life. "Blow up your TV," he crowed, "Go to the country, build you a home."

John's gently listing waltz "Illegal Smile," another signature song from his debut album, is at once hilarious and sad. Unlike Arlo's hipster dope-smuggler, Prine's protagonist is no freewheeling hippie brazenly waving his freak flag in the face of the establishment. On the contrary, he's not interested in making waves. He's just a weary workin' man hoping for a moment of repose from a world he can neither control nor understand. Most of us assumed Prine's "Illegal Smile," was inspired by the cheap thrill of smoking an occasional joint. As he sang, "Won't you please tell the man I didn't kill anyone, / No, I'm just tryin' to have me some fun."

But Prine's perspective is rarely obvious. "I have to confess, the song was not about smokin' dope," John told Lydia Hutchinson of *Performing Songwriter* magazine. "It was more about how, ever since I was a child, I had this view of the world where I can find myself smiling at stuff nobody else was smiling at. But it was such a good anthem for dope smokers that I didn't want to stop every time I played it and make a disclaimer. When I first started singing it, I went on this underground TV program, and the only stage set they had was two chairs and this fake marijuana plant. I came on and sang 'Illegal Smile,' and they kept having the camera pan in, real psychedelic-like, on the plant. On top of that, I got fined by the Musicians' Union for not taking any money to do the show."

Cab Calloway's palpable references to dope and sex in his 1931 hit "Minnie the Moocher" escaped few at the time, although the public may have wondered what the madcap bandleader meant when he sang of "kicking the gong around," an obscure reference to smoking opium. Meanwhile, the song's heroine, "Poor Min," tried to scrape the bail money together for her old man, "Smokey," whom Calloway described as being "cokey," undoubtedly a reference to his habit of regularly powdering his nose with cocaine. Nefarious as Calloway's tale of the jazz age was, its sassy lyrics didn't stop the song from selling more than a million copies and later becoming a vehicle for a Betty Boop cartoon.

A swing tune written and recorded in 1936 by jazz violinist Hezekiah Leroy Gordon "Stuff" Smith and his Onyx Club Boys, "You'se a Viper" celebrates smoking "a reefer five feet long, not too fat and not too strong." The song was popularized by Harlem pianist Fats Waller in 1943 as "The Reefer Song." The rambunctious remake featured Fats jabbering a line of jive over his trademark stride piano, while imitating the sound of hissing snakes as he strenuously tokes on a joint. As the song explains, when you're a "viper"—a hemp-head—you "don't give a damn if you can't pay the rent." Just as long as there's some good weed on hand.

Few cared whether black jazz musicians smoked dope, just as long as they kept it in their own backyard. That was until 1947, when "Handsome Harry the Hipster" Gibson cut "Who Put the Benzedrine in Mrs. Murphy's Ovaltine?" The way-out jive-talking pianist/singer had crossed some invisible line that, most likely, he wasn't even aware of. Apparently Ovaltine, a favorite chocolate drink of kids everywhere, and speed did not mix, not even in such an obvious novelty number. Suddenly Gibson found himself blacklisted and headed for skid row, until making his comeback many years later, in 1975, when Dr. Demento's radio show put the song back in rotation. Updating ragtime riffs into rock 'n' roll, and overhauling his lyrics to fit a new generation, Harry the Hipster suddenly found new fans amongst the hippies. He cut two more albums before "getting his hat" in 1991.

The film *Reefer Madness*, with its over-zealous warning about the effects of "marihuana" (as it was spelled on the stylish movie poster), resembled a comedy more than the public service message it was intended to be. Financed by a church group and originally titled *Tell Your Children*, the 1938 film portrays a group of unsuspecting college kids who fall prey to a depraved pusher and find themselves under the spell of the evil weed, which induces bizarre paranoid visions that instantly drive them to acts of rape, murder, and suicide. In short order, everyone either winds up dead or in the lunatic asylum, due to the unpredictable powers of cannabis.

By the early 1970s, *Reefer Madness* had become a cult favorite of the very "degenerates" it attempted to warn America's fair citizenry about in the first place. Hippie "dope fiends," stoned out of their heads, packed movie theaters from coast to coast over the next decade to view midnight showings, laughing hysterically at the film's obsessive paranoia and heavy-handed production values.

Ever since the Beatles' "I Want to Hold Your Hand" soared to No. 1 in the winter of 1964, the watchdogs from the Federal Communications Commission (FCC) had become increasingly suspicious about songs containing drug references, no matter how silly or subliminal. Bob Dylan, America's weathervane of hip, always seemed to know which way the cultural wind was blowing; he thought the Fabs were sending out some sort of smoke signal when they sang "I get high" repeatedly. Upon closer scrutiny, the lyrics turned out to say "I can't hide." But that didn't stop Bob from turning the Beatles onto pot in August 1964, at the Delmonico Hotel in Manhattan. Hesitant at first, Lennon ceremoniously appointed Ringo as his "royal taster" before taking that fateful toke.

Two years later, Ray Charles, fresh out of rehab after kicking his heroin habit, gleefully crowed "Let's Go Get Stoned." Most folks assumed the sentiment exalted the highs of hooch, while somehow having little or nothing to do with the nefarious effects of narcotics or reefer. But Joe Cocker and his sprawling ensemble Mad Dogs and Englishmen made sure the reference was clear with their 1970 raucous remake.

Although stumbling up the charts to No. 2, Dylan's "Rainy Day Women #12 & 35" was banned from dozens of radio stations in the US and Britain. Dylan himself was said to be under the influence while recording the tune in Nashville in March 1966. Over a plunky tack piano, blaring trombone, and a rowdy crowd of wasted pals, "the voice of a generation" howled the lyric, a double entendre that bounced between the joys of getting high and the drag of being torn down by dim-witted critics and backstabbing friends. Dylan's message is simple. You can't win, whether you're "trying to make a buck" or "playing your guitar," so you might as well enjoy yourself, no matter what you do.

A few weeks later, the first strange rumblings of a new psychedelic music could be heard when the Byrds released their new single "Eight Miles High," a rambling jam inspired by Ravi Shankar's sitar and John Coltrane's modal jazz musings. The song's heady imagery was, according to the group's leader Roger McGuinn, inspired by an intercontinental flight to England for the Byrd's first European tour. The *Gavin Report*, a radio trade magazine that decided what was decent and indecent, interpreted its murky cryptic verse, "rain grey town known for its sound, in places small faces abound" (a shout out to Steve Marriott and Ronnie Lane of the Small Faces and their hometown of London), to be some sort of opium-induced vision concocted to corrupt the youth of America.

One of the few American bands to claw their way to the top of the charts while the British Invasion was in full throttle, the Byrds suddenly found themselves at the center of controversy. McGuinn, who was soon to become a born again Christian, attempted to balance out the ensuing nonsense by explaining that the inspiration for "Eight Miles High" had nothing to do with drugs and that commercial airliners usually flew at an altitude of six miles above the earth's surface. He then changed six to "eight," simply because it sang better.

The song's coauthors, the notoriously outspoken stoner David Crosby and Gene Clark (who ironically quit the band due to his fear of flying), eventually confessed that the lyrics actually had a quite lot to do with their habit of getting high.

Yet plenty of songs managed to slip by in this atmosphere of suspicion and scrutiny, including the Beatles' "children's song" "Yellow Submarine," which some claimed was a thinly veiled metaphor for a popular barbiturate of its day. Although "White Rabbit" teemed with drug references from its famous opening line, "One pill makes you larger and one pill makes you small," sung by Jefferson Airplane's Grace Slick in a trance-like incantation over a creeping Ravel-like bolero, its obvious association with the children's classic *Alice in Wonderland* magically protected it from the censors. Even the Rolling Stones' "Mother's Little Helper," a snide swipe at pill-popping housewives who get stoned in order to cope with the boring drudgery of their lives, made it to No. 8 on the pop charts without much fuss. Once again, the Beatles artfully dodged any controversy in their cute and coy way, while they (and everyone else) got high with "A Little Help from [their] Friends." The cheerful toe-tapping ditty (as with "Yellow Submarine" before it) was sung, after all, by the loveable Ringo, so how "bad" could it be?

In complete defiance of everything decent and moral that middle-class white American society stood for, the Velvet Underground dragged the drug scene into the safe, secluded suburbs with the noise-drenched jams of "Heroin" and "I'm Waiting for the Man." Mortified parents forbade their kids to listen to that godforsaken album with the banana on its cover (designed by the band's producer, pop art super-star Andy Warhol). The Velvets' guitarist/singer Lou Reed told the press repeatedly that he was not glorifying or advocating intravenous drug use but was presenting it objectively, without passing any moral judgment. Reed claimed that he personally delved into an underworld of darkness and depravity in order to exorcize his own self-destructive demons; perhaps in doing so he might save someone else from the sort of hell he'd experienced. Of course, it all seemed terribly cool and romantic to his young, impressionable audience.

Nobody stuck it to "the establishment" quite like the New York Yippie street busker (and self-proclaimed "rock 'n' roll outlaw") David Peel, a one-note wonder who thrashed away on an acoustic guitar while shouting his knuckle-headed dope anthems in a hoarse roar. After witnessing Peel and his motley crew the Lower East Side, live in Washington Square Park in 1971, John Lennon (who was undoubt-edly stoned himself) was captivated by David's raw, irrepressible spirit, and signed him to a recording contract with the Beatles' record company, Apple. Lennon then produced Peel's highly controversial and widely banned album *The Pope Smokes Dope*. When asked by the *Tampa Tribune* what inspired his blasphemous ditty, David quipped, "He's the highest head in the church, isn't he?"

Overnight the image of the pot-puffing pontiff appeared every-where, on posters, T-shirts, and buttons, as Peel (who'd previously sold close to a million copies of his 1968 album, *Have a Marijuana*) was suddenly thrust into the mainstream, performing on *The David Frost Show*, thanks no doubt to his association with Lennon. Backed by a hodgepodge hippie orchestra that featured John gleefully thumping away on a washtub bass, with his wife, Yoko Ono, slapping a tabla, and radical rabble-rouser Jerry Rubin clumsily strumming something that resembled an autoharp or zither, Peel proudly crowed about the joys of "living in a garbage can" in "Hippie from New York City," a hilarious satire on Merle Haggard's "Okie from Muskogee."

Booked on bills at clubs and rock festivals with everybody from Alice Cooper and B. B. King to Dave Brubeck, Peel soon headed for Hollywood, playing bit parts in a handful of low-budget counter-culture flicks. Between his populist pot odes and ragged hippie image (with his tinted granny glasses and long hair parted down the middle, the FBI allegedly mistook a photo of the Yippie street punk for Lennon), David became a "household name" in crash pads from Cambridge to Santa Monica.

In a surreal twist that defies both reason and imagination, the Vatican official newspaper *L'Osservatore Romano* chose David Crosby's *If I Could Only Remember My Name* in its list of "Top 10 Pop Albums of All Time" in 2010. It's not surprising to learn that holy ears deeply appreciated David's heavenly harmonies on tracks like the evocative "Song with No Words (Tree with No Leaves)," but someone within the organization obviously hadn't done their homework before adding David's name to the roster. After all, Crosby was the "pervert" who wrote "Triad," a song detailing a hippie love triangle, which so irked Roger McGuinn that he refused to release it on a Byrds' album. (David then personally delivered the tune to the Jefferson Airplane, whose lovely, lazy version is a highlight of their 1968 album *Crown of Creation*.) In 1982, Crosby had been busted for cocaine and heroin and spent nine months behind bars in a Texas jail. Three years later he faced another run-in with the law when he was charged with drunk driving, packing a pistol, and more coke. Beyond its surprising taste in music, the Catholic Church has had a legendary reputation for forgiveness and a deep belief in redemption, which Mr. Crosby must undoubtedly have appreciated.

By the early 1970s, a new soundtrack had begun to reflect the increasingly strange times, as longhaired troubadours sang the praises of a new breed of "heavy" heroes in anthems like "Willin'." Written by Lowell George, Little Feat's slide guitarist extraordinaire, "Willin'" tells of a renegade trucker and his wild adventures smuggling dope from Mexico. Although bedraggled, our hero will not be discouraged, and is still "Willin'" as long as there's plenty of "weed, whites, and wine."

By the time "Willin'" appeared on Little Feat's self-titled 1971 debut album, the song had already become an underground hit by Sea Train, whose lead singer Peter Rowan would later compose his own glorious odes to dope, like "Panama Red" and "The Free Mexican Airforce."

Whether these counterculture bards were aware of it or not, they'd been following the hot and dusty trail of the *narcocorrido*, Mexico's traditional folk ballads that romanticized the lives of drug smugglers known as *contrabandistas*. Traced back to the 1930s, and said to have been played as early as the 1910 Mexican Revolution, these songs were passionately sung over rhythmically strummed guitars and Norteno-style accordions that percolated with an up-tempo polka beat.

"The *corrido* had always been based on recounting real events, with all the names and dates right, and most *corridos* gained their popularity from the importance of their subjects," author Elijah Wald points out in *Narcocorrido* (published in 2001), his exhaustive investigation into the tradition of Mexican outlaw songs. The book recounts Wald's travels to Ciudad Guerrero in Chihuahua to interview Angel Gonzalez, father of the Corrido genre and composer of the sensational "Contrabando y Traición," originally recorded by Joe Flores and made famous by Los Tigres del Norte in 1971 after a slow, eight-month rise to the top of the charts. The song, unlike typical *corridos*, was a jumble of fact and fiction. It told the story of Emilio Varela and Camelia la Texana, a pair of likeable desperados whose escapades were soon fashioned into the plot of a "flashy modern action film," *Camelia La Texana*. Gonzalez's popular ballad, Wald explains, was "very much in tune with the current events. The early 1970s were a peak period for Mexican drug trafficking, and the public was eager for tales of daring border smugglers."

As an art form the *narcocorrido* is alive and well in the twenty-first century, thanks to the daring adventures of the violent and powerful "Shorty," better known as "El Chapo."

The infamous Mexican drug lord, real name Joaquin Guzmán Loera, had a personal fortune that was once appraised by *Forbes* magazine at approximately $1 billion. In 2001, El Chapo miraculously escaped by slipping past the guards of Jalisco's Puente Grande prison hidden in a laundry cart; whether through cunning or influence, he managed to remain at large until he was apprehended once more in February 2014. He escaped again in July 2015, through an underground tunnel from Altiplano maximum-security prison outside Mexico City; *Billboard* magazine subsequently published an article on the many *narcocorridos* that quickly sprang up glorifying him. They included Lupillo Rivera's "El Chapo Otra Fuga Mas" ("El

Chapo, Yet Another Escape"), which was written within weeks of his latest daring escapade. Meanwhile, "The King of *Corridos*," Gerardo Ortiz, penned "El Primer Ministro" ("The Prime Minister") once more lionizing *el enemigo público numero uno*. Los Canelos de Durango's "El Señor de la Montaña" (which translates to "The Mountain Man") took another approach. It revealed how the massively powerful El Chapo bribed corrupt officials to turn a blind eye to his ongoing criminality and the whereabouts of his alleged eighteen hideouts.

The massively popular bilingual hip hop track "El Chapo," released by The Game & DJ Skrillex in October 2015, began with a boast: "I am the God, El Chapo." While the rap is narcissistic to the point of absurdity, the lyric quickly turns from humorous, as he brags of knocking off Donald Trump's toupee, to ugly and brutal as he fantasizes about spilling his brains "on the sidewalk" with his .38.

In January 2016, the *New York Times* reported that El Chapo had been captured once more by a squad of "gun-toting marines." It turned out that the notorious kingpin had been hiding in the sewers of Mexico City, "stripped to his undershirt and covered in filth."

With two previous escapes to his credit, it will be interesting to see how long the high security prisons of Mexico can hold El Chapo, whom the *Times* called "a Robin Hood figure for modern times."

That rings true for the burgeoning counterculture to the north, in the US. On their 1971 self-titled debut, *The New Riders of the Purple Sage*, the San Francisco Grateful Dead spin-off band, who took their name from a Zane Grey novel, recount the misadventures of "Henry," a likeable, hapless dope-runner who's "comin' down the mountain, drivin' fast, fast, fast . . . " With its good-time country-rock feel, "Henry" could have been the perfect theme song for Gilbert Shelton's underground hippie comic book *The Fabulous Furry Freak Brothers*.

But it was the title track from their sophomore album, *The Adventures of Panama Red*, originally written and sung by bluegrass crooner/ psychedelic cowboy Peter Rowan, that became the band's biggest hit, and for which they also earned a gold record in 1973.

In Rowan's dope opus, the outlaw "Panama Red" (whose name was inspired by a particularly powerful strain of marijuana) came blazing into town, "on his white horse Mescalito," looking to "steal your woman" at first and then to "steal your head." In the hippie slang of the day, the "head" that Rowan sang of was either one's prized dope stash or peace of mind, which everyone was seeking, whether by smoking pot, chanting mantras, or practicing meditation.

"'Panama Red,'" Rowan recalled, "was written during the summer of Woodstock [August 1969], when I was playing on the streets of Cambridge, Massachusetts. Back then pot was everywhere. It was the people's buzz. Everybody was smoking, carrying, and giving it away. We had a crop in our back yard. It grew in ten-foot stalks. But Panama Red was a different kind of high. It had a warm and jovial feeling. It put everything in a new light. We got it from the jazz musicians. I never saw herb like that again. The song 'Panama Red' was simply the personification of the herb. In songs like that and [Rowan's western opus] 'Land of the Navajo,' I was somewhat aware that I was helping to create a new mythology for my generation. Sadly, it seems that every-thing about that time has a huge onus on it these days. The virtues our generation originally inherited from Henry David Thoreau, like inde-pendent thinking and civil disobedience, are all too often seen today as scabrous instead of noble behavior."

Rowan's "Free Mexican Air Force," written in 1978 at his Texas hideout Camp Howdy, came, he said, as "an end of an era." The hero of the song, Beauregard Hooligan, was based on a friend who started out selling nickel bags of pot, until the day he pulled off what Peter dubbed "The One Man Short" when he swam across the Rio Grande River, smuggling marijuana in big plastic garbage bags. "Herb floats!" Rowan said with a laugh. "It was a time of mythologizing, of creating the story. Each day was like living a page right out of your book, or a scene from your own movie. Getting high was very cinematic in some ways. Then there was the image, being in character and wearing all the gear."

By the end of the 1960s, bands like the Byrds, Joe Walsh's James Gang, the Flying Burrito Brothers, and the Eagles all posed for album covers done up in satin Nudie suits, vintage boots, and dusty old hats, with shotguns by their sides. The image of the outlaw, down to his six-shooter, had seemingly been kidnapped, hogged-tied, and held for ransom by the rock star.

"Although I took the persona of the LA Cowboy at that time, I wasn't really livin' that life, but I certainly knew plenty of people who were. I actually wrote that song about a Tibetan lama named Chogyam Trungpa Rinpoche (the founder of Shambala Buddhism), who was famous for his tremendous wisdom and charisma, as well as his sense of humor and penchant for sake. He was an outlaw. In a way, he was really Panama Red! See, underneath all of this drugging was the sense that enlightenment was imminent."

8

RUDE BOYS AND REGGAE RENEGADES

Originating in Jamaica in the late 1960s, reggae is an amalgam of musical styles and spirituality, with far-reaching roots from Ethiopia to Detroit (perhaps the two greatest influences being Emperor Haile Selassie and Motown bassist James Jamerson). Although the infectious funky rhythm was a product of Trenchtown, the Kingston ghetto, the message of black struggle spoke to people of African descent worldwide. Whether fighting "Babylon" in the guise of apartheid in South Africa or the legacy of colonialism in Jamaica, reggae created a unity reaching beyond geographic boundaries.

"'Black Jack Davy,' 'Stagger Lee,' and 'Johnny Too Bad' are all-encompassing everymen that move through all kinds of societies," blues and roots singer Taj Mahal explained. "They're somebody whose story gets told again and again until it reaches the point of mythology. These songs have been passed down from generation to generation. When *The Harder They Come* [the 1972 film starring Jimmy Cliff] first came out, that was a real groundbreaking movie which brought people into a whole 'nother scene that was happening in Jamaica and the Caribbean at the time."

There have been plenty of Jamaican outlaw anthems inspired by the ongoing battle that marijuana smokers and growers have fought with the authorities as their Rastafarian culture stands in resolute defiance to their country's laws. They include songs like "Johnny Too Bad" (written by T. Wilson, W. Bailey, H. Beckford and D. Crooks, originally recorded by the Slickers and later popularized by Taj Mahal on his 1974 exploration of Caribbean music, *Mo' Roots*) and "I Shot the Sheriff," the centerpiece of the Wailers' second album, *Burnin'* (1973), in which Bob Marley's protagonist pleads his case of self-defense: "I shot the sheriff," he cries, "But I didn't shoot no deputy."

When Sheriff Tom Brown takes dead aim at him, the narrator shoots first in self-defense, claiming that his "reflexes had got the better of [him.]" His crime, of course, was growing marijuana, an herb sacred to all followers of the Rastafarian cult. "Every time I plant a seed, he said kill it before it grow," Marley pleads in frustration.

Eric Clapton's famous cover of the song, from his album *461 Ocean Boulevard*, which soared to No. 1 on the Billboard charts for a week in September 1974, instantly popularized reggae worldwide.

While Jimmy Cliff's personal story parallels that of "Ivan O. Martin," the protagonist of the independent Jamaican film *The Harder They Come*, the character is actually based on Vincent "Ivanhoe" Martin, an actual outlaw from Kingston, who was also known as "Rhygin." As a teenager, Cliff left his home in the country and moved to the slums of Shanty Town in Kingston. Later that year (1962), he recorded his first single, "Daisy Got Me Crazy." In 1969, his song "Many Rivers to Cross" would inspire director Perry Henzell to offer Cliff the starring role of Ivan Martin in *The Harder They Come*. Young and naïve, fresh from the countryside, Ivan comes to Kingston and is quickly divested of all his earthly possessions. He turns to his mother, who offers no help, and soon finds himself living rough, hustling in the ghetto, commonly known as Shanty Town. Ivan eventually finds a job doing chores for a preacher, but predictably the preacher wants no blasphemous "boogie" music played or listened to in his house. The preacher becomes irate, tearing up Ivan's collection of *Playboy* magazines after discovering that he's been "skylarking" with Elsa, his adopted daughter.

Enraged upon finding Ivan rehearsing in his church, the preacher accuses him of fornicating with Elsa. Emotionally distraught, Ivan then winds up in a knife fight over his bicycle, slicing up a bully who taunted him. In lieu of doing jail time, Ivan is repeatedly beaten with a switch by the authorities. Somehow, after all of this, he still manages to make it to his recording session where he sings a funky, chugging version of the film's title song, which asks the lord to forgive his oppressors as "they know not what they've done." But it's not just the church or the cops hanging him up; Ivan's record producer Hilton offers him a mere twenty-dollar contract, which he proudly refuses.

Ivan soon discovers that Hilton controls the entire scene, with the record stores and DJs in his back pocket. He finally acquiesces and takes the lousy twenty bucks, then finds work in the ganja trade, running spliffs to local bars as his song hits the radio. When he refuses to pay off his "protectors," they rat him out and the police are soon on his trail. Things quickly turn from bad to worse. As his theme song "Johnny Too Bad" plays, Ivan runs reckless with his pistol, killing anyone who has slighted him. Then he heads to the rock for rescue, but as the song goes, "there is no rock."

Meanwhile, his record keeps climbing the charts. Hilton hopes to get Ivan back in the studio once more to cut another record and cash in on his soaring popularity before the authorities "string him up." Ivan makes a pretty good run, stealing a Cougar convertible from a fancy hotel while getting a few laughs out of zig-zagging up the fairways of a golf course. Stopping by a photo studio, he poses in a pimpy hat and leopard-print shirt with his six shooters drawn. But after catching a couple bullets in the gut, he fails to board the boat to Cuba and make his escape, as Cliff's own song "You Can Get It if You Really Want" plays in the background. In the meantime, the entire Jamaican army (in a scene obviously inspired by the climax to *Butch Cassidy and the Sundance Kid*) surrounds Ivanhoe and, in a blinding round of gunfire, creates a hero and a martyr.

Despite its deep rhythmic groove, "Wanted Dread and Alive" by Peter Tosh (1981) is something of a cardboard cut-out, lyrically speaking. "They," the "evil forces," are after him, for no apparent reason other than that he lives the Rastafarian lifestyle. While the lyric comes off as somewhat paranoid, Tosh's persecution complex had some basis in reality. It seems that he had every reason to be constantly looking over his shoulder. On 1977's "Stepping Razor," Tosh growls "If you wanna live, treat me good . . . I'm like a stepping razor, don't you watch my size, I'm dangerous," as a stinging lead guitar break backs up his threat.

Tosh, who was invited by his ex-partner Marley to perform at the One Love Peace Concert in 1978 (after he had left the Wailers in 1974), defiantly fired up a spliff on stage and pontificated on the many merits of marijuana while chastising Jamaica's Prime Minister, Michael Manley (who was seated in the crowd at the time) for failing to legalize the sacred weed. Defiant? Yes. Smart? No. Months later it came as no surprise when Tosh was arrested on a trumped-up charge and beaten up by the police.

In the end, ironically, it wasn't the authorities or a member of the "shitstem" (as he often referred to the establishment) who did him in. After returning from a trip to the States, on September 11, 1987, Tosh was met at his home by a trio of thugs standing outside his door demanding money. After Peter explained that he was momentarily "light," Dennis "Leppo" Lobban, an old acquaintance whom Tosh knew and had tried to help after getting out of jail, put a gun to his head and squeezed the trigger. In the panic that ensued, Leppo's buddies gunned down Tosh's friends, DJs Doc Brown and Jeff "Free I" Dixon.

There had always been a strong rivalry between Marley and Tosh as to which of them would fulfill the role of reggae's prophet and martyr. Unfortunately, they both died much too young, Marley at thirty-six and Tosh at forty-three. In Marley's case, death perhaps might have been postponed but he chose to seek no help for his worsening medical condition, leaving it up to the will of Jah (the Rastafarians' name for God) to heal his infected toe (a melanoma that eventually led to brain cancer). To this day Marley's message continues to travel worldwide, thanks to reggae's irresistible beat, while Tosh, a soulful singer/songwriter and guitarist in his own right, sadly remains a footnote, forever standing in his former bandmate's shadow.

From the song's gooey wah-wah groove to Junior Murvin's velvet smooth falsetto, the influence of Curtis Mayfield on "Police and Thieves" is unmistakable. (Murvin, a fan of Mayfield, would later help popularize his signature gospel song "People Get Ready" in Jamaica as "Rasta Get Ready.")

Produced by the always-innovative Lee "Scratch" Perry at his legendary Black Arc Studio, "Police and Thieves" (the title track of his 1977 debut album), while hot in Jamaica, eventually caught fire in England, where it climbed to No. 23 on the charts.

Well-received on both sides of the Atlantic, Junior's song was a gentle plea for peace, appealing to both cops and gangs to chill out in the face of mounting violence taking place on the streets of Kingston.

Although his soothing voice and bouncy beat had a way of taking the bite out of his socially poignant lyrics, Junior would continue to explore themes of criminality with his 1982 album *Bad Man Posse* and again two years later with *Muggers in the Street*.

The Clash would bring some crunch and attitude to Murvin's smooth style with their cover of "Police and Thieves," from their 1977 self-titled release. The decision by Joe Strummer and Mick Jones to record a reggae tune (particularly one which promoted peace) came at a significant time, as the raging British punk scene was often viewed as an aggressive (some might even say "fascist") expression of angry, unemployed white youth, who sometimes blamed their troubles on the influx of immigrants from Pakistan and Jamaica.

A number of reggae artists would adopt outlaw handles, including the 1980s Jamaican dancehall DJ Joseph Winston Sterling, who became better known as Josey Wales, having named himself after Clint Eastwood's character in the gritty Western *The Outlaw Josey Wales*.

Dennis Smith became "Dennis Alcapone" after his friends had bestowed the moniker on him in honor of his love of old gangster movies. Over a buoyant bass groove, his 1971 hit "Guns Don't Argue," produced by reggae pioneer Bunny "Striker" Lee, featured Alcapone's expressive voice. Hard and gravelly one minute, a sweet falsetto the next, and saturated in reverb, his voice leapt octaves as he namechecked notorious bad boys from "Pretty Boy" Floyd and "Baby Face" Nelson to his namesake Al "Scarface" Capone. Following in Smith's footsteps was the reggae singer known to his mother as Lester Bullock, who first went by "Young Alcapone" before producer Lee "Scratch" Perry convinced him to strike out on his own as "Dillinger."

Whether he first heard the phrase "Cocaine, running around my brain" sung by the Piedmont blues man Reverend Gary Davis, or was inspired by later cover versions recorded by Bob Dylan, Jackson Browne, or the Grateful Dead, Dillinger fashioned "Cocaine Blues" into his own funky reggae version called "Cocaine in My Brain," which featured a wah-wah-laden guitar riff and some foot-fooling dropped beats.

Born in Rhodesia (later Zimbabwe) in 1945, singer/songwriter/guitarist Thomas Mapfumo grew up in the country, living the traditional Shona lifestyle. As a teenager, he played guitar and sang a mix of songs in his native language, along with covers of Otis Redding and Elvis Presley tunes. Inspired by the infectious groove of Bob Marley and the Wailers and the burgeoning creed of Rastafarianism, which celebrated the Emperor of Ethiopia, Haile Selassie, as a modern-day prophet, Mapfumo soon concocted his own unique brand of pan-African reggae that helped to spiritually and culturally unite the rastas of Jamaica with their African brothers, thousands of miles away.

In response to the endemic racism of Rhodesia's white government, Mapfumo forged a percolating message music, which he dubbed "Chimurenga" (which translates to "struggle"), rather than performing banal pop songs. The controversial "Lion of Zimbabwe," as Mapfumo became known, sang his revolutionary ideology in a gentle, prayer-like voice over an infectious groove comprised of plunky, reverb-drenched electric guitars and melodic horns. While his song, "Hokoyo" (meaning "Watch Out!") sounds less like a threat than a heartfelt chant for peace, it led to his incarceration without any formal charge in 1979. After the arrival of black majority rule in 1980, Mapfumo soon found himself at odds with the government of Robert Mugabe. He emigrated to Eugene, Oregon, in the 1990s, where he lives and continues to make music to this day.

In August 1993, the body of Adesanwo Shokoya was found outside of Fela Anikulapo Kuti's home in Lagos. The electrician had allegedly been beaten to death by the singer's bodyguards after arguing over a bill for $138. Nigeria's biggest pop star, an outspoken critic of the military controlled government, was immediately arrested and charged with murder and conspiracy.

Mr. Shokoya, it seems, had been accused by Kuti's bandmates of embezzling funds. According to the police, Kuti had ordered his posse to teach his disloyal employee a lesson. But Shokoya unexpectedly died as a result of their excessive manhandling. While a Lagos newspaper editor considered Kuti nothing more than "a nuisance," he clarified to a *New York Times* reporter that the singer was "no murderer. . . . He's being punished not for what he's done, but for who he is."

The controversial musician, whose famously blunt and accusatory remarks and decadent lifestyle made him constant fodder for the tabloid newspapers, seemed remarkably unfazed throughout the whole ordeal. "It's just another one of their ploys to trap me," he remarked, while dressed in what the *New York Times* described as his "standard press interview attire—bikini underwear." Kuti, a ringmaster of the first degree, had already begun to grow weary of the circus. As the *Times* reported, Kuti was "arrested, jailed, charged with murder and released on bond," for allegedly ordering the death of the electrician. The trumped-up claims, which he denied as "ludicrous and politically motivated," were eventually dropped, but harassment by the corrupt Nigerian authorities would continue for the rest of his life.

In 1974, originator of a highly infectious style of music he dubbed "Afro-Pop," he opened a Lagos club called the African Shrine. As Kuti began to dig deeper into his Yoruba roots, he started incorporating mystical rituals into his band's musical performances. Archaic magicians from Ghana allegedly performed miraculous feats, while shamans chanted cryptic incantations from the Ifá religion and dancers with painted faces and bodies swooped and twirled in zoomorphic gesticulation. A Cameroonian priest was said to have sacrificed a man and then raised him moments later from the dead.

After meeting a young African American woman named Sandra Isodore at The Shrine, Kuti would quickly become radicalized, devouring books by Malcolm X and Eldridge Cleaver, and learning the backstories of the Black Panthers Huey Newton, Angela Davis, and Bobby Seale. Fela's blend of volatile politics and cultural pride, which he expressed not in his native Yoruba but in Pidgin English (in hopes of reaching a broader audience) over a James Brown-inspired funk groove, soon exploded all over Lagos.

Located across the street from the Shrine, Kuti's musical commune, which he named "Kalakuta" (after the notorious Indian dungeon known as the "Black Hole of Calcutta"), had become the constant target of police raids. Inspired by the Black Panthers' attempt to establish themselves as an independent entity in the face of what they deemed a tyrannical and racist empire, Kuti built a tall fence around his compound and declared it a self-governing state, which immediately raised the ire of the authorities.

In 1977, a squadron of soldiers surrounded Fela's house and burned it to the ground, beating everyone inside while destroying everything they could get their hands on, including irreplaceable instruments and tapes (Kuti's song "Unknown Soldier" recounts the entire debacle). Then came the greatest tragedy of all, a few days later, with the death of his seventy-seven-year-old mother, Funmilayo Ransome-Kuti. A well-known women's rights advocate, she died from injuries incurred after she'd been pushed from a second-story window.

From that point on there was no turning back for Fela. His mounting anger could not be tamed or muzzled. Dropping his middle name, "Ransome," which he considered no more than "a slave name," Kuti adopted "Anikulapo," which translates to "He who carries death in his pouch." Fela likened the name to a powerful talisman that he wore proudly to show everyone, from the authorities to the various enemies he'd made along the way, that he alone was the master of his fate and only he would decide when the time was right to surrender to death's beckoning.

As his scathing criticism of the government grew, Kuti was routinely harassed by the police. Courtroom and jailhouse doors revolved with a tiresome regularity. With his popularity reaching new heights, Kuti attempted to run for president in two elections in Nigeria, but found his name had been kept off the ballot by his adversaries in a nefarious attempt to stop him from returning democratic rule to his countrymen.

In November 1984, Fela was arrested for carrying the sum of 1,500 British pounds while he and his band and entourage attempted to board a plane in Lagos, bound for America to play a concert tour. Convicted and sentenced to five (sometimes reported as ten) years behind bars, Kuti, who was feted as a hero by his cellmates, wound up serving only eighteen months until he was freed when General Ibrahim Babangida's coup overthrew the Buhari government.

As legendary in his homeland as Robin Hood or Jesse James, Fela Anikulapo Kuti was not an outlaw in the traditional sense. Although he most likely carried firearms (for self-protection) and routinely instigated confrontation with the authorities, he never kidnapped anyone or robbed banks, nor, as a modern day griot, did he sing romanticized ballads of brigands of yore. Instead, Fela continually challenged society's norms by his example. His outrageous lifestyle, which included marrying twenty-seven women on one day (many of whom were singers and dancers in his band), and his relentless "in your face" attitude, flamboyant clothes, and unrestrained radicalism, profoundly resonated with his fellow Nigerians. Kuti's popularity soon spread to the rest of Africa, and then to London and Europe, whose youth at the time were in the throes of rebellion, sparked by a devastating recession and the thrash of punk rock. Like Bob Marley before him, who found inspiration in the Rastafarian creed for the message-filled lyrics he fused to an irresistible beat, Kuti created music with the power to free people (at least momentarily) from their daily grind. He inspired them to look beyond the grim circumstances of their lives, rise up and shake off oppression ("By any means necessary" as Malcolm X said), and create a better tomorrow.

In 2009 the Broadway play *Fela* opened. Featuring Bill T. Jones's magnificent choreography, it celebrated Kuti's life and music, twelve years after his death at age fifty-eight.

9

LITTLE CRIMINALS AND LOVEABLE LOSERS

By the late 1960s and early 1970s, the image of the outlaw as a rugged individual battling an unjust, impersonal system seems to have devolved into that of a somewhat harmless, likeable loner, a sad sack who appealed to our sense of sympathy rather than a valiant hero fulfilling our need for righteousness and sense of adventure. He'd become declawed and defanged and posed little or no danger to society.

Written by Robbie Robertson and Richard Manuel and sung by Manuel on the Band's self-titled 1969 second album, "Jawbone" portrays a comical small-town, small-time crook who loves his work. "I'm a thief and I dig it!" Manuel crowed gleefully.

Ultimately Jawbone is more of a nuisance than any real threat to society. No one takes him too seriously and the townsfolk who populate the imaginary frontier of the Band's "Invisible Republic," as Greil Marcus dubbed the dispossessed generation of baby boomers who rebelled against the establishment in hopes of getting themselves "back to the garden" (as Joni Mitchell once sang), only taunt and goad him to "go on home!"

Guitarist/songwriter Robbie Robertson once explained that the comical "Jawbone" was inspired by the shady characters and barflies who regularly frequented the Band's early gigs, back when the group played in seedy Canadian nightclubs.

Kicking off with corny gunshot sound effects and a bouncy mandolin, the Bonzo Dog Doo-Dah Band's "Bad Blood" (from their 1972 reunion album *Let's Make Up and Be Friendly*) is a brilliant parody of the outlaw ballad genre, built on a shamelessly absurd lyric about a half-blind and totally crazy amputee who spends seven years seeking revenge on the scoundrel who did him wrong.

"Bad blood will drive you crazy," intones Vivian (formerly known as Victor Anthony) Stanshall in his best macho Johnny Cash imitation, framed by a reverb-saturated twangy guitar and tinkling barroom piano. But before our bitter and dilapidated narrator has a chance to settle his old score with the bastard who's to blame for his lifetime of misery, a lumberjack suddenly appears out of nowhere and kills him first, robbing him of the sweet revenge he's sought for decades.

Battling the Bonzos for first (or last, depending on your perspective) place for the most outlandish outlaw song of all time is the Incredible String Band, an eccentric batch of Scots who showed a flair for theatricality with their earlier recording of the Gilbert and Sullivan–inspired "The Minotaur's Song" (from their milestone 1968 album *The Hangman's Beautiful Daughter*). *U*, their double-album/stage extravaganza, which featured the artful flouncing of the hippie dance troupe known as the Stone Monkey, included the curious "Bad Sadie Lee." Warbled by Janet Shankman (founder Robin Williamson's future and former wife), the tune was a good-natured parody of old-time American folk music, on which the Incredibles employed a plethora of instruments, including a rollicking tack piano, a clickety-clacking washboard, a boinging Jew's harp, a twangy banjo, and a squeaky fiddle, as Shankman recounts the misadventures of a spunky gunslinging girl from "wild Wyoming" who "can shoot better than Annie Oakley." In fact, the slug from her gun can do just about anything, from killing buzzards to breaking whiskey glasses in bars she's never been in. "Sadie" recounts her sorrowful tale of how she was jilted by the famous pioneer Daniel Boone, who left her for "a ginger-haired ornery raccoon, and that's what turned me bay-ad!"

U also included Mike Heron's whimsical ballad of "Hirem Pawnitof," the famous highwayman, and his "motley crew," who ride "from Leeds to Carter Bar." While ordering the occasional traveler to "stand and deliver," Hirem and his scruffy band are, for the most part, a harmless bunch who have clearly "been taking too many trips."

"The Holdup," written by multistring wizard David Bromberg and George Harrison, appears on Bromberg's 1972 album *Demon in Disguise.* It portrays a rowdy gang of Latinos, who, like Hirem Pawnitof's "motley crew," are just out for a good time. "We were having dinner at my manager's house when I started playing an old nylon gut-string [guitar] that loaned itself to a Mexican feel, which inspired the lyric," Bromberg recalled. "We wrote the song in about twenty minutes." It's all good fun, as a gang of desperados head into the sunset, stopping at Rosa's Cantina where "We'll spend all your money / Just getting our nose wet."

"Robbin' Banks," by Oregon-based singer/songwriter Jeffery Frederick and his band the Clamtones, from *Have Moicy!*, released in 1976, also brought in Holy Modal Rounder Peter Stampfel and the eccentric folk singer/painter Michael Hurley. "Robbin' Banks" portrays another good-timing crook who loves "bein' illegal." Being an outlaw thrills the singer to the point where it is "makin' my bone wiggle, / Every time I see the law." The song evokes a *Butch Cassidy and the Sundance Kid*–type "buddy movie," in which "Boone" and his sidekick "Jocko" (the names that Michael Hurley gave to the half-wolf/half-man cartoon characters that illustrate many of his album covers) guzzle whiskey by the bottle and stick up banks from Argentina to Alaska without ever having to face the firing squad.

"Michael and Jeffrey got extremely drunk one night," Jeffrey's widow Kathryn Frederick recalled with a laugh. "And Michael said, 'Let's make a movie about Boone and Jocko in Argentina.' And Jeffrey thought, 'What a great idea.' So Michael fell asleep while Jeffrey stayed up and wrote a song about robbin' banks, chicken coops, and bein' chauffeured, and havin' Alaska in their eyes. Jeffrey got up the next morning and said, 'Here's the song, where's the movie?' And Michael said, 'What movie?' He'd totally blacked it out. And that's how 'Robbin' Banks' was written."

Probably the best known of these fictitious fugitives is "Rocky Raccoon," from the Beatles' self-titled 1969 album, a.k.a. *White Album*, written and sung by Paul McCartney. McCartney recounts the tale of a pathetic Old West gunfighter, who winds up shot full of holes in a sudden draw over his floozy girlfriend, who goes by a bevy of names from Lil to McGill to Nancy.

Country rock was a tricky matter back in its early stages in the mid-1960s. The Beatles were one of the first pop bands to blend these styles when Ringo, who unabashedly adored Buck Owens, tried the Bakersfield, California, cowboy's song "Act Naturally" on for size. There always seemed to be a campy, tongue-in-cheek element whenever a British band, whether the Beatles or the Rolling Stones, played anything with a country flavor. Although the Beatles' original "What Goes On" features some fine Chet Atkins–style picking by George Harrison, it was handed to Ringo to sing, as no one was going to take the song too seriously when it was warbled by their loveable "dumb" drummer.

Jim Croce's "Bad, Bad Leroy Brown," on his second album, *Life and Times*, was a catchy old-time ditty. One of the most famous outlaw ballads in recent time, the song was ubiquitous on AM radio. With bubbly covers by everybody from Frank Sinatra to Sonny and Cher to Jerry Lee Lewis, "Bad, Bad Leroy Brown" would forever leave its mark on the American cultural landscape. Croce, a former construction worker who turned coffeehouse singer in the late 1960s, based the song on the adventures of a fellow soldier at Fort Dix, New Jersey, who went AWOL and was dragged back to the brig in handcuffs. One has to wonder whether Croce was inspired to name his leading character after Lee Brown, who previously "blowed Little Sadie down." While Croce compares Leroy to "old King Kong" and claims he's "meaner than a junk yard dog," Brown is really nothing more than a boldly drawn cartoon character. *Life and Times* spent two weeks at No. 1 in the charts in July 1973. Two months later, on September 20, Croce was tragically killed in a plane crash.

Like a series of snapshot portraits, these quirky ballads recall the misadventures of a variety of small time ne'er-do-wells who are more a danger to themselves than society. Famous for his rolling New Orleans piano style, satirical lyrics, and tender ballads, Randy Newman sings skewed portraits of rednecks, slave traders, and pin-headed politicians. In his song "Little Criminals" (from the 1977 album of same name), Randy recounts a small time crook's plan to knock over a gas station and make it "to the top."

In a similar vein, the gravelly throated iconoclast Tom Waits paints a mug shot portrait of a small time hustler named "Small Change," who winds up getting "rained on with his own .38." Brimming with sexual innuendo, Joni Mitchell's "Raised on Robbery" is a character sketch of a boozy floozy hanging around a small-town dive, looking to lure any loser into her web. In a line worthy of Mae West, Mitchell sings "I'm a pretty good cook, / Sittin' on my groceries." But everybody's hip to her routine, and she goes home frustrated, with only her sordid past to keep her company. The song features Mitchell's fellow Canadian Robbie Robertson on some smoldering lead guitar work.

Richard Thompson's "Shane and Dixie" (from his 1994 release *Mirror Blue*) is a lighthearted Chuck Berry–style romp about a pair of bumbling bank robbers out for "fame and love." Seeking adventure and fast cash, this pair of clueless crooks (a caricature of Bonnie and Clyde) are no more than a couple of bored thrill-seekers out for kicks.

Not surprisingly, everything goes wrong right from the get-go. When Shane sees Dixie sprawled on the floor after catching a bullet, he turns the gun on himself and blows his brains out, hoping to reserve his place in the history books. But the twist comes when they find Dixie still alive, although barely. She quickly recuperates and falls in love with the journalist who comes to write her story. Meanwhile Shane is soon forgotten and a pack of vandals spray-paint his headstone as weeds grow tall around his grave.

Released in 1969 as a single from their second album, *Town and Country,* Humble Pie's roots rocker "Sad Bag of Shakey Jake" is another boldly drawn caricature of a small-time outlaw, recited by Steve Marriott over the funky grind of his guitar. The lyric makes little attempt to disguise its inspiration, which boldly borrows from the legend of Billy the Kid, who "shot a man when [he] was just eighteen." The song's hero, Jake, was not only "born under a bad sign" (thank you Albert King) but believed himself to be "the devil's own son" (undoubtedly a reference to Peetie Wheatstraw, better known as "The Devil's Son-In Law"). Although we never learn what led him to a life of crime, we do know that Shakey Jake was on the lam, trailed by the Texas Rangers, for the sin of committing just "one mistake."

"I don't want flowers and nobody's gonna weep," Marriott sang, as if admitting that neither Jake nor his ambiguous ballad was particularly memorable. While few sing the praises of "Shakey Jake" these days, Marriott (the front man for the original Small Faces and Humble Pie, who tragically died in a fire in April 1991) will live forever in the annals of rock 'n' roll for his smoky voice and impressive guitar chops.

The romantic image of the outlaw hits an all-time low in 1993 with King Missile's "Take Stuff from Work," in which front man/poet John S. Hall shamelessly advises abused wage slaves everywhere that the only way they'll ever feel better about their lousy jobs is to help themselves to whatever office supplies they can carry out the door without their boss noticing.

Hall's petty thievery doesn't stop with mere pens, pencils, and paper clips. He invites his disgruntled, disenfranchised workers to think bigger:

> *Why buy a file cabinet?*
> *Why buy a phone?*
> *Why buy a personal computer or word processor?*
> *Take 'em from work.*

I took a whole desk from the last place I worked.
They never noticed and it looks great in my apartment. . . .

It's your duty as an oppressed worker to steal from your
  exploiters. . . .
I wrote this at work.
They're paying me to write about stuff I steal from them.
Life is good.

"It's basically a communist diatribe," Hall explained. "I was walking into work one day, and this guy Dave saw me, and he looked both ways, sneaky like, and then he tried to stuff his computer keyboard into his shirt. I went to my desk and wrote 'Take Stuff from Work,' in about five minutes."

"It's a one-chord song and one of my favorite John S. Hall lyrics," recalled Stephen Tunney (a.k.a. "Dogbowl," the song's coauthor). "'It's your duty as an oppressed worker to steal from your exploiters,' is a great line. I think we wrote it in his family's living room or on the 59th Street Bridge. But it's just one chord chugged out, with the occasional punk ska thing and some pseudo free-jazz thrown in."

Beck's pathetic/hysterical epic folk ballad "Mexico" begins with the anti-folk singer/songwriter turned rock star loosely strumming his acoustic guitar in a minor key, recalling how he and a couple of his drunk and sullen buddies came to lose their way. "Mexico" is essentially a clever parody of the old "The Buffalo Skinners" (a.k.a. "The Hills of Mexico"), a traditional song collected by John Lomax for his famous 1918 songbook *Cowboy Songs, and Other Frontier Ballads*, which recounted the gruesome details of a deadly buffalo hunt on the Texas plains.

"Come gather 'round me people," Beck warbles in a weary voice, recalling his lousy job working the late-night shift at a local McDonalds drive-thru when he was held up by a bandit demanding money and "and three big Macs to go."

Our antihero's angry boss gives him the boot, once he discovers his unreliable employee didn't call the police because he was afraid that he might go to jail over a couple of outstanding Jaywalking tickets. Hoping to avoid the wrath of his fed-up and frustrated parents, with whom he still lives, he heads over to his pal Dave's house. They are soon joined by their buddy Steve and spend the next few hours getting stoned, calling girls, and being depressed, until Steve goes looking for his dad's hunting rifle. The despondent trio then tramp over to a local 7/11, where they attempt to pull their first stick-up. But the clerk only stands there laughing at these sorry slackers, as he pulls out an Uzi submachine gun from behind the counter while the boys frantically scramble for their lives. Their sorry saga continues as the protagonist recounts how they return to the McDonalds where he was previously employed. Having no car, they saunter up to the drive-thru window and demand a bag full of cash and burgers to go. "Suck on this you weasel" our antihero says as he blows his boss away. Like the swindled "Buffalo Skinners" of Woody Guthrie's famous ballad, they also head south of the border to Mexico, where they are quickly plagued by a bad case of diarrhea and homesickness. Dave and Steve call their parents, who soon appear to retrieve their wayward boys, only to leave their friend on his own in Mexico where he eventually finds a job . . . working at McDonald's once again.

The likeable slacker is one of the many guises that the chameleon-like Beck wears best. The only crime committed by the protagonist of his 1994 Generation X anthem "Loser" is simply existing, taking up space, breathing. "I'm a loser baby," he groans, "so why don't ya kill me?" While most of his surrealist verse is wide open to interpretation, Beck's poetry resonated with his disenfranchised generation in a big way.

Perhaps the greatest loser anthem of all was the Beastie Boys' "High Plains Drifter," from their classic 1989 album *Paul's Boutique*, about an obnoxious juvenile delinquent who name-drops Clint Eastwood's Dirty Harry and Dr. Hunter S. Thompson in hopes of achieving one iota of credibility. Over a crunchy beat, the Beastie Boys, in their unmistakable New Yawk accents, spit out the adventures of the "High Plains Drifter," spray-painting a portrait of a modern day desperado on a high-speed cross-country adventure of misdemeanors. He gets his kicks grooving to the tunes on his eight-track tape deck, while chain-smoking Kool cigarettes as he runs over mailboxes and shop-lifts at K-Mart. He only takes a break from his obnoxious spree long enough to watch porn in his lonely motel room. Sticking up a 7/11 makes him "feel like Steve McQueen." Not surprisingly the cops soon catch up with him and he winds up in jail with Otis, the town drunk (an obscure and amusing reference to *The Andy Griffith Show*). But this irrepressible punk's adventure doesn't end here; he claims to have "Houdini'd" his way out of his handcuffs and the Brooklyn House of Detention, grabbing the jailor's billfold on his way to Off Track Betting, where he immediately doubles his loot on some long shot. Then he steals another car and disappears into the American night, to annoy whoever he chooses.

Sometimes the persona of a songwriter is as colorful as those of the characters found within their lyrics. As is the case with David Allan Coe, whose shit-kickin' redneck romp "Fuzzy Was an Outlaw" portrays a backwoods hillbilly who rides his motorcycle down to Kentucky, where he joins a gang of outlaws. Donning faded, ragged blue jeans, Fuzzy quickly settles down to a life of homesteading, driving his tractor through bucolic fields each morning at sunrise. What makes this long-hair farmer an outlaw isn't exactly clear, other than perhaps living the back-to-nature/off-the-grid hippie lifestyle that became popular in the wake of the Woodstock Festival in August 1969. Fuzzy teaches the song's narrator how to live off the land, which implies that he might be growing something more exotic than corn and potatoes. As the author of Johnny Paycheck's No. 1 hit "Take This Job and Shove It," David Allan Coe has never been known for subtlety.

For better or worse, the outlaw singer has always spoken his mind freely. With one look at his wild wardrobe—a mosh of redneck down-home togs and tacky Vegas glitz (Kid Rock, for whom Coe later opened, didn't have to look any further for a role model for his metal/ hillbilly image)—it's clear that Coe doesn't give a damn what you think. Neil Strauss of *The New York Times* considered Eminem's music "tenderhearted" when compared to Coe's controversial lyrics, which he deemed "racist, misogynist, homophobic, and obscene." His tacky and tasteless album covers (the jacket to his 1977 release *Texas Moon*, on which "Fuzzy" appeared, depicted Coe and company unabashedly mooning the camera) are trashy and blunt as a butter knife.

Born in Ohio in 1939, David Allan Coe seemed to have a proclivity for trouble from the start. Landing in reform school by the age of nine, he would spend the next twenty years in and out of jail, where he once crossed paths with Screaming Jay Hawkins, the one-time middle-weight champion of Alaska, alleged father of somewhere between thirty-three and seventy-five children, and lunatic patriarch of the musical genre that later became known as "shock rock." Coe claimed Hawkins encouraged him to pursue his musical career.

By 1967, Coe was free and heading for Nashville, where he lived for a while in a hearse parked outside of the legendary Ryman Auditorium, until recording his first album *Penitentiary Blues* in 1970. There is little doubt that the enormous success of Johnny Cash's albums *At Folsom Prison* and *Live at San Quentin* helped the former jailbird turned troubadour to find his musical niche. Coe, who built his image on his criminal past, claimed he'd done hard time for murder, when he was actually convicted for armed robbery. Eventually the truth surfaced, causing him to be shunned by his fellow outlaws, no matter how many names he dropped in his self-serving elegy "Willie, Waylon, and Me."

While some fans may have felt that Coe lacked integrity, he warmly glorifies Fuzzy as "a man above all others," who "never was the kind to turn his back upon his brothers."

Critic Stephen Thomas Erlewine of Allmusic.com maintained that David was "the purest honky-tonk and hardest country [singer] of his era. . . . He may not be the most original outlaw but there's none more outlaw than him."

Even more than his controversial lyrics and boilerplate blues rock, Coe's reputation as an outlaw is of ultimate importance to his fans. Hyping the rerelease of *Penitentiary Blues* in 2005, Hacktone Records distributed a much-coveted bumper sticker depicting the outlaw rocker's mug shot with stenciled letters boasting "I did time with David Allan Coe." The album, which was advertised as "so outlaw, it was written behind bars," included a twenty-page booklet, excerpted from Coe's self-published memoir *Ex-Convict*, offering tips "on how to survive in (and out of) prison."

No one summed up the plight of the forgotten small-time felon in a few words better than Danny O'Keefe (best known for his 1972 hit "Good Time Charlie's Got the Blues") with the droll lyrics to his song simply entitled "Outlaw": "You can't be an outlaw when you're not wanted anymore."

10

FULL OF LONESOME AND REGRET

Whether they're looking through the noose, facing a firing squad, or approaching the electric chair, the true character of outlaws often comes into play in their final moments. The age-old adage "crime doesn't pay" has come back to haunt many criminals faced with retribution for the wrongs they've done. "Gallows Pole," a song that stretches back to fifteenth-century England, is a fine example of this type of heavy-handed morality. The song is also known as "Hangman" or, in the 1940 recording by folk singer John Jacob Niles, "The Maid Freed from the Gallows." Niles's unearthly voice moans and wails the tale of a wayward lass condemned to death; we are never told exactly what the poor girl's crime was. Most often the song is sung from the viewpoint of a young man waiting upon the gallows, about to hang because of his outstanding unpaid debts. He hopes (in vain) that someone will arrive in the nick of time and buy back his freedom before he winds up "swinging high from this hangman's tree." One by one, each member of his family appears after "travelin' many a mile"; the singer repeatedly begs the executioner to "slack [his] line" just a little longer, only to realize his family and friends have all arrived empty-handed, just to watch him die. Time is running out fast yet no one is willing or able to help the doomed narrator, who can only feel betrayed in his last moments as he is preparing to face his cold, dark grave. No one does a thing to save him, until suddenly his "sweetheart" appears:

> *"Sweetheart, sweetheart, sweetheart,*
> *Did you bring gold*
> *   For to pay this hangman's fee?*
> *Or did you come to see me swingin'*
> *   High from this hangman's tree?"*

> *"Darlin', darlin', darlin',*
> *I brought you that gold*
> *   For to pay that hangman's fee,*
> *'Cause I don't want to see you swingin', swingin'*
> *   High from no hangman's tree."*

Whether sung as "Gallows Pole" or "Gallows Tree," the tune was covered by everyone from Lead Belly (the "King of the Twelve-string Guitar", who first recorded it in 1939 as "Gallis Pole") to Jimmie Rodgers, who believed the song's subject matter was too macabre to sing for his audience on his 1958 television show. Instead, Rodgers chose to perform it for the stagehands, who were said to have "greatly enjoyed it."

"Gallows Pole" eventually found its way into many a folk singer's repertoire during the folk revival of the late 1950s and early 1960s, from the Kingston Trio (pasteurized) to Peter, Paul, and Mary (earnest) to Odetta (weary and haunted), before winding up on Led Zeppelin's rootsy third album in 1970.

Robert Plant, whose shrill shriek of a voice often brought to mind the emotional histrionics of Janis Joplin, pleads for the life that is about to be snuffed out, crying:

> *"Brother, did you get me some silver?*
> *Did you get a little gold?*
> *What did you bring me my brother,*
> *   To keep from the gallows pole?"*

Led Zeppelin's version of the age-old song offers a few unexpected twists: Jimmy Page's chiming 12-string guitar; a finger-picked banjo; drummer John Bonham's propulsive beat; and Plant's sly lyrical reinterpretation. While the brother manages to bring a "little gold" and "a little of everything," it's still not quite enough to placate the insatiable executioner. The protagonist then pleads with his sister to take the hangman "by the hand" and lead him off to "some shady bower" and warm his "blood to boiling hot" in order to save him "from the wrath of this man."

Having defiled his sister, the hangman returns with a big smile on his face. "Pray tell me that I'm free to ride, ride for many a mile," the desperate criminal pleads. Although the hangman agrees that his prisoner has "a fine sister," he reneges on his side of the bargain. Whether it is bloodlust on the corrupt official's part, or a personal vendetta, is never explained as he laughs and "pull[s] so hard" on the rope until the protagonist is at last "swinging on the gallows pole."

Despite his siblings' gallant efforts, the convict's hopes are suddenly dashed as the rope tightens around his neck and chokes the life from him. The song then busts wide open into a mad celebration, driven by Page's searing leads, as Plant, now in the guise of the executioner, shouts "Swing!" while ad-libbing a macabre nursery rhyme as he gleefully watches the prisoner's body see-saw wildly back and forth.

Perhaps in the end it was best that he was hanged. After all, the criminal was willing to bankrupt his family, both financially and morally, by prostituting his poor sister in order to gain his freedom. The details of the song are vague about the nature of the debt he owes, but whatever he did, it must have been substantial, as capital punishment was meted out rather than hard time in a debtor's prison.

It seems that nearly every country around the world has a Robin Hood figure of its own making. In France that honor goes to Louis Mandrin, born in 1725 to a reputable family who fell on hard times. Following the death of his father, a successful horse trader, Louis, at age seventeen, was thrust into the role of the breadwinner for his mother and eight siblings. At the time, much of the populace had been under the thumb of corrupt tax collectors who, although in the service of the king, were known to fill their own coffers by extorting exorbitant fees on basic necessities such as salt and tobacco.

At age twenty-three, Mandrin had been commissioned to deliver a pack of ninety-seven mules to the French army, which was stationed in Italy. But everything went suddenly awry as they crossed the Alps. Nearly eighty of the animals died of exposure to the harsh weather conditions. Louis and the remaining mules arrived in terrible shape. Despite his best efforts, he was not paid. This insult, along with the trauma he'd just endured, only exacerbated Mandrin's already growing disdain for authority.

Then, in July 1753, Mandrin and his pal Benoît Brissaud were arrested following a brawl in which their combatants died. While Mandrin managed to escape, his friend Brissaud was hanged. Louis' brother Pierre, a convicted counterfeiter, would meet his fate on the gallows on the very same day. The combined effect of losing his brother and Brissaud pushed Mandrin over edge. He joined a band of tobacco smugglers and quickly became their leader, organizing them into a small militia of guerilla fighters whose numbers eventually swelled to approximately 300. Mandrin and his fearless posse soon became a cause célèbre, after the locals learned of his defiant stand against the tax collectors. Louis and his crew were said to smuggle tobacco, herbs and spices, textiles, and hides across the border from Switzerland, which they generously distributed to the masses while blatantly refusing to acknowledge the crooked officials' jurisdiction.

Informed upon by two members of his own gang, Louis Mandrin was arrested and tried on May 24, 1755. Two days later, he was condemned to be broken upon the wheel before a dismayed crowd, said to total 6,000. Louis allegedly endured the barbaric treatment for nearly ten minutes, while being repeatedly struck with iron rods. Torn apart, yet still miraculously alive, he was finally put out of his misery by strangulation. Apparently both the French economist Turgot and writer/philosopher Voltaire were appalled by Mandrin's savage treatment and vociferously protested the unforgivable way that he and his band had been abused.

"La Complainte de Mandrin" or "Mandrin's Lament," composed by an unknown bard, was soon heard throughout France and parts of

Switzerland. A first-person account of the brigand's career, the song began by describing his gang of twenty to thirty bandits: "All dressed in white, just like merchants." But we never hear anything again about his men as the narrator goes on to describe his "first little theft" when he "make[s] off with the purse of a priest." Mandrin discovers the extravagant sum of "1000 écus" and then piles up three carts with a load of "robes and coats" that he takes to sell cheap at a fair in Holland. As if to rub it in, he boasts that "they didn't cost [him] a thing." Louis's little crime spree does not last long and he is soon apprehended and put on trial by the "Sires [of] Grenoble [in] their long robes, and their square hats [who] would soon judge [him]." "They sentenced me to hang," he moans. "Oh! That is hard to hear!"

Brought in chains to the market square, Mandrin describes his last moments on earth, as he "climbed up onto the gallows [and] looked at France." He sees his "companions in poverty" (note that in the original French lyric "misère" means "poverty," not "misery") barely existing "in the shadow of a shrub." With his imminent death comes an outpouring of regret: "Please tell my mother that she will never see me again. I am a child. Do you hear me? I am a child who is lost!"

As the song has no chorus, it's interesting to note that each verse is punctuated with the repeating phrase—"Do you hear me?"—which can be interpreted in a number of ways. It may be intended to provoke the listener's sympathy for Mandrin, or perhaps the songwriter wanted to add a moral tone, to warn whoever heard this tragic ballad not to do "what I have done," as Lead Belly, Bob Dylan, and Eric Burdon would later sing in "House of the Rising Sun."

Louis Mandrin died in 1755, which makes him a revolutionary *before* the French revolution began in 1789. With frustration and anger against corrupt authorities and the monarchy certainly evident by 1755, Mandrin's cry of "Do you hear me?" might have been be a call to revolt as easily as a plea to dissuade others not to follow his path to oblivion.

Just a few years after Mandrin's death, Johannes Bückler, the "German Robin Hood," was born in Miehlen in 1778. From a young age, Bückler was branded with the less-than-glamorous nickname "Schinderhannes," as his father and grandfather were both "schinder," which meant they dealt in the cadavers of dead animals. By age sixteen, Johannes was arrested for stealing hides from the local tannery where he was employed. He soon escaped from jail and turned to larceny and armed robbery, leading a small band of thieves around the Hunsrück Mountains of the Rhineland. The local peasants sympathized with Bückler and his gang and were said to have aided Schinderhannes as an act of rebellion against the French, who occupied the territory at the time. After repeated scrapes with the law, the young outlaw eventually disappeared and enlisted in the Austrian Army under the alias of Jakob Schweikart, but his true identity was soon discovered and he was incarcerated. His paramour Juliana Blasius, better known as "Julchen," performed with her father, a musician, and her sister in the street and at fairs, where she sang ballads and played violin. She was soon arrested, interrogated, and charged as his accomplice. Attempting to free her, Schinderhannes, caught between a rock and a hard place, informed on nineteen former members of his gang, who were then systematically tracked down and executed. Having cooperated with the authorities, Bückler hoped to escape the guillotine himself, but had no such luck and was beheaded on November 21, 1803, before a crowd of 40,000 protesters and gawkers outside the gates of Mainz.

Over the centuries, the young outlaw's legend has mushroomed, beginning with Carl Zuckmayer's play *Schinderhannes*, which first opened in Berlin on October 13, 1927. A year later, a film called *The Prince of Rogues* was directed by Curtis Bernhardt with Hans Stüwe in the lead role. Bückler has also been the subject of dozens of songs, whether sung to the accompaniment of accordions and tubas at beer festivals or interpreted by the atmospheric electronic German neo-folk duo Belborn (their rendition comes complete with the sound of a head being chopped off on the downbeat).

Meanwhile, the traditional ballad "Schinderhannes" is a first-person account, describing the capture of the young outlaw "in the deep woods," and recounting how he was "led into the city, where [he] was to be hanged."

According to the song, Bückler was interrogated "two or three times" and "every word was written down." He was then imprisoned in a "deep tower" where, not surprisingly, he discovered the jail food they served to be inedible. As the lyric tells, Schinderhannes was forced "to eat bad meals" until "the time came when [he] could eat no more." Whether it was the lousy chow, or the sense of impending doom, Bückler soon broke down in remorse, and religion finally got the best of our young, brazen outlaw as he began to obsess:

> *Oh, what will my mother say,*
> *When she hears of all the accusations*
> *That I had done so much bad*
> *In my young years?*

Although his exact birthdate is unknown, the song claims Johannes Bückler "lived twenty-two years," and like many a scoundrel before him (and since), he sought forgiveness and redemption in his final hours. As the song tells: "two nights before my end, I received the sacrament."

Repenting wholeheartedly, the protagonist begins to plead:

> *Farewell dear father, farewell dear mother,*
> *Farewell dear sister, farewell dear brother,*
> *Wash your hands in my blood,*
> *So that you know how much it hurts.*

The lyric "wash your hands in my blood" clearly evokes Christ's last supper, when Jesus asked his disciples to share a cup of wine, saying it represented his blood. Bückler's last-minute regret, coming from an outlaw of "Robin Hood" stature, seems disappointing and out of character and may have been the work of the songwriter after the fact, determined to tack on a moralistic ending to discourage young men from following in Bückler's wayward footsteps.

In stark contrast to this traditional folk ballad stands the Neo-Nazi pagan band Absurd's interpretation of "Aufruf des Schinderhannes," which was growled, screamed, and shrieked over a deafening onslaught of guitar, bass, and drums. While the lyric itself is a romantic ode to defying the establishment, the hardcore tonalities of the music perfectly evoke the oppression that Johannes Bückler brazenly battled, as well as the harsh punishment he suffered in response to his brief rebellious life:

> Up, up comrades, while the night is dark,
> Show your heroic acts, all are sleeping at the ready.
> All judges and henchmen and anyone else who can scare us,
> You may not conceal yourselves when you attack coura-
>   geously.
>
> Don't spend too much time pondering, hurry and go to the
>   place
> Where in filled cabinets there lies a concealed treasure.
> Break down the door and locks where the large palace is,
> Drill through the brimming barrels and drink the best
>   wine.
>
> But hear the pleas of the poor, help them in their misery,
> Have mercy on them, with them share your bread.
> Let the wanderer on the road go in peace,
> Only attack those who look down on poverty.

The next verse seems rather ironic as we hear Bückler remind his crew that if they are captured and face torture or death, they are to endure it, and remain faithful to him and their fellow gang members, no matter what befalls them. But once his lovely Juliana is captured and faced with torture and incarceration, Schinderhannes, forced to choose between loyalty to his men and chivalry to his paramour, "unlocks his mouth" and begins naming names:

> Should you feel the pressure, the torture of jail,
> Don't save your own back, once and forever,
> If after all the lashes, the lock of your mouth doesn't stay
>   shut,
> Then you are pale corpses, you're headed to the gallows.

In some versions Bückler is hanged, while in others he is beheaded, which is historically correct.

As with Robin Hood or Jesse James, just the utterance of Cole Younger's name inspires a range of emotions, from sympathy for the hardships he endured to deep respect for the heroic life he led. Although James remains America's ultimate outlaw (most likely as he was murdered, while Cole went to jail and repented for his wild deeds), the Younger brothers actually once had top billing in what sounds like a now-forgotten 1970s rock band, the Younger-James Gang. No outlaw ever teemed with remorse like Cole Younger. One must wonder how Jesse James would have felt about such bellyaching. As Peter Rowan admonished, "Once you stand up against the norm, you can't ask for mercy." Or, like it says somewhere in the outlaw's unwritten code book, "If you hang, you hang alone. Just don't cry about it."

Cole Younger's perspective was decidedly different: "The man who chooses the career of outlawry is either a natural fool or an innocent madman. . . . The term outlaw has a varied meaning. A man may be an outlaw, and yet a patriot. There is the outlaw with a heart of velvet and a hand of steel; there is the outlaw who never molested the sacred sanctity of any man's home; there is the outlaw who never dethroned a woman's honor, or assailed her heritage; and there is the outlaw who has never robbed the honest poor."

Younger offers a shopping list of regrets and lessons learned the hard way: "Come with me to the prison, where for a quarter of a century I have occupied a lonely cell. When the door swings in on you there, the world does not hear your muffled wail. There is little to inspire mirth in prison. For a man who has lived close to the heart of nature, in the forest, in the saddle, to imprison him is like caging a wild bird. And yet imprisonment has brought out the excellences of many men. I have learned many things in the lonely hours there. I have learned that hope is a divinity; I have learned that a surplus of determination conquers every weakness; I have learned that you cannot mate a white dove to a blackbird; I have learned that vengeance is for God and not for man; I have learned that there are some things better than a picture on a church window; I have learned that the American people, and especially the good people of Minnesota, do not strip a fallen foe; I have learned that whoever says 'there is no God' is a fool;

I have learned that politics is often mere traffic, and statesmanship trickery; I have learned that the honor of the republic is put upon the plains and battled for; I have learned that the English language is too often used to deceive the commonwealth of labor; I have learned that the man who prides himself on getting on the wrong side of every public issue is as pernicious an enemy to the country as the man who openly fires upon the flag; and I have seen mute sufferings of men in prison which no human pen can portray.

"And I have seen men die there. During my twenty-five years of imprisonment, I have spent a large portion of the time in the hospital, nursing the sick and soothing the dying. Oh! the sadness, the despair, the volcano of human woe that lurks in such an hour. One, a soldier from the North, I met in battle when I wore the gray. In '63 I had led him to safety beyond the Confederate lines in Missouri, and in '97 he died in my arms in the Minnesota prison, a few moments before a full pardon had arrived from the president."

After wasting away in a jail cell for a quarter of a century it is understandable how one might become somewhat sanctimonious. Younger's heavy-handed moralizing doesn't hold back:"There is no heroism in outlawry," he wrote. "And the fate of each outlaw in his turn should be an everlasting lesson to the young of the land. And even as Benedict Arnold, the patriot and traitor, dying in an ugly garret in a foreign land, cried with his last breath to the lone priest beside him: 'Wrap my body in the American flag'; so the outlaw, from his inner soul, if not from his lips, cries out, 'Oh, God, turn back the universe!'"

"The Prisoner's Song," recorded by Vernon Dalhart in 1925, is a classic lament of loneliness and regret. Dalhart got the mournful tune from his cousin Guy Massey. He learned it from his brother Robert, who apparently overheard his fellow inmates singing its yearning verse while serving time in the state penitentiary. Dalhart was already famous for his recording of "The Wreck of the Old 97," which sold in the neighborhood of seven million copies the previous year. Although he'd studied voice at the Dallas Conservatory of Music, Dalhart stuck with the vernacular style of the Lone Star cowboy, which, combined with a weepy fiddle and rudimentary strummed guitar, spoke to down-home folks across the West and South. With its sorrowful lyrics telling of "cold prison bars" and sleeping on "a pillow of stone," "The Prisoner's Song" (credited to Guy Massey) became a favorite of everybody from country crooner Hank Snow, who warbled it to a loping beat, to the "Father of Bluegrass," Bill Monroe, who cut an up-tempo version featuring his famous high/lonesome style vocal style and a smoking mandolin solo.

Written and sung by Reverend Gary Davis, "Bad Company," is another moralistic ballad that spills with regret. Blind since childhood, Gary was a virtuoso guitarist and impassioned preacher who could be found singing the glory of his Lord on city-street corners from Durham, North Carolina, to Harlem. A master of the devil's music, Davis toured America and England playing the blues in coffeehouses, festivals, and concert halls, inspiring and teaching firsthand a new generation of guitar pickers that included everyone from Dave Van Ronk, Jorma Kaukonen, and David Bromberg to Ry Cooder and Taj Mahal.

In "Bad Company," Davis's gravelly voice (which Eric von Schmidt once described as "God's own bullhorn") gives the chilling testimony of a boy who is about to be executed in the electric chair. Regretful for not heeding his mother's warning, the protagonist is unable to eat a bite of his last supper. "I couldn't eat either," the song's narrator adds. "Bad company, children," Davis moans wearily, "Bad company brought me here."

Another classic outlaw song that teems with lonesomeness and regret is Roy Acuff's "Lost Highway," as recorded by Hank Williams. In it, he recounts a tale of woe about a lost soul, just twenty-two, who has led a sinful life for which he's already "paid the cost." Not surprisingly, he bemoans his life as a gambler, drinker, and womanizer who wanders aimlessly, alone, in shame and bewilderment. The protagonist knows he is a goner, convinced nothing can save him and that it's already "too late to pray."

Written and sung by Johnny Cash, "Folsom Prison Blues" is a classic jailhouse ballad, sung from the perspective of a regretful inmate serving a life sentence after he "shot a man in Reno just to watch him die." In his husky baritone, Cash bemoans failing to listen to the advice of his dear mother, who warned him as a young boy not to "play with guns" (a theme he would later revisit in "Don't Take Your Guns to Town"). The song brims with heartbreaking remorse as Cash laments that he hasn't "seen the sunshine since I don't know when." Worse than that is the damn train that keeps rolling by his window, taunting him with visions of plush dining cars packed with fancy folks sipping coffee and puffing on big fat stogies.

The "Man in Black" often sang from first-hand experience. Although he never went so far as to kill a man (as both Skip James and Lead Belly allegedly had), he still knew a thing or two about prison walls. While Cash never actually did any hard time, he'd been arrested on seven occasions over a seven-year period, mostly for public drunkenness. Once he was picked up at two o'clock in the morning in Starkville, Mississippi, with a belly full of beer, for the crime of picking flowers. Then he was busted in El Paso, after having crossed the border into Mexico to buy amphetamines and barbiturates. The final time came in Lafayette, Georgia, in October 1967, for pills once again. After a powerful lecture from a spiritually minded sheriff, Cash returned to Nashville where he voluntarily submitted to a detox program that allowed him to finally kick his habit.

During the mid-1950s, images of the antihero, as portrayed by Marlon Brando in *The Wild One* and James Dean in *Rebel Without a Cause*, dominated Hollywood. While Elvis Presley was the poster boy for teenage sex and rebellion, Cash was truly antiestablishment in both his image and his unbridled compassion for the downtrodden. His simple yet poetic verse spoke directly to honest working folks who felt disenfranchised and alienated by a cutthroat capitalist system. They related to his simple stories, his plainspoken populist politics, his unpretentious delivery, and his world-weary grin. And although he was hardly Hollywood handsome, women found his rugged features, animal magnetism, and piercing dark eyes strangely seductive.

Cash had also unknowingly won the hearts of a cross-section of America that he never imagined was listening. In Teresa Ortega's essay "Johnny Cash as Lesbian Icon," she recalled her grade-school fantasy of standing before the mirror, "repeating 'Hello, I'm Johnny Cash' in the lowest voice [she] could muster—singing along with him, trying to play the harmonica as well as guitar like him, and eventually dressing like him, in all-black men's clothes and heavy black boots."

Ortega describes Cash as "mysterious, sexy, and perverse," pointing to the "dangerous appeal" of his 1968 classic album *At Folsom Prison* to state her case. She's grateful to the Man in Black for "his notable contributions to the world of lesbian fashion. With his homely face, starkly cut hair and [at that time] unfashionably black clothes, Cash's star image is determinably anti-aesthetic, a style that owes more to folksiness than to artiness. Cash's unapologetic self-presentation symbolizes many lesbians' view of their own relationship to ideals of physical beauty both masculine and feminine."

All in a day's work it seems, for an American folk legend. . . .

In 1968, Cash's remake of "Folsom Prison Blues" shot up the charts to No. 1 once again for four weeks. The album *At Folsom Prison* was Johnny's first platinum record and would inspire another prison outing the following year: *Live at San Quentin*.

With Keith Richards's twangy acoustic guitar and Mick Jagger's chugging harmonica driving the rhythm, the Rolling Stones delivered a down-home acoustic reading of "Prodigal Son," a remake of "That's No Way to Get Along," Reverend Robert Wilkins's tale of a poor boy who robs his father's money and heads off down the road seeking adventure. But the Prodigal Son's new-found freedom is short lived. The next thing he knows a famine has stricken the land and the only job he can manage to scrounge is feeding some farmer's swine. In no time he's standing with his head hung down and crying, "That's no way to get along." Hightailing it back home, he begs forgiveness from his dad, who falls to his knees praising the Lord for the return of his wayward son. It's an emotional reunion, and the entire family all sits down to a sumptuous feast, where the grateful father proclaims "my son was lost but now he is found." In Wilkins's morality play the prodigal son actually finds forgiveness and redemption once he faces his father and admits to his wrongdoing. This is definitely an exception to the old rule that you can't go home again.

Perhaps more than any other rock star in history, Keith Richards embodies the image of the incorrigible outlaw, artfully blurring the boundary between reality and myth. Searching for words to describe Richards, British music journalist Nick Kent borrowed a phrase previously used to describe the equally debauched poet Lord Byron: "mad, bad, and dangerous to know." Cutting it a little closer to the bone, the gravel-throated poet/singer Tom Waits once likened his friend to "a killer at a gas station." Keith's fabled drug habit and frequent showdowns with the law (amounting to five arrests and trials in all) have been the stuff of legend since his initial bust at his Redlands estate in February 1967, which led to a brief incarceration at the infamous Wormwoods Scrubs Prison. The experience of spending the night in a cold, lonely cell would inspire the alienated anthem "2000 Light Years from Home," from the Stones' *Their Satanic Majesties Request*. Much to the chagrin of the authorities, Richards and Mick Jagger gained overwhelming support from the public, who felt the Stones had been unjustly persecuted. The furor prompted William Rees-Mogg of *The Times* of London to write an audacious editorial entitled "Who Breaks a Butterfly on a Wheel?" There was little doubt the police were out to make an example of England's bad boys when the plan backfired royally.

Ten years later, in February 1977, the Royal Canadian Mounted Police nailed Keith for narcotics in his hotel room at the Toronto Hilton. Charged with "possession of heroin for the purpose of trafficking," the guitarist was suddenly faced with a sentence of seven years to life behind bars. Once more, Richards miraculously dodged the bullet. He was put on probation for a year and handed a suspended sentence after promising to go for treatment and performing for a pair of benefit concerts in April 1979.

Millions of his fans continue to live vicariously through Keith's misadventures, while copping his unique style (no one more so than Johnny Depp, who used him as the basis for the character of Jack Sparrow in the film *Pirates of the Caribbean*), from his swaggering guitar stance to his skull ring and shark's tooth earring. Richards has likened his well-worn image to "a long shadow" that still hangs over him decades later, despite having settled down (to some extent) to raise a family in Connecticut.

Keith Richards wasn't the only famous musician targeted by the cops for his incorrigible ways. Like Frank Sinatra's alleged ties to the mafia, Waylon Jennings's notorious coke habit fueled his "Outlaw" mystique, while helping to sell plenty of records and concert tickets. Along with Willie Nelson, Tompall Glaser, and Jessi Colter, Jennings would achieve unprecedented success with the 1976 release of *Wanted! The Outlaws*, the first country album to go platinum. But a year later, in 1977, Jennings was busted when a posse of federal agents came barging in "through the back door" of his Nashville recording session looking for a package of cocaine. Before they could nail Jennings with the goods, he flushed the bundle of blow down the toilet. His quick response managed to cripple the prosecution and the charges were eventually tossed out due to a lack of evidence. The only regret Jennings seemed to have over the whole affair was the loss of his stash and the headache of dealing with the authorities.

The bust would inspire Jennings's next hit record, in October 1978. Over a percolating boot-stompin' beat, he growled wearily, "Don't You Think This Outlaw Bit's Done Got Out of Hand?" As Telecasters snarled and twanged, Jennings recounted the recent chapter of his personal mythology, after he and his band were described as "outlaws in some old magazine," which led him to getting "busted by the man" for the crime of "singin' through [his] nose." The song talks about the forces of law and order "protecting you from me," but at this time Jennings was harming no one but himself as he ran himself ragged with coke. Unable to sleep, Jennings chain-smoked while playing pinball for days on end. The song soared to No. 5 on the country charts, branding Waylon's outlaw image (defined by his black leather vest, perpetual black cowboy hat, and shaggy goatee) into the public's imagination.

Jennings would later recut "Outlaw Bit" as a tender ballad, complete with a string section, while exchanging the lyrics' "bit" for the more bitter "shit."

In comparison to the punk-rock explosion of the late 1970s and early 1980s, the "Outlaw" image seemed rather tame. But the metaphor of the country singer as incorrigible brigand continued to flourish in 1985 when Jennings joined a new gang, comprised of Willie Nelson, Kris Kristofferson, and Johnny Cash. The first Highwaymen album included a cover of "Desperados Waiting for a Train" by Guy Clark (considered "The Fifth Highwayman" by many fans) as well as Jimmy Webb's "The Highwayman."

While the melody to "The Highwayman" is both simple and bold, Webb (author of such 1960s epics as "MacArthur Park" and "Wichita Lineman") takes the song beyond the typical outlaw ballad we've come to identify with any one of these singers. Instead it follows the path of one man's reincarnation from one life to the next, speculating on what this "old soul" might become next.

"The Highwayman" begins with Willie Nelson singing of his life as a rapparee, who once robbed many a young maiden's baubles as they traveled along the old coach roads. But he soon faced the gallows for his crimes, which included killing the gallant soldiers who tried, but failed, to capture him. The Highwayman's spirit is eternal and cannot be killed by something so mundane as a bullet, knife, or rope.

Kris Kristofferson sings the next verse in the guise of a sailor, followed by Waylon Jennings, who plays a dam builder who died in an accident. The song's final verse was a bit of a leap for Johnny Cash, who always managed to maintain his credibility, no matter where a song lyric took him. Here he sings in the unlikely guise of a pilot from the future, guiding a rocket ship across the Milky Way. Webb wraps up his poetic parable by implying that one day his protagonist will reincarnate once more as a bold-spirited brigand or perhaps "a single drop of rain." And then the Highwaymen boldly chant together: "And I'll be back again, and again."

Webb's whimsical lyric would trigger a rash of satirical verse on YouTube, inspiring hundreds of comments ranging from the hilarious and imaginative to the cheap and smutty, parodying the song with opening lines such as "I was a Canadian, / On a moose I did ride," "I was a Mongol, / In the fearless Golden Horde," "I was a ventriloquist dummy, / Always had a hand right up my back," and "I was a porn star, / Among the porn skanks I did ride."

But no matter how the public might have mocked Webb's whimsical lyric, "The Highwayman" clearly spoke to millions of country music fans.

Listening to Bob Dylan's 1975 album *Desire*, one has to wonder where the former "spokesman of his generation" was getting his advice at the time: a bookie, the CIA, a waitress in Little Italy? "Hurricane," his epic ballad about boxing great Ruben "Hurricane" Carter, was unquestionably a powerful song, cowritten with Jacques Levy and told in eleven verses, all lovingly embroidered by Scarlet Rivera's swooping violin. Bob did a noble thing, trying to get a fair trial for a man he believed was innocent, with his life rotting away in a prison cell. He even got some of his cool friends together to play a big benefit concert at Madison Square Garden to help the Hurricane out. How was he to know that Carter was guilty?

"Joey," on the other hand, an ode to mob boss Joey Gallo, was a bad idea from the start with its disturbingly naïve refrain: "Joey, Joey, what made them want to come and blow you away?" In a Cliff Notes musical version of *The Godfather*, Dylan tells Gallo's tale with cinematic detail nearly equal to that of director Francis Ford Coppola. "Born in Red Hook, Brooklyn," Joey "opened up his eyes to the tune of an accordion." After Gallo avenged a gang of thugs who came to rub out his brother, he did "ten years in Attica, reading Nietzsche and Wilhelm Reich." Not only was Joey a jailhouse scholar but a fashion plate of the first order. Upon his release from prison, Bob tells us, he "dressed like Jimmy Cagney." From that day on, according to Dylan, Gallo went straight, refusing to carry a gun as "too many children" could get hurt. But then one day, for no apparent reason, his enemies returned and murdered him in cold blood in a Lower East Side clam bar.

What's so aggravating about the song is not that it's poorly written or performed. On the contrary, the problem is Dylan's perspective. In his attempt to canonize Gallo, he actually robs the man of the outlaw's inherent karma. What goes around comes around. You live by the gun—you die by the gun. There's something righteous about that. It doesn't matter that Joey served his time. The seeds of Gallo's revenge were planted years before he hung up his weapon. Joey knew why they came to blow him away. So why couldn't Dylan figure it out?

"Mama Tried" is another classic tale of misadventure and regret, written and performed by Merle Haggard, from his 1970 album *Okie from Muskogee*. Later popularized by the Grateful Dead, the song portrays a convict surrounded by the four lonely walls of his cell, with his past weighing heavily upon his guilty conscience. "Mama tried to raise me better," a young Bob Weir confesses, as he hangs his head in shame, "but her pleading I denied."

In a similar vein is Weir's earnest recitation of "Me and My Uncle" by John Phillips (of the Mamas and the Papas). In it the Dead's rhythm guitarist recounts the calamity he encounters with a band of young, drunk cowboys on a hot, dusty day in Santa Fe. Fueled by flowing liquor, "a friendly game" of poker quickly turns sour when one of the cowboys accuses the protagonist's uncle of cheating. "Oh no, it couldn't be," he sings:

> *"I know my uncle, he's as honest as me,*
> *And I'm as honest as a Denver man can be."*

A moment later all hell busts loose as one of the cowboys reaches for his gun. Our young storyteller draws first and shoots him dead. In the heat of the moment, he grabs a bottle and cracks another cowpoke on the jaw, before blasting the last of the bunch. In the midst of this bloody spree, he manages to stand back just long enough to lament the fate of his final victim. "Oh damn, he won't grow old," he sighs, before blowing him away.

With the much-coveted gold in tow, he and his uncle (who must have been both proud and stunned by his nephew's lightning-fast, cold-blooded response) hop on their horses and head for Mexico, crossing the border, which seems to represent something more than a mere geographical boundary. With the fresh blood of three young cowboys resting heavily on his soul, the nephew finds the doors to hell have suddenly been thrown wide open. Life is cheap to our fallen hero. Laws have become meaningless and now anything seems possible.

"I love those cowboys," he says with a modicum of regret. He also "loves" his uncle as well, but not nearly as much as that bag of gold, and in short order kills him too, leaving "his dead ass there by the side of the road." It seems whatever sorrow our protagonist offers for his murderous ways is, in the end, only lip service at best.

Best known for mid-1960s chart-topping hits like "California Dreamin'" and "Monday, Monday," John Phillips also wrote "San Francisco (Be Sure to Wear Flowers in Your Hair)," in June of 1967, for Scott McKenzie. It helped to lure hordes of hippies in search of peace, love, and music to the Monterey International Pop Festival (which Phillips coproduced). Phillips, we later discovered, harbored a nefarious side, fueled by heavy drug use, and there were posthumous allegations of taboo-breaking sexual behavior. Amongst his catalog of bubbly folk-rock hits, "Me and My Uncle" stands as a particularly dark portrait of the human spirit, revealing what even the most innocent among us is capable of under dire circumstances.

Similar themes can be found in Steve Earle's moralistic rocker "The Devil's Right Hand," the story of a wayward lad who is enchanted by a gun he finds down at the local general store. Aghast, his "Mama" warns her son "the pistol is the devil's right hand." The song unfolds like an American fairytale, as Earle's cocky protagonist buys the firearm and soon discovers it "can get you into trouble but it can't get you out." Before long he winds up in a card game and catches "a miner cheating." Before he knows it he "shot the dog down."

The tale comes to an end with a clever twist as the protagonist stands trial, denying any wrongdoing. Denying his guilt he claims, "Nothing touched the trigger but the devil's right hand."

Written by former Buddy Holly guitarist Sonny Curtis (whose best known song was "Love Is All Around," the theme to the popular TV sitcom the *Mary Tyler Moore Show*), "I Fought the Law (And the Law Won)" reached No. 9 on the Billboard charts in early 1966 thanks to El Paso rockers the Bobby Fuller Four. Covered by Hank Williams Jr. in 1978, the song was roughed up a year later by the Clash, who best embodied the rebel image of the British punk scene. True to form, the Clash kicked out the jams, howling of the joys of "Robbing people with a six-gun" over a pair of grinding guitars. Joe Strummer sings of the hard life of a chain gang convict, with a heart (and beat) nearly as heavy as the sledgehammer he wields to break up big rocks in the summer sun. Sympathizing with the plight of Sex Pistols bassist Sid Vicious, who was on trial at the time for murdering his girlfriend Nancy Spungen, Strummer changed the lyric from "I left my baby and it felt so bad" to "I killed my baby," adding a darker dimension to the already tragic and regretful tale.

A Clash rarity, "Bankrobber" was released as a single in the UK in the summer of 1980. Its irresistible bass-driven dub groove, played by Paul Simonon, propels Joe Strummer's tale of a man whose father was a benevolent brigand who "loved to steal your money" but "never hurt nobody." As with most of Strummer's songs, "Bankrobber" is a vehicle for the unvarnished truth: "Some is rich, and some is poor, that's the way the world is," he sings in a gruff London burr. But, as Joe firmly believed, no matter what life hands you, you don't just sit around complaining about "how bad your luck is."

While shooting an accompanying video for the song, outside a bank, a pair of the band's roadies, wearing bandanas, were stopped and interrogated by the police for looking suspicious.

"Bankrobber" was later covered by Hot Tuna in 1992. The band's guitarist/vocalist Jorma Kaukonen thought it was originally "a reggae song" that the Clash had covered. With the help of Michael Falzarano's choppy mandolin he turned it into "an Appalachian mountain folk song." Either way, Hot Tuna's laidback rendition of the obscure Clash tune featured some slinky slide guitar work and rippling accordion riffs by keyboardist Pete Sears.

Even though Merle Haggard's "Branded Man" (the title song from his 1967 album) does his time and pays his debt to society, he still finds himself alienated and "out in the cold" following his release from prison. No matter how he tries to walk the straight and narrow, the "black mark" of his past, "the secret" of having done time for committing a felony, relentlessly hounds him wherever he goes. Haggard perfectly nails the dilemma that every ex-con faces: no matter how he tries to walk the straight and narrow, he still has to face his checkered past and "tell 'em where I've been."

On his album *I'm a Lonesome Fugitive*, from March 1967, Haggard croons the hard-knocks "Life in Prison" as a pedal-steel guitar riff frames his every word. Its slippery tone seems to mock the bewitched con who, "insane with rage," took "my darlin's life." As the song ends, he cries piteously, "If I could die, my pain might go away."

Following Gene Clark's abrupt departure from the Byrds in 1966, at the height of their popularity (the troubled singer/songwriter ironically quit due to his fear of flying), and the subsequent firing of their outspoken and outrageous harmony singer/second guitarist David Crosby, the Byrds quickly filled the void with the doomed angel of country rock, Gram Parsons. A longhaired scholar of country music, Parsons soon spirited the band from LA to Nashville and replaced the trademark jingle-jangle chime of Roger McGuinn's twelve-string Rickenbacker with a gaggle of banjos, mandolins, fiddles, and pedal-steel guitars.

In the late 1960s, rednecks stood resolutely on one side of the barbed-wire fence, while hippies hung out on the other. There just was no in-between. While Merle Haggard's "Okie from Muskogee" took pot-shots at the counterculture, Peter Fonda and Dennis Hopper's film *Easy Rider* (1969) helped fuel stereotypes and widen the chasm between the two polarized groups. That lasted until the early 1970s, when the New South began to rise with the arrival of the Allman Brothers and Lynyrd Skynyrd. It's interesting to note how closely *Easy Rider*'s pair of motorcycle outlaws, played by Fonda and Hopper, resembled the Byrds' Roger McGuinn and David Crosby (right down to his droopy Yosemite Sam mustache).

With the release of *Sweetheart of the Rodeo* in August 1968, the Byrds once again changed the course of rock 'n' roll. (They'd done it twice before, creating the folk-rock sound of "Mr. Tambourine Man" and "Turn, Turn, Turn" and, more recently, forging psychedelic rock by mingling elements of John Coltrane's free-jazz improvisation with the transcendental drone of Ravi Shankar's sitar for "Eight Miles High.")

Although sounding more Pat Boone than George Jones, Gram Parson's rendition of Merle Haggard's "Life in Prison" (along with the band's cover of the Louvin Brothers' "I Like the Christian Life," which most people assumed was a joke until Roger McGuinn became a born-again Christian himself) stands as a powerful testimonial for country music as an indelible component of rock 'n' roll. While there is no doubting the credibility and authenticity in Haggard's performance, the Byrds' earnest cover appealed to a generation of hippies who were not yet ready or able to handle genuine country music straight-up.

With the help of an uncredited Bob Dylan, Roger McGuinn would write and sing "The Ballad of Easy Rider" for Hopper and Fonda's film. In the early days of the Byrds, McGuinn and Crosby had effectively reworked the traditional ballad "He Was a Friend of Mine" into a breath-taking lament for the martyred President Kennedy. "The Ballad of Easy Rider," which reveals a similar cadence, became a haunting eulogy for Dennis Hopper's character "Billy," who is blown off his motorcycle after flipping some trigger-happy redneck the finger. "All he wanted, / Was to be free, / And that's the way, / It turned out to be," McGuinn sobs. The song was later covered by Richard Thompson on his 1976 collection, idiosyncratically titled *(guitar, vocal)*.

Pennsylvania singer/songwriter John Gorka's "Jailbirds in the Big-house" is another somber epitaph for the wasted lives of those gone wrong.

> They built a prison by the freeway,
> Just to rub it in.
> It's a gentle reminder
> Of the wages of sin. . . .
>
> There's a hundred stories
> For every man in there,
> There's marks on the cell walls,
> There's marks on the men.

In the song's chorus, Gorka sings:

> Jailbirds in the big house,
> Jailbirds on a spree,

Some of them coulda looked like you,
Some of them used to look like me.

Gorka boldly makes the point that inmates doing time are not all that different from himself, nor his audience. "'Jailbirds' came out of years and years of passing by the Rahway State Prison on the way to see relatives as a kid, and years later driving into New York from Pennsylvania," Gorka recalled. "As a grown-up I wondered who was in there that I might know and I thought of [the song's protagonist] 'Teddy.' I was sitting at a bar in Portland, Oregon, after a show, having a sandwich, and overheard a conversation a young woman was having on the pay phone nearby. I thought I heard her say that her uncle was getting out of prison and they were having a party for him. I don't know if that is what she said or if it was my imagination but that was the beginning of the song." Gorka's quirky sense of humor is in fine form in the opening verse:

Teddy was a bad kid,
From a bad family tree.
He was voted most likely
To commit a felony.

But the hard reality of the criminal's life and his sad fate quickly sets in as the song turns from whimsical wordplay to a realistic portrait:

His face was waiting for a number,
His fate was aching to be sealed . . .

And if you should run across him,
He could shorten your life,
With the butt of a pistol,
Or the edge of a knife.

Texas songwriter Kevin "Blackie" Farrell's "Sonora's Death Row" begins by celebrating the free mescal on the flow down at "Amanda's

Saloon," where we find the song's protagonist, a carefree gambler, enjoying himself amidst a clutch of lovely senoritas.

After having "won some silver at seven-card stud," he takes a break from the action to step outside for some fresh air, but "the whiskey and the mescal and peso cigars" begin to fog his head. A moment later he is approached and held up by some gun-wielding figure standing in the shadows. "Somebody whispered 'Your life or your money,'" Farrell sings. Reaching for his pistol to defend himself, he finds it gone. He wakes some indeterminable amount of time later, "face down in Amanda's back alley." Scrambling over to his horse, he pulls his Winchester rifle from its holster and storms back into the saloon where he finds his friends drinking and laughing while "twirlin' [his] pistols and throwin' [his] money around."

Overcome with rage, he starts shooting recklessly until someone suddenly falls to the floor, jarring him back to his senses. Suddenly the song's protagonist discovers his "six-gun" had been tied to his hip all along, and the wad of bills he'd won had been shoved deep down into his pocket of his jeans where he'd left it. Realizing he'd been bewitched by hallucinogenic hooch, the protagonist "fell to [his] knees and cried."

> For a nightmare of mezcal was all that it was,
> No one had robbed me at all.
> I wish I was dreamin' the sound of the gallows
> They're testin' just outside the walls,
> And I'd give a ransom to drink there today,
> And be free of Sonora's Death Row.

Texas songwriter Tom Russell considers "Sonora's Death Row" "the best cowboy twist-of-fate song ever written." The song has also been recorded by Robert Earl Keen and Richard Shindell.

Strains of the seventeenth-century ballad "Patrick Fleming," which recounts the exploits of a "valiant soldier" who, out of desperation, becomes a daring bandit until he's captured and executed, in 1650, can be found in "Whiskey in the Jar." Musicologist Alan Lomax once described the enduring tune that glorifies the fate of highwaymen in Ireland and Scotland as "a rollicking ballad." "The gentlemen of the roads robbed English landlords [and] were regarded as national patriots," wrote Lomax, who first collected "Whiskey in the Jar" for his book *The Folk Songs of North America.* Lomax's fine field recording of the song came from a performance by the great uilleann piper and song collector Séamus Ennis in 1951 and was released on his compilation *World Library of Folk and Primitive Music, Vol. 2: Ireland.*

"Highwayman and outlaw songs are found in the folk music of countries the world over," explained the New York–based antifolk singer/guitarist Kirk Kelly. "These stories always draw on timeless themes of class struggle, but in the long and brutal English occupation of Ireland, class struggle was always intertwined with the struggle for independence and more recently, the establishment of a democratic republic. While many celebrate the story of a specific individual like Jack Doogan [a.k.a. Donahoe or sometimes Doolan] of "The Wild Colonial Boy," or Willie Brennan from "Brennan on the Moore," the protagonist of "Whiskey in the Jar" is most likely a real person or based on the stories of various individuals from the same region, around the same time, whose campaign ended with betrayal but whose actual identity has been lost to time and revision. Amidst the country's rich repertoire of songs, chronicling generations of martyrs until the Easter Uprising, the rapparee stands as a timeless and tragic but boldly unique hero."

As with Blackie Farrell's "Sonora's Death Row," "Whiskey in the Jar" was another song, perhaps one of the first, in which alcohol was an accomplice to murder. Most often credited to "Traditional," it has withstood countless lyric and melodic makeovers for centuries. Recorded by everyone from the folk singer/actor Burl Ives to platinum-selling thrash gods Metallica (who won a Grammy in 2000 for their version), "Whiskey in the Jar" was originally popularized by the Dubliners on their 1967 album *More of the Hard Stuff,* which was comprised of a variety of drinking songs. Over the years, "Whiskey in the Jar" has appeared under various titles, including "The Sporting Hero," "Kilgary Mountain," and "Gilgarra Mountain," as well as "Whiskey in the Bar." In 2014, controversial Uruguayan group El Cuarteto de Nos put a Latin spin on it, recording the tune in Spanish as "Whisky en Uruguay."

The song is most often set in the Emerald Isle, anywhere from Cork to Kerry to Sligo (while American versions of the song frequently take place in the Appalachians or occasionally in the Ozark Mountains). It recounts the robbing of a military man, usually a captain (who frequently goes by the name of Farrell) but sometimes a colonel, and the subsequent betrayal of the brigand by his sweetheart, who is known as Molly, Ginny, or Jenny.

The saga begins as the hapless Captain Farrell sits counting a pile of money and is confronted by the song's protagonist, who suddenly produces both a pistol and a rapier and firmly yet politely instructs him to "stand o'er and deliver" his "pretty penny," while warning him not to try any funny stuff "or the devil, he may take ya."

The chorus follows the end of each verse, chanted like a nonsense mantra or drunken incantation. Impossible to decipher, it's not exactly clear who is singing it, whether it is the drunken mumble of the perpetrator of the crime or the nervous chatter of his victim. Is it Captain Farrell offering a dram to the man who is holding him up, perhaps in garbled Gaelic? "Musha ring dum a do dum a da," goes the chorus, "Whack for my daddy-o" (whatever that means, it is repeated again). And then, we learn, "There's whiskey in the jar."

With his pockets bulging with booty, it's off to his fair Molly our impulsive narrator does ride. "She swore that she'd love me, never would she leave me," he confides but her shallow promise vanishes by the next verse as he curses her wicked soul: "But the devil take that woman, for you know she tricked me easy."

Our "drunk and weary" leading man now enters Molly's chamber, seeking sanctuary from the crime he has committed, but he is not safe. "I never knew the danger," he confesses. "For about six or maybe seven"—we are not sure if he's talking about minutes or hours later—in walks Captain Farrell, whose name conveniently rhymes with "both barrels," with which our pickled protagonist immediately blasts him.

Following the shooting, and another refrain of "Musha ring dum a do dum a da, / Whack for my daddy-o," the thief and murderer finds himself dejectedly behind bars, attached to "a ball and chain," wishing he was sleeping once more in sweet Molly's chamber. The song ends with him singing "I got drunk on whiskey-o" which is rhymed with "I love my Molly-o," despite the fact that she allegedly turned him in to the authorities (while undoubtedly keeping all the loot).

One additional question remains. Did the Captain knowingly follow his assailant to Molly's chamber to confront the culprit, or did he suddenly come upon him when he also was expecting to sleep in her chamber that fateful night?

With our protagonist in prison and the captain robbed and shot full of holes, "Whiskey in the Jar" teems with regret. Only Molly (or Jenny or Ginny) seems to have made out all right in the end.

"'Whiskey in the Jar' lends itself perfectly to rock," Kirk Kelly pointed out. His rough and tumble Lower East Side Irish roots-rock band Paddy on the Railway plays a driving arrangement with a strong backbeat that is "always appreciated."

Phil Lynott, an anomaly as a black man in fronting the Irish rock group Thin Lizzy, recorded a rocking version of "Whiskey in the Jar" as the band's first top-ten hit in 1973. Accompanied by Eric Bell's soaring lead guitar work, Lynott's raspy soulful voice belied a strong feeling of melancholy as he recounted the misadventures of the ill-fated rapparee over a steady rocking 4/4 beat. Thin Lizzy would continue to mine the outlaw image with the title track of their 1976 album *Jailbreak*.

In 1990, the Pogues joined forces with the Dubliners, bringing their punk-rock edge to their aging heroes' sound and melding two generations of Irish music to create a surging remake of "Whiskey in the Jar," which climbed to No. 4 on the Irish pop charts and No. 63 in the UK. With the silver-bearded Ronnie Drew and snaggle-toothed Shane McGowan growling in tandem there's little doubt of the strength of the whiskey they so wholeheartedly praise.

Eight years later Metallica made the song their own. The video that accompanied their 1998 recording of "Whiskey in the Jar" opened with long shot of a house party going full throttle. James Hetfield lets loose a feral scream as shapely babes in bras flounce about like delirious marionettes in a debauched ballet, rapaciously guzzling booze from bottles and suggestively sucking on ciggies, while the band grinds a grungy anthem, venerating the lost souls of yore. While musically Metallica's "Whiskey in the Jar" is a great update of the centuries-old song, the video, which depicts a drunken lesbian bump and grind session in a glaringly lit bedroom, leading to a panty-clad pillow-fight, is no more than a pointless exercise in hedonism. Meanwhile the song's refrain, "There's whiskey in the jar," remains something of an enigma:

Is the whiskey the cause of all of our antihero's troubles? Does it drive him to commit robbery and murder? Or is it the only antidote capable of soothing his sorry soul?

Elton John and Bernie Taupin's outlaw fantasy "Ballad of a Well-Known Gun," from their 1970 album *Tumbleweed Connection*, was a brilliant slice of Americana, written ironically by a pair of Brits (Taupin had yet to visit the US when it was composed). Over his punchy piano, a funky rhythm section, and the stabbing guitar riffs of Caleb Quaye, Elton recounts the remorseful tale of "a well-known gun," as a gospel choir, which included the blue-eyed soul goddess Dusty Springfield, sings the haunting refrain, "Now they've found me / Well I won't run." Surrounded by a throng of Pinkerton agents who tracked him down, our gunslinger/ hero can now barely manage to stutter and hang his "head in shame," as he recounts how he was driven to a life of crime in a desperate effort to save his "starving family," who tragically wound up in the "poor house."

As the British rock journalist John Tobler wrote in the liner notes to the album's rerelease in 1995, "Nearly all of the songs [on Elton's second album] seemed to reflect Bernie Taupin's preoccupation and fascination with the American West, outlaws, sheriffs, the great outdoors, etc."

As a young man, Taupin was inspired by Marty Robbins's classic gunslinger ballads, "El Paso" and "Streets of Laredo." He later confessed to having been "totally influenced" by the Band's 1968 debut *Music from Big Pink*. The specter of "Virgil Caine," the famed protagonist of Robbie Robertson's "The Night They Drove Old Dixie Down," is all over Elton and Bernie's epic "My Father's Gun." The impact of The Band's second album (simply titled *The Band*) inspired much of Elton's *Tumbleweed Connection*, from its down-home country/funk feel to the sepia-tone record jacket, and the series of old-fashioned portraits of the musicians on the inside sleeve. The song seamlessly captures the battered but indomitable spirit of the Confederacy. Having laid his father's "broken body down below the Southern land," the song's bedraggled hero proudly dons the grey Rebel uniform, loads his father's hallowed pistol, and takes a solemn oath never to rest until "the cause is fought and won."

11

(S)HE'S A REBEL

No matter where or when the outlaw's drama unfolds, women are intrinsically involved, playing a crucial role, whether as outlaws themselves or as the romantic interest, pining away for their unruly yet terribly charming beaus. At some point (whether in ballad, story, or movie) the heroine may either pick up a harp or sit down at a spinet to sing a lilting catalog of his many virtues; or she may lift a dram glass and curse him for many of the same reasons. She might be portrayed as a stoical plainswoman, like Etta Place (Katharine Ross), the bewitching schoolmarm of *Butch Cassidy and the Sundance Kid*, who is expected to "hold down the fort." She must fend off everyone from encroaching savages to federal agents while her man pillages the countryside, either driven by desperation or on a noble mission to redistribute the wealth of an unjust society. On the other hand, there is the gangster matriarch, as personified by Ma Barker, fiercely devoted to her wayward sons and turning a blind eye to their most heinous crimes.

In the rock 'n' roll songs and country ballads of the late 1950s and early 1960s we hear again and again of the dedicated girlfriend, who, beyond all reason, is willing and prepared to stand by her man despite the outcome.

Sung by the Shangri-Las, a group comprised of two pairs of sisters from Queens, New York, "The Leader of the Pack" was a novelty number written by George "Shadow" Morton, Jeff Barry, and Ellie Greenwich. Released by Red Bird Records, the song, which shot to

No. 1 for one week in November 1964, came with a plethora of kitsch production touches, including revving engines and screeching tires, culminating in an enormous crash.

The simple lyric recounts how a pair of teenagers meet down at the local candy store one day; all is swell until her parents discover he comes from "the wrong side of town." Not surprisingly, they forbid their daughter from ever going out with the likes of him. The next thing she knows, her father demands she tell Jimmy they can no longer see each other. A quick kiss goodbye, a gush of tears, and her dreamboat roars off into the rainy night on his motorcycle. A moment later she lets out a shriek as he wipes out on his bike. Although he is dead and gone, she will forever remain faithfully his.

Like a romantic ode from another century updated and sung by a clutch of fair maidens done up in stockings and bouffant hairdos, "He's a Rebel" (written by Gene Pitney and produced by Phil Spector) is a classic anthem of teenage nonconformity. In under three minutes the song manages to evoke the indescribable allure of the antihero, as portrayed by James Dean in *Rebel Without a Cause* or Marlon Brando as "Johnny," the drop-dead cool leader of a motorcycle gang, in *The Wild One*.

> *He's a rebel and he'll never ever be any good.*
> *He's a rebel 'cause he never ever does what he should.*

Over the decades "He's a Rebel" has continued to show enormous staying power. Despite Spector's blunder of crediting the vocal performance to the Crystals (it was actually sung by the Blossoms, featuring a young Darlene Love), *Rolling Stone* ranked it No. 263 among its Top 500 Best Rock Songs of All Time.

"He's a Bad Boy," written by Gerry Goffin and Carole King and recorded in 1963 by King, was later updated as "Bad Boy" by the Holy Modal

Rounders, New York's Lower East Side anarchist string band. Their version (which borrows the first verse and chorus from Goffin and King) contains some additional bizarre lyrics about creepy drug dealers on St. Mark's Place. It's interesting to note that Neil Young would later borrow most of the song's melody for his enchanting Native American fantasy "Pocahontas."

Written by Glenn Frey and Don Henley, "Desperado" was the title cut of the Eagles' 1973 sophomore (and somewhat sophomoric) concept album of the same name.

"This was a very macho scene in the Burt Reynolds sense of the word," wrote Joe Harrington in *Sonic Cool*. "Fueled by coke, it was the Great Western Myth of the Rock-Star as Outlaw, epitomized by the Eagles' lame concept album *Desperado*."

No matter how rough and rustic the band tried to appear on their album cover, draped in leather gun-belts and wielding pearl-handled six-shooters, this was ultimately wimpy stuff. As "Desperado" builds towards its melodramatic climax (whether in Don Henley or Linda Ronstadt's version), the singer pleads "let somebody love you;" it suddenly becomes clear why this tortured fellow would rather be out "riding fences" than allow himself a moment of intimacy with the person handing him such an ultimatum.

Parodied by "Weird Al" Yankovic, it was also lampooned by comedian Larry David in the 141st episode of *Seinfeld*, entitled "The Checks," in which Elaine's new boyfriend gets a distant, misty look in his eyes every time he hears "Desperado" on the radio. She wants to share the song with him but he, like the heralded desperado, only remains distant and aloof.

"The Eagles' music is bubblegum," the "Father of Country Rock," Gram Parsons, once groused. "It's got too much sugar on it. Life is tougher than they make it out to be." Parsons's own search for credibility and authenticity led to him quitting the Byrds just six months after having forged their masterpiece of Americana, *Sweetheart of the Rodeo*. He then formed the short-lived Flying Burrito Brothers, whose musical brew magnificently merged soul with country. Gram may have followed in the footsteps of legendary honky-tonk heroes Hank Williams and George Jones, but those steps tragically led him to an early grave, dead at twenty-six from the lethal combo of booze and morphine.

"They learned their Southern culture second-hand," English critic Peter Doggett said of the Eagles. "Country [in the 1970s was] perched precariously between transforming America in its own image and sacrificing its soul to Hollywood."

These days country music bears little resemblance to its former self, beyond the obligatory cowboy hat and perhaps an acoustic guitar, whose presence is often a prop at best.

Over jangling acoustic guitar and a big Texas beat, Waylon Jennings delivers Lee Clayton's "Ladies Love Outlaws" in his trademark rugged-but-earnest voice. Clayton's lyric delves into the relationships of three couples, beginning with the lovely Bessie and her beau Leroy, who, despite his wild ways, makes her yearn to have children someday; children who undoubtedly will grow up to be just like him. Next comes Bennie, a country-rock barroom guitarist who is something of a fugitive. He loves Linda, a well-built blonde with a heart of gold, who is determined at all costs to make the relationship last. The last verse describes Jessi (undoubtedly referring to Jessi Colter), who is as fond of shiny cars and diamonds as she is of her man, Waymore (Waylon's nickname), who, although in love with Jessi, is trying his best not to get tied down.

The song's catchy chorus cleverly sums up why these couples continue to stay together despite their apparent differences. Perhaps the reason, as Clayton reveals, is that "outlaws touch the ladies somewhere deep down in their soul."

Bristol, Tennessee, songwriter David Massengill was originally inspired to write his epic outlaw ballad "On the Road to Fairfax County" while experimenting with a new tuning on his Appalachian mountain dulcimer.

"Suddenly I found this melody," David explained. "It had two parts: one line answered another, like a call and response type thing. I had the melody for about two weeks and was trying to find the lyrics. At first I figured it was a prison-break song, or maybe it took place in Ireland because it was an old traditional-sounding melody. It was a ballad and didn't need a chorus.

"There was a songwriter night coming up at the Cornelia Street Café (a popular folk and jazz club in Greenwich Village) and it was time to get this down. It was like five o'clock in the morning and I said to myself, what's the oldest story that you know? And I thought about an outlaw western and I wrote, "Oh once I loved an outlaw" . . . and that was the opening line. Then the responding line was, "He came and stole my heart."

Over the years "On the Road to Fairfax County" has been covered by a handful of singer/songwriters, including Joan Baez, David Bromberg, and the Roches.

"I've always been conflicted about the song," Suzzy Roche confessed. "If you really think about it, it's deeply disturbing. The girl gets robbed twice: first he steals her heart and then he steals her money. Outlaws have a certain romantic allure, but I wonder if she might have been better off if she'd never run into him in the first place. But what a beautiful melody though!"

"I feel sorry for the audience when they're going to hear a long story song with like twenty verses," David laughed.

"'The Maiden and the Convict,' tells the story of my mother's marriage to her first husband, a South American flamenco guitarist with a hot temper," explained Mat Hagar of the Brooklyn-based country, folk, and rockabilly trio Outlaw Ritual. "That song was written in the spirit of Vladimir Vysotsky."

At that time singer/guitarist/poet/actor Vysotsky was deemed "anti-Soviet scum" by the Russian government. His own father informed on him to the KGB. A legend of Moscow's 1960s folk underground scene, Vysotsky recorded his early songs at home on reel-to-reel tapes and circulated them on cassettes as "anonymous" or "traditional" for the sake of self-preservation. In hard-knocks Brechtian ballads, delivered in a gravelly, thunderous voice, Vysotsky frequently took aim at corrupt and cruel communist government officials, who routinely kept him under surveillance, and romanticized the burgeoning criminal underground. The self-proclaimed "soul of bad company" became the toast of ex-prisoners, who assumed he'd done hard time, so convincing was his portrayal of the hardships they'd endured. (The truth was, he'd never seen the inside of the Gulag, contrary to statements broadcast in the TV show *60 Minutes* in 1977.) Although stating publicly that his songs were not autobiographical, Vysotsky was nonetheless adored by macho Russian boxers, soldiers, and soccer stars alike.

Hagar's "The Maiden and the Convict," delves into the dynamic of his mother's relationship with a fleeting man who not only "stole" her heart but threatened to steal her life as well:

> *Here's something you should know,*
> *Know about the wind and which way it will blow.*

Hagar sings, alluding to the coming trouble:

> *Be it in the dead of night,*
> *Or the silence of day bright,*
> *Find a place that you can hide,*
> *Lock the door from the inside,*
> *Take only what you need,*
> *And pray that he don't find you,*
> *In your dream.*

> *You never could decide,*
> *What it was about him*
> *That made you want to run and hide,*
> *That day you gazed into his old and beady eyes,*
> *As if he came out of the sky.*

> *He's meaner than an old dog bite,*
> *He took the apple from your eye,*

The brightness from your light,
But he taught you how to sing,
And he even gave you a ring.

Although the convict inspires the maiden to sing, it was not a love song springing spontaneously from her heart but a deep and troubling blues or old folk ballad that relentlessly haunts her soul.

"Sovay" (a name most likely derived from "Sophie" or "Sylvie") is a romantic English ballad that tells the story of a woman who dons male attire, masquerading as a highwayman in order to hold up her fiancé to test his love before they are to be married. Disguised as a man, she draws a pair of pistols and demands that her lover stand and deliver his money and gold watch, along with the gold ring upon his finger (which she had given him). "Deliver it, deliver it your sweet life to save," she sings. Her betrothed flatly refuses, telling the outlaw that "he" would have to kill him first before he would willingly hand over the ring.

The next time he sees Sovay, he tells her of his encounter with the bandit, upon which she confesses her prank, adding that if he'd surrendered the ring she would have plugged him full of lead:

"For if you'd have given me that ring," she said,
"I'd have pulled the trigger,
I'd have pulled the trigger,
And shot you dead."

"Sovay," a standard among British folk-rock groups of the 1960s, has been recorded by Martin Carthy, Bert Jansch and his band Pentangle, and Jah Wobble, bassist with Public Image Ltd.

A wild woman who drank wine and brewed moonshine, "Darling Corey" (a.k.a. "Darling Cory" and "Darling Cora") played banjo, frolicked in her bare feet, and wielded firearms (sometimes two at a time) as well as any man. The opening verse to the ballad alerts us that the "revenuers are a'comin'" to "tear [her] still house down." By the second verse Corey is out of the bootlegging business and brandishing a pair of pistols along with "a banjo on her knee" (a very familiar phrase, undoubtedly inspired by Stephen Foster's popular song "Oh Susannah," whose wandering beau was headed for Alabama, holding a similar instrument in a similar manner).

There are many versions of this song. The earliest known recorded version is by B. F. (Benjamin Frank) Shelton, a banjo-picking barber from Kentucky who traveled to Bristol, Tennessee, in July 1927, and cut four tunes for Victor Records, including "Darling Cora."

The song soon became a standard across the American South, found in the repertoire of country, folk, and bluegrass singers, including Bill Monroe, whose high/lonesome holler pleaded:

> Wake up, wake, darling Corey,
> And go get me my gun.
> I ain't no man for trouble,
> But I'll die before I run.

You can almost smell the moonshine on Roscoe Holcomb's breath when he howls "Darling Corey." While his clanging banjo and keening voice warn of the highway robbers a-comin', we never learn how or why Corey dies and winds up "laid down in the meadow." We can only listen as her life continues sliding downhill. With each passing verse Corey becomes a little less "darling." She's next seen "drinking away her troubles with a lowdown gambling man" (a lyric clearly borrowed from the ballad of the doomed "Little Maggie," famous for clutching "a dram glass in her hand" and drinking for all the same reasons and in similarly bad company). The fourth verse hints that "Darling Corey" has become a complete wretch as the singer (who confesses that "bad liquor has destroyed [his] body") implores her to "stop hanging around [his] bed." The time is not long before he must "lay darling Corey down."

Despite the song's dark lyrics, the version of "Darling Corey" played in recent years by the duo of pianist Bruce Hornsby and multi-string wizard Ricky Skaggs seems incongruously cheerful. Its bouncy square-dance rhythm belies the tragic fate of the fallen heroine and ultimately becomes a vehicle for Hornsby's prodigious keyboard riffs. Their jubilant jam makes you wonder if the musicians, as well as their enthusiastic crowd, haven't forgotten why the singer needed to "dig a hole in the meadow" in the first place.

The real Arizona "Ma" Barker was nothing like the cokey disco queen portrayed in the accompanying video to Boney M's 1977 hit song "Ma Baker." Born in 1873 in Ash Grove, Missouri, Arizona Barker would raise a clutch of ill-mannered, illiterate hooligans with her shiftless husband, George. According to J. Edgar Hoover's FBI files, "Ma," the husky, square-jawed moll, was "the most vicious, dangerous, and resourceful criminal brain of the last decade," while those who knew her personally denied she had any control over her offspring's felonious activity. In his autobiography, the bank-robber Harvey Bailey, a friend of the Barker family, laughed at the notion that Ma was the gang's shrewd strategist, claiming she "couldn't plan breakfast!" Alvin Karpis, who later joined forces with the Barker boys, described their mother as "an old-fashioned homebody" whose worst crime was being "cantankerous." According to Karpis, "Arrie," as she was sometimes known, was simply a front "when [they] traveled together" in the guise of a mother and her sons. "What could look more innocent?" Alvin claimed the charges were "ridiculous," pointing out that "there is not one police photograph of her or set of fingerprints taken while she was alive."

Either way, her image as the gang's mastermind fueled the public's imagination, selling thousands of newspapers and inspiring a slew of songs, books, and movies for more than eighty years, including *Ma Barker's Killer Brood* (1960), B-movie master Roger Corman's 1970 film *Bloody Mama* (starring Shelly Winters in the title role, with Bruce Dern, and an unknown Robert De Niro as Lloyd Barker), and *Public Enemies* (1996).

Following a robbery in 1910, their eldest boy, Herman, reportedly mowed down a small child while driving off in his getaway car in Webb City, Missouri. In August 1927, he allegedly killed a cop in cold blood at point-blank range. A year later, Herman would turn the gun on himself, after having been seriously injured in a high-speed chase. Loyal to the end, the Barkers' eldest son chose to die rather than face the law and risk informing on the family. The surviving three brothers, Lloyd, Arthur (a.k.a. "Doc"), and Fred, would all soon be viewing the world through iron penitentiary bars. A study of their mug shots reveals a series of inscrutable faces that appear more aggravated by the inconvenience of incarceration than even slightly remorseful over the offences that led them there in the first place.

It seems their father, George Barker, wasn't cut out for a life of crime. While disapproving of his sons' unlawful lifestyles, he was willing for the most part to keep his mouth shut and live off the bounty of his boys' bad behavior. Journalist Miriam Allen deFord speculated that George eventually "gave up completely and quietly removed himself from the scene." He may indeed have left for the reasons given by the FBI, who portrayed "Ma" as a loose woman who, they claimed, regularly had "outside dates with other men." With her husband out of the picture and her boys either dead or "up the river," Ma, left to her own devices, quickly fell on hard times and is said to have turned to prostitution between 1928 and 1931.

While in prison, Fred befriended Alvin Karpis, with whom he formed a new gang upon their release. Their proficiency at bank-robbing and kidnapping wealthy business tycoons would make them famous from coast to coast. Things had begun to look up momentarily for Ma Barker and her new beau, Arthur Dunlop (a.k.a. Dunlap), until his body was found, floating in a Minnesota lake, naked, with a bullet in his head, after he had got drunk and blabbed about his outlaw pals' latest exploits. From then on, it is said that the boys regularly installed Ma in her own hotel room, just down the road from wherever they were holed up, as she tended to be jealous and suspicious of any of the young ladies that her sons befriended along the way. Apparently there was only room for one woman in the Karpis/Barker gang.

Following "Doc" Barker's arrest in Chicago on January 8, 1935, the FBI, thanks to a stack of letters Doc had foolishly kept, managed to track down Ma and Fred's hideout in Ocklawaha, Florida. Ma's mention of "Gator Joe," an enormous alligator that lived in Lake Weir (the hometown of Gator Joe's, a restaurant named in the famous beast's honor), had tipped off the Feds to their location.

Eight days later, on January 16, the FBI surrounded their rented house. A four-hour shoot-out ensued. Following a long eerie silence, the agents cautiously entered the home to find Doc's body riddled with bullets, while Ma had apparently died of a single gunshot wound.

Plenty of gossip and controversy ensued. Over the next nine months the public was invited to view the outlaws' bodies on display. Many wondered if Ma was really the ruthless ringleader that J. Edgar Hoover had made her out to be. While stories circulated that she was found clutching a Tommy gun in her stiff fingers, several believed her death was an act of wanton violence on part of the FBI, who could have taken more care to bring the notorious gangster matriarch in alive. In the end, the capture and killing of these treacherous villains put quite a feather in the cap of the FBI's high-profile director.

Over the years, Ma Barker's legend has been enshrined in songs of every imaginable style, from opera and rock to rap and disco. In 1957 John Eaton, best known for his microtonal compositions and work with synthesizer pioneer Robert Moog, composed an opera, named for and inspired by the misadventures of *Ma Barker*. In 1996 the Swiss-born avant-garde jazz pianist Michel Wintsch teamed up with the Geneva-based playwright Gérald Chevrolet (whose script was inspired by the great French novelist, Marguerite Yourcenar) to create another opera about the misbegotten Ma.

Formed in 2004, the Southern metal band Maylene and the Sons of Disaster based their image and songs upon the story of the Karpis/Baker gang. Bearded, tattooed, gravel-throated vocalist Dallas Taylor explained the "crazy backwoods theme" behind the Alabama-based group, comprised of "five dudes who play the role of the Barker sons." Over grinding guitars and a slamming jackhammer beat Taylor shouts his morality tales to a mostly white, male, baseball-capped crowd who thrust their fists into the air while jerking spasmodically to the music in what appears to be the modern equivalent of a tribal antelope dance. "Life lived unjustly," Taylor warns, "will meet divine justice on the other side."

It's no surprise that a rapper would adopt Ma Barker's name as her handle, a move that no doubt loaned a bit of gravitas to her image. That dubious honor goes to Satina Pearce (a.k.a. "Shaqueen"), the ex-wife of gangsta rapper Kool G Rap, a self-described "street chick" who "spit gutter" along with her hip hop husband on the 2003 album *5 Family Click*. "I know the street life," the rapping Ma Barker assured Melanie J. Cornish of allhiphop.com in a 2006 interview. "I didn't just sit home and go to school and then go to the movies. I had a lot of run-ins with the streets and the cops. That was my life and that was what I saw."

Ironically, the chart-topping song that memorialized Ma Barker world-wide failed to even get her name right. In 1974, the German producer Frank Farian (known to his grammar school teacher as Franz Reuther) was suddenly pressed to form a group after his dance track "Do You Wanna Bump?" took off in the discotheques of Holland and Belgium. Teaming up an exotic bunch of singers and dancers from Montserrat, Jamaica, and Aruba, he dubbed them Boney M., inspired by the popular Australian TV show *Boney* (the nickname of Napoleon Bonaparte, a half- Aboriginal detective). After their song "Daddy Cool" hit No. 1 in the Fatherland, Boney M. released their second chart-topping album, *Love for Sale*, which featured the stylish (and remarkably vapid, yet popular) tribute to the 1920s gang-leader Ma Barker, called "Ma Baker." Farian's reason for changing her name was simply "because it sounded better." The song opened with a voice commanding everyone, in a raspy hillbilly twang resembling that of Irene Ryan, "Granny" of the popular TV Show *The Beverly Hillbillies*, to "Freeze! I'm Ma Baker, put your hands in the air and gimme all your money!" It had little to do or nothing with the legendary outlaw.

Fragments of truth can be found within the verses. Ma *did* have four sons. She *did* break up with her husband as he (allegedly) "wasn't tough enough." And the "man she liked," Arthur Dunlop *did* unintentionally "inform" on the gang, for which he paid the ultimate price. No matter what takes place in this cardboard cut-out version of her life, Ma Barker is once more painted as a cold-hearted woman, who, it is stated in the refrain, "never knew how to cry . . . but she knew how to die."

As a form, the ballad limits songwriters to employing only the essential details of the story they must tell. This is mostly due to the restrictions of their chosen rhyme scheme. Yet it remains the challenge of the bard to create a work of clarity and artistry under such conditions. While the lyrical expectations of a disco dance track are admittedly low, one must wonder just how far writers are willing to distort their subject matter in hopes of knocking off a song. Like its real-life counterpart, "Ma Baker," written by Frank Farian, Fred Jay (a.k.a. Friedrich Alex Jacobson), and George Reyam (a.k.a. Hans-Jörg Mayer), is guilty as charged!

12

STREET FIGHTING MAN

Outlaws come in a variety of styles, but looks are often deceiving. Back in the day, people might have assumed that the Hells Angels were lefties, due to their outlaw image—motorcycles, wild hair, beards, leather, and blue jeans. Nothing could have been further from the truth. They were at the opposite pole, ideologically, to the hippies of the day: but both groups were decidedly antiauthoritarian. They stood, or more like slouched, in solidarity against "The Man" (and most likely for free love and dope as well). In the same way, gangbangers battling over their turf and fist-waving anarchists hurling Molotov cocktails against an oppressive government share similar outcomes—incarceration or death.

Although possessing a deeper, more realistic understanding of the harsh reality of the streets, inner-city bards are not alone in fashioning the zeitgeist into popular song. With the intensifying political atmosphere of the late 1960s and early 1970s, rock stars like John Lennon, the Rolling Stones, and Lou Reed all felt compelled to sound off about pressing issues (admittedly from a safer, more comfortable vantage point) rather than exploring the foibles of love or making poetic allusions to getting high.

Following the Paris riots of May 1968, Mick Jagger and Keith

Richards's rough-and-tumble "Street Fighting Man" quickly became the anthem of disenfranchised longhairs, disillusioned and frustrated with the peace movement and the slow, step-by-step approach to changing "the system." Mick's uncanny question—"What can a poor boy do, 'cept sing for a rock 'n' roll band?"—still rings true to inner city kids with no way out other than the slim prospect of playing professional sports or taking the mic in their hands to speak about the unjust condition of their lives.

"It was uncanny how popular music framed the political events of the time. The Beatles single 'Revolution' was released just as the 1968 Chicago riots kicked off, while the Stones' 'Street Fighting Man' followed immediately after," said Pat Thomas (author of *Listen Whitey*, the 2012 survey of pop music and the Black Power movement). "It was the first and only time a counterculture reached such an elevated level of political awareness. While the bands had their ear, the Yippies' political rhetoric, particularly the outrageous pranks of Jerry Rubin and Abbie Hoffman, really caught the attention of suburban kids across the country."

Taking a stand against the establishment was all in a day's work for a young Bob Dylan. "How much do I know to talk out of turn? / You might say I'm that I'm young, you might say I'm unlearned," he snarled in his 1963 protest song "Masters of War." Words blasted from Bob's mouth like bullets. The scruffy Minnesota folk singer didn't need a gun; his mercurial mind *was* his weapon, a rocket launcher aimed at the glaring hypocrisies of President Johnson's "Great Society." Before Dylan eventually abandoned politics for poetry and rock 'n' roll (and later country music and, even more surprisingly, Christianity), he incited black musicians, from Stevie Wonder and Marvin Gaye to Sly Stone and his funky Family, to start writing and singing about serious issues challenging African Americans.

"A lot of people never connected the dots between Marvin Gaye's *What's Going On* and Sly's *There's a Riot Goin' On*," Pat Thomas pointed out. "Sly [whose album was released six months after Marvin's epic, in May 1971] was just answering his question. The song 'What's Going On' was actually inspired by the People's Riot in Berkeley in the spring of 1969, when Renaldo Benson of the Four Tops was on tour in San Francisco and became enraged over a protest that turned violent between hippies and the police. There was a vacant lot which the hippies wanted as a public park, while the University planned on turning it an athletic field."

The lot soon became a battleground as the police began beating and arresting a bunch of obstreperous kids. Benson, with the help of Al Cleveland, who occasionally co-wrote with Smokey Robinson, quickly worked up a sketch of "What's Going On."

"The Four Tops refused to record it, as it was too political," Thomas said, "while Joan Baez considered it." Benson and Baez, who had previously crossed paths in Paris, fell out of touch and Marvin Gaye wound up recording the song.

While Gaye shot to No. 2 on the charts, the Supremes momentarily dropped the sticky-sweet sentiments of songs like "Baby Love" to address the problems faced by young unwed inner-city mothers in "Love Child." Initially their producer Berry Gordy equated such viewpoints with insubordination and mutiny, until he realized the record-buying public was hungry for something with a bit more edge than Motown's smooth harmonies and dance steps.

But it was the startling message-music from Harlem's proto-rap group, the Last Poets, that best captured the grim atmosphere and overwhelming hopelessness that pervaded America as cities burned from coast to coast in the wake of Martin Luther King Jr.'s assassination. Featured in the soundtrack to 1970's *Performance* (which starred Mick Jagger as a debauched and forgotten rock star), the Last Poets' "Wake Up, Niggers" exploded like a Molotov cocktail in the consciousness of anyone who came within earshot of the record. (While the song received zero airplay, the soundtrack to *Performance*, which featured the Rolling Stones, was the perfect vehicle for the Last Poets to get the word out.) Over the tribal groove of conga drums and a chorus of exacerbated voices chanting "Wake up, wake up," the message came across loud and clear. The time had come to take a stand and demand equal rights, as Malcolm X said, "by any means necessary." As street poet/proto-rapper Gil Scott-Heron revealed in "The Revolution Will Not Be Televised," we could no longer look the other way and ignore the hard truths. The day will come, Gil assured us, when everyone will have to stand and fight for what they believe (which ultimately is the fate of every outlaw): "You will not be able to stay home, brother, / You will not be able to plug in, turn on, and cop out."

Whether one credits (or blames) Abbie Hoffman, Jerry Rubin, or David Peel, John Lennon upon his arrival in New York in 1971 suddenly became a politically charged lefty.

"Rubin's influence on John and Yoko cannot be underestimated," Pat Thomas emphasized. "Every day Jerry would go down to see John and Yoko when they lived on Bank Street, in the Village. It was Jerry who introduced Elephant's Memory to John when he needed a sympathetic, politically charged rock band to back him up."

Throughout most of the 1960s the Beatles had remained aloof on matters of war, poverty, and human rights (most likely due to their manager Brian Epstein's tight control of the Liverpool lads' image). Love, beginning with the girl/boy variety and later the universal power capable of saving the world (along with the occasional message about getting high), had been the Fabs' all-purpose answer to everything. But now Lennon, who only a few years earlier had been chauffeured around London in a garishly painted Rolls Royce, had traded in his psychedelic Silver Cloud in hopes of gaining a bit of street cred. The working-class hero and his Japanese conceptual artist wife cut their hair (which they then donated to charity), donned fatigues, and chanted simple three-chord agitprop anthems to get the word out on Angela Davis, the Attica State jail riots, and the problems facing Northern Ireland. Bullhorns, raised fists, and slogans quickly became their M.O.

Slumming with revolutionaries soon led Lennon into a nasty battle with J. Edgar Hoover, who now reserved for the ex-Beatle the kind of personal vendetta that he'd formerly held for the criminals who topped his most wanted list. The F.B.I compiled a file on John that was allegedly more than 5,000 pages long. It is said that President Nixon feared Lennon's participation in anti-war demonstrations might possibly cost him the re-election in 1972. The US immigration authorities immediately went to work, citing Lennon's previous arrest for possession of a small amount of cannabis in London in 1968 as their motive to deport him. John and Yoko then spent the next three years fighting for his green card, which was finally awarded on October 8, 1975 (one day before his thirty-fifth birthday), proclaiming "the courts will not condone selective deportation based upon secret political grounds." (The sad irony remains that if Nixon had succeeded, and Lennon had been deported, he might not have been assassinated on the streets of New York in 1980.) Tricky Dick's paranoia ultimately loaned more credence to the power of Lennon and Ono's peace campaign, which included such benign forms of protest as recording and releasing in 1969 a melancholy sing-along (produced by Phil Spector) called "Happy Xmas (War Is Over)." It was accompanied by a series of "War Is Over! If You Want It" billboards mounted in cities around the world, as well as their honeymoon Bed-In for Peace (which took place not in the US but in Amsterdam and Toronto).

Years later, Yoko Ono explained the couple's strategy: "The War Is Over! Campaign was once a tiny seed, which spread and covered the Earth." Ono described their use of power as pop stars to wage peace and raise consciousness as nothing more than "small pebbles": "[But] when they're dropped in the ocean, [they] will immediately affect the ocean of the whole wide world." Ono added, "Don't throw a big stone. It scares people and creates repercussions." In hindsight it seems preposterous that the leaders of the free world felt so threatened by (what many deemed) such naïve actions by a pair of gentle Zen tricksters.

With Lennon (and Ono) suddenly taking the lead in the political arena, Dylan, who'd gone country in the meantime (releasing the much-maligned *Nashville Skyline* in 1969 and the disastrous double-album *Self Portrait*, the following year) was briefly inspired to return to his old protest songwriting ways, recording an aching lament for "George Jackson" after the Black Panther was slain by guards at San Quentin Prison when a failed escape attempt turned into a horrible bloodbath.

On May 4, 1970, in what became known as the Kent State Massacre, the Ohio National Guard killed four college students and wounded nine (one of whom was permanently paralyzed) at an anti-war rally. Crosby, Stills, Nash, and Young responded swiftly to the tragedy by recording the haunting broadside "Ohio," written and sung by Young. His bandmates chanted the haunted mantra, "Four dead in Ohio," while his guitar groaned and screamed in the face of the senseless and brutal killing.

Graham Nash (Young's sometime bandmate in Crosby, Stills, Nash, and Young) released his first solo album, *Songs for Beginners*, in 1971. It included the song "Chicago," an urgent plea to America's youth to come to the midwestern mecca and "change the world." Although heartfelt, the song seemed a bit twee and naïve in the wake of the vicious riots at the Democratic Convention in Grant Park, which left many bewildered, with cracked skulls and bloody shirts, and wondering what became of free speech and the right to assemble. After all, if the CIA could track down and kill Che Guevara in the jungles of Bolivia, what chance did an idealistic white, middle-class college kid from the suburbs have?

On the other hand, the Buffalo Springfield's "For What It's Worth" was one of the most powerful protest songs of the 1960s, reflecting the gulf between America's alienated youth and the establishment, who were happy and determined to keep things status quo. Sounding world-weary beyond his barely twenty years, Stephen Stills sighed heavily, "There's battle lines being drawn, / Nobody's right if everybody's wrong."

The summer of 1971 also saw the release of the Who's kick-ass anthem "Won't Get Fooled Again." While its mesmerizing Terry Riley-inspired keyboard intro and lead singer Roger Daltrey's rip-the-roof-off scream ignited the passion of their fans, the song, heard these days in heavy rotation on oldies stations, TV shows, and commercials, rings with the hollow promise of a failed revolution. Even notorious stoner Hunter S. Thompson, the wacky genius of Gonzo journalism, had enough wherewithal to see right through all this populist posturing when he claimed that Lennon's "Power to the People" unfortunately came "ten years too late." Even Lennon himself (who had written and sung the grungy rocker "Revolution," the Beatles' first foray into agit-prop) felt compelled to agree with Thompson later. In a 1980 interview he confessed that "Power to the People" was no more than "a quickie" that "didn't really come off." But that didn't stop his proletarian anthem from going gold and hanging around the charts for nine weeks.

Hailing from "Trench Town" (as the ghetto of Kingston, Jamaica, is known) the Wailers released their first album, *Catch a Fire*, in 1972. It was a collection of irresistible reggae tunes written by Bob Marley and Peter Tosh, built on syncopated bass lines and accented by crisp timbale shots. The Wailers sang of the grim realities their people faced in the "Concrete Jungle" where "burning and a-looting" were a nightly occurrence. The ominous "Slave Driver" reminded the island's long-time oppressors, the British colonizers, that the tables had turned and payback for the abuse they'd suffered was not far off. The Wailers' follow-up album, *Burnin'*, from 1973, featured the powerful anthem "Get Up, Stand Up." Over a funky clavinet Tosh introduced the world to the band's Rastafarian creed, while inspiring people worldwide to take action and "stand up for your rights."

These odes of political struggle soon spread beyond the battlegrounds of the inner city to the suburbs, igniting the passions of a generation of (predominantly white) kids who yearned not to follow the middle-class paradigm.

The twisted tale of "Tania," from Camper Van Beethoven's break-through fourth album, *Our Beloved Revolutionary Sweetheart*, portrays a slacker's obsession with an heiress turned outlaw: Patty Hearst.

"To start with, the band was originally called Camper Van Beethoven and the Border Patrol," the band's lead singer and primary songwriter David Lowery pointed out. "All of our friends and fans started calling us CVB for short—which sounded like a pseudorevolutionary, fake-terrorist group. Greg Lisher (the group's guitarist) came up with this vaguely Eastern European sounding piece of music which was the impetus for 'Tania.' It was intended to be an instrumental at first. We were going to name it after some Russian girl's name like Nahnatchka. Somehow Tania, as in Patty Hearst, came about, which was perfect. It went with the whole CVB persona. So I started to look up some stuff about her. It was a really interesting story. She was brainwashed [by her kidnappers] and goes over to the other side. There's that really great, iconic picture of her in the bank where she is holding the automatic rifle. It's a great image. I didn't romanticize it, although we did in the song:

> *Oh, my beloved revolutionary sweetheart,*
> *I can see your newsprint face turn yellow in the gutter.*
> *It makes me sad, how I long for the days,*
> *When you came to liberate us from boredom,*
> *From driving around from five to seven in the evening.*

My beloved Tania, we carry your gun deep within our
*   hearts,*
For no better reason than our lives have no meaning,
And we want to be on television.

"It was a play on the bad man ballad and the band's fake revolutionary persona. All that crazy stuff that went on in California in the early seventies, like Patti Hearst, Angela Davis, and the Zodiac Killer, got all mixed together in my head," Lowerey explained.

"I think we focused on Patti Hearst because the whole SLA [Symbionese Liberation Army] thing seemed so ridiculous; and the process of 'brainwashing an heiress' was so fake it seemed like reality was being written by TV writers," said Jonathan Segel, Camper's violinist/organist/guitarist. "Especially since there were actual movements going on at the time, like the Black Panthers. Certainly, TV benefited greatly from Patti and the SLA. Now that scenario is as cliché as a biker in a black leather motorcycle jacket or a hippie cult leader."

A mad/hilarious tirade against society and the ills of rock 'n' roll, "Burn and Rob" by antifolk singer Paleface topped college radio charts in 1991. The song was originally inspired by the 1990 arrest of the British heavy metal band Judas Priest, who were accused of inciting a pair of drunk, alienated Nevada teenagers to blow their heads off with a 12-gauge shotgun. The refrain of "Do it!" (employed by everybody from Yippie rabble-rouser Jerry Rubin to Nike, to sell sneakers) from their song "Better by You, Better Than Me" (a remake of an old Spooky Tooth tune) allegedly drove these two lost souls to suicide. Primitively strumming an acoustic guitar, Paleface recounts (with a couple extra syllables tossed in whenever he feels like it) a total delinquent's fantasy of drugs, theft, and murder, all due to the evil influence of rock 'n' roll.

Well I bought my favorite record at my local record store.
I woulda bought a lot but I had a rotten job.
I took it home and I put it on the turntable,
It made me wanna kill everybody in the neighborhood.

It made me wanna burn and rob, burn and rob,
Rock 'n' roll made me wanna burn and rob,
Burn and rob, burn and rob,
Kill everybody and quit my stupid job!
I already had my dad's checkbook, so I ran off to the bank.
I took out all the money and I loaded up on crank,
Then I went across the country spreading fire and disease,
I prayed to the devil down on my bloody knees,
Then I bought another record and I committed suicide.

While a mock condemnation of heavy metal, Paleface's "Burn and Rob" is a fierce portrait of contemporary disaffected youth and the damage a little skewed ideology can do. One of the saddest examples in recent times is the story of the "American Taliban," John Walker Lindh.

There comes a time for most musicians when deteriorating social conditions no longer allow them to continue writing what Steve Earle refers to as "chick songs." And Earle, having been married seven times, is a master of the "chick song," of both the sweet and bitter variety. But with the release of his 2004 album, *The Revolution Starts Now*, it was clear that Earle felt the time had come to take a stand. The collection of songs, he explained, was written and recorded in a matter of days as an urgent telegram to the American people to wake up and reclaim what's left of our dwindling democracy. Earle employed a straight-ahead, grindin' rock band (The Dukes) to drive home his populist message, with fuzz-drenched guitars that recalled many of the great 1960s bands like Credence Clearwater Revival and the Velvet Underground. The album, a rockin' political hot potato, captured a similar spirit to that found in Neil Young's strongest political statement, "Ohio," which was written and recorded live in one day. Earle's brand of agitprop, with its raw unpolished sound, also suggests John Lennon's early 1970s protest songs, like "Power to the People," "The Luck of the Irish," and "Attica State."

Earle's "unapologetic leftist" stance was prominent again, in "John Walker's Blues," from his 2002 release *Jerusalem*, a moving ballad about John Walker Lindh, the Marin County teenager who went looking for something to believe in beyond the vapid lifestyle he saw represented in *Rolling Stone* and on *MTV*. The song of the lost American kid who became a Muslim fundamentalist, fighting in the Jihad, brought a storm of controversy down on Earle, as the press immediately branded him "a musical Michael Moore."

"The reason that Michael Moore scares the living fuck out of people is because he is not an elitist," Earle countered. "He comes from working people. He's not spouting political theory on an abstract level."

"I totally believe Pete Seeger when he said that all songs are political, because lullabies are political to babies. We're living in politically charged times, so these last few records I've made are really political. But when I die, if you do the math you'll probably find I have written more songs about girls than I did politics," he laughed.

Busted for possession of heroin and cocaine in the early 1990s, Steve was sentenced to a year behind bars. But after two months he was freed on the condition that he participate in an outpatient program until he cleaned up. Since then, Earle, despite his stormy relationships with women and right-wing politicos, has become a full-time peace warrior, playing benefits for everything from the right to abortion to the abolition of the death penalty.

13

STOMP SOME RUMP

For hundreds of years, troubadours, griots, or bards—as singer/ songwriters and poets are known in various cultures worldwide— have recounted the daring exploits of outlaws. Then, in the last quarter of the twentieth century, the legends (whether heroes or anti-heroes) seized the stage themselves, took the mics in their hands, and stood before their audience, unabashedly rapping the highlights of their own résumé.

"Love has been the traditional component of songs for 1400 years. Rap has covered a lot more ground than we have ever dealt with before," singer/songwriter Randy Newman told author Paul Zollo. "They're talking about life. There's more interest to those lyrics, all in all, than the bulk of pop music has produced, ever."

No matter how you feel about rap, love it or loathe it, Newman was right. If you really want to know what's going on in the inner city from the Bronx to Compton and points in between, it can all be found within the high-gear spontaneous flow of the street poet.

"The earliest recordings of gangster hip hop came in around 1981, 1982," explained Andre Torres, former editor of the cutting-edge black-culture magazine *Wax Poetics*. "The Golden Flamingo label recorded a band with the unlikely name of the Land of Hits Orchestra. This was low-budget stuff, recorded live, but mind-blowing. It's where funk ends and hip hop first begins. Then along came Schoolly D, one of the first East Coast gangstas . . . pre Ice-T. He really pushed the feel and the look of the Philly street gangs."

"The first record that came out along those lines was Schoolly D's 'P.S.K.' [Park Side Killers]," Ice-T explained, giving props to the man who helped to catapult his career. "When I heard that record I was like, 'Oh shit!' . . . I *dug* that record. . . . All he did was represent a gang on his record. I took that and wrote a record about guns, beating people down, and all that with '6 in the Mornin'.'"

Over the sound of a slammin' metallic drum-machine, Schoolly D. spits his story straight from the streets. The sparse production gives way to a raw voice saturated in reverb, accented by angular, rhythmic record scratches. While the typically narcissistic posturing of today's emcees is there, it's kept to a minimum in "P. S. K." as Schoolly D. represents real street life, rapping about money, "fly ladies," and the ever-present atmosphere of violence.

Ice-T then took Schoolly D's message to the next level, triggering the beginning of gangsta rap with his "6 in the Mornin'," a B-side that packed a stronger criminal element as well as a candidly provocative view of the pimp life. As Torres points out, "It's a very important record." Kicking off with an easy groovin' snare beat, Ice-T, the "self-made monster," leads us through the grim realities of his 'hood, where "just living in the city is a serious task." Listening back years later to the track, his simple sing-songy delivery resembles a degenerate jump-rope song. His story, on the other hand, is anything but lightweight.

Recounting how his car was pulled over by the LAPD, he is shaken down by "the pigs," who not surprisingly find some heavy artillery stashed in the trunk, including "an Uzi, .44,. and a hand grenade." Although our hard-boiled protagonist manages to maneuver through an ever shifting maze of prison, guns, sex, and death, he is constantly confronted by the bleak existential prospect of living in a world where "life has no meaning and money is king."

Released in 1987, Ice-T's debut album *Rhyme Pays* was the first hip hop LP to merit a Parental Advisory sticker, which carried a warning of explicit lyrics. This flagrant attempt to muzzle "the filthy mouths" of many rap, metal, and R&B artists by Vice President Al Gore's wife, Tipper, and her posse of puritanical "Washington Wives," was known as the PRMC, the Parents Music Resource Center. Ice-T soon retaliated against this free-speech lynch mob with his 1989 release *The Iceberg/ Freedom of Speech . . . Just Watch What You Say*, in which he name-checks Ms. Gore, referring to her as a "dumb bitch" and equating her self-righteous campaign with censorship. "The Constitution," Ice-T reminded all involved, "says we all got a right to speak."

Ice-T's benchmark "Cop Killer" hit the streets in 1992 on *Body Count*, an album by the rap/thrash band of the same name. Cowritten by Ice-T and guitarist Ernie-C, the song was actually performed while Body Count made the rounds on the Lollapalooza festival circuit in 1991. Shortly after the record's release, the video of Rodney King's savage beating by the LAPD swept from coast to coast. In a horrendous failure of justice, the offending cops were acquitted and riots immediately broke out in South Central LA.

In a show of solidarity with their fellow lawmen, a group of Texas police officers demanded an immediate boycott of the song. Ice-T, who had ironically played a cop in the film *New Jack City* in 1991, attempted to squelch the escalating controversy when he replied, "I'm singing in the first person as a character who is fed up with police brutality. I ain't never killed no cop. I felt like it a lot of times. But I never did it."

Mounting death threats and the backlash of offended stockholders threatening to sell their shares prompted Warner Brothers to take the song off the album and drop both Ice-T and his group from their roster.

In his 1994 book *The Ice Opinion: Who Gives a Fuck?*, Ice-T reiterated his position on the issue, reinforcing the fact that the song was a work of fiction: "If you believe that I'm a cop killer, you believe David Bowie is an astronaut," he quipped, referring to Major Tom, the tragic hero of Bowie's song "Space Oddity."

Outrageous as it seemed at the time, a song like "Cop Killer" was nothing new and can be traced back to "Duncan and Brady," which was originally recorded in 1929 by Wilmer Watts and his Lonely Eagles in Chicago for Paramount Records. Commonly known as "Been on the Job Too Long," the song recounted the alleged shooting of an arrogant beat cop named James Brady by the bartender, Harry Duncan, following a barroom brawl in Charles Starkes's Saloon in St. Louis on October 6, 1890. Watts, who apparently heard the song second-hand before recording it, confused the two main characters, portraying Duncan as the cop and Brady as "a worker on the telephone wire."

But those details were soon ironed out in both Blind Jesse Harris's and Lead Belly's versions of the song, which revealed that the corrupt and violent underbelly of America's cities was far grittier than most people suspected at the time. By the 1960s, "Duncan and Brady" would make the rounds through the repertoires of folk singers, from Dave Van Ronk, Spider John Koerner, and Tom Rush to the New Riders of the Purple Sage and Bob Dylan. No matter how each artist put his own personal stamp on it, the basic plot of the song remained the same. Brady incites a shootout after he brazenly comes into the saloon:

> *Walkin' in the room when the game was goin' on,*
> *Knockin' down windows and breakin' down the door.*

Smugly sporting his "shiny star," it's clear that Brady had "been on the job too long." When the crooked cop tries to arrest Duncan (for what crime we are never told in the original version of the song), the short-tempered bartender immediately draws his pistol and blows "a hole in Brady's chest." His knee-jerk response was also chalked up to Duncan also having "been on the job too long." Brady, it is said, "knew he done wrong," and is now "lyin' dead on that barroom floor," while Duncan is immediately fingered as the prime suspect in the law-man's murder. In real life, many believed the fatal bullet had actually been fired by Charles Starkes, the saloon's proprietor. No matter how he protested and proclaimed his innocence, the bartender's appeal was ultimately ignored by the Supreme Court and he was hanged by the neck until dead on July 27, 1894.

The New Riders of the Purple Sage recorded a bouncy good-time version of "Duncan and Brady" on their debut album, complete with a plunky banjo and a mocking pedal-steel guitar riff played by Jerry Garcia. With tongue in cheek they gleefully sing the song's refrain, "Been on the job too long," evoking the feel of the Grateful Dead's tragic/comic ballads "Dupree's Diamond Blues" and "Casey Jones."

A surprisingly abstract take on "Duncan and Brady" comes from singer/songwriter Tom Rush, who claimed to have learned it from the roots and blues guitarist Spider John Koerner. As Tom told his crowd one night before launching into a nine-minute rendition of the tune, the scatological Spider John had "put his own twist on it."

In Rush's vivid retelling, the song's bridge explodes into an absurd talking blues (second only to Arlo Guthrie's "Alice's Restaurant Massacree"), in which he recounts how Duncan, a first-rate hustler, runs a store that sold everything from potato chips to used cars. Duncan holds a monopoly on all the action that goes down in the town of "Duncanville" (which just happened to be named after him). The all-powerful Duncan also owns a hotel as well, where the whole town lives, except for Brady and his long-suffering wife. Over a gingerly strummed ragtime rhythm, Rush weaves his surreal tale of wild all-night parties with copious amounts of booze, gambling, and wild women. Everybody is having a ball except for Brady, who "as the town's sheriff, is compelled to remind them, 'It's illegal.'" Brady, who can't stand to see people enjoying themselves, reaches for his "pearl handled, hair-triggered .44 and climbs the stairs of Duncan's hotel with the intent to blow down the door." But Duncan and his pals are one step ahead of him, waiting with a high-power cannon that splatters the pesky lawman "all over the east side of town." Ironically Brady's wife doesn't seemed too disturbed upon hearing the news of her husband's sudden demise. In fact, as in Lead Belly's version, she is relieved he's finally gone and is happy to receive his pension. Once the word is out that Brady is dead, the women of Duncanville "all dress in red," which is traditionally considered a flagrant display of disrespect to wear to anyone's funeral.

"I think what hooked me into the song was the line about having 'Been on the job too long,'" Tom Rush explained. "I could relate to it, even fifty years ago. Now I've *really* been on the job too long! I think these old murder ballads and outlaw songs continue to appeal to us and hold the same attraction that most TV series do nowadays. We like to imagine all these exciting things that never happen in our own boring lives, if we're lucky."

Like Robert Johnson (the Mississippi bluesman who dodged the voracious jaws of hellhounds, gangs of good ol' boys out to lynch him, and even ol' Satan himself, waiting for him down at the crossroads with a contract to sign over his soul), the star-crossed Tupac Shakur knew his time on earth wasn't long. In "If I Die 2Nite," the weed-puffin' Makeveli of rap—to use one of his stagenames—desperately sought refuge from America's deranged and brainwashed lifestyle. Although he struggled to rise above his conditioned, media-poisoned brain, Tupac inherently understood the odds had been stacked against him from the start. Running with criminals through the ghetto streets, "duckin' cops and clutchin' his Glock," his brain swirled with the nightmarish visions of doing time in retribution for all the fools he's "dusted."

Following the drive-by assassination attempt on his life, on September 6, 1996, Shakur died of multiple gunshot wounds a week later in a Las Vegas hospital. Although his legend thrives twenty years after his murder (whether the crime was carried out by Orlando Anderson of the Compton-based gang known as the Southside Krips or his nemesis, Notorious B.I.G.), hip hop had lost a true master and innovator of the form.

Beyond the swaggering sensationalism and titillation of rap, Shakur's spontaneous lyric flow was a brutal but authentic reflection of ghetto life. As 50 Cent later acknowledged, "Every rapper who grew up in the nineties owes something to Tupac. He didn't sound like anyone who came before him."

"All I can think about is fame," Shakur once mused. Despite the desperation and determination of most hip hop emcees to free themselves from the galling conditions of inner city life, the joyride of sensual pleasure and crass materialism to which many fall prey is all too often fast and fleeting. Whatever fame is ultimately achieved is sadly short-lived, usually lasting no more than a day, taking the form of a front-page headline or gossip spilling from the lips of some well-groomed news anchor, and managing to hang in our collective attention-deficit memories for at best (as Andy Warhol once predicted) fifteen minutes.

On his 1993 release "Sound of da Police," Bronx-born rapper KRS-One equates the ever-present police siren to the scream of "the beast." The actual criminals, he proclaims in the song's accompanying video, are the cops. KRS-One then recites a litany of abuse that stretches back to his great-grandfather and great-great-grandfather. "When's it gonna stop?" he begs, exasperated, as images flash behind him of African Americans assailed by the forceful spray of firehoses turned on them during the 1960s civil rights riots.

Released in March 1987, *Criminal Minded* sported the first hip hop record jacket to openly glorify weaponry, depicting a heavily armed KRS-One and his partner DJ Scott La Rock (a.k.a. Scott Sterling) wielding pistols and draped in cartridge belts. Found within that provocative sleeve was "9mm Goes Bang," arguably hip hop's first song based on a first-person crime narrative. Yet on the album's title track, KRS-One takes a surprisingly peaceful stance: "These days I'm tryin' to give back," he says. "Stopping the violence is what I'm all about."

KRS-One, whose name is an abbreviation of that of the blue Hindu flute-playing god Lord Krishna (also spelled KRSNA), has, with the help of his spiritual practice, always tried to take the high road, helping his fans to rise above the violence and chaos of the ghetto.

KRS-One's struggle to keep the peace doesn't imply that he is weak or willing to look the other way when things get rough. On the contrary, he (like his namesake Lord Krishna, who fervently drove the reluctant General Arjuna's chariot into the epic battle of Kurukshetra) remains true to himself, his 'hood, and the world at large.

Over the punchy snare groove of "Black Cop," he calls out his fellow African Americans, whom he believes have betrayed their own people by joining the police force. "Thirty years ago there were no black cops," KRS-One roars. "Shootin' black people . . . You don't even get paid a whole lot!"

Time and time again we have witnessed how everyday people are transformed into outlaws when the conditions of their lives force them to take a stand, whether as a matter of philosophy, morality, or survival. Under such dire circumstances one must choose to "Live Free or Die," as the compelling motto on the state of New Hampshire's license plates implores.

Nowhere has that slogan seemed to ring truer than the South Bronx, home to DJ Kevin Donovan, who dubbed himself Afrika Bambaataa in honor of the fearless Zulu chief Mbata Bhambatha, who in 1906 summoned his tribe to fight the South African government, which had imposed oppressive tax laws upon his people. Having made the transition from warlord to peace warrior, Donovan (commonly credited as the originator of the term "hip hop") would use the music as a vehicle to bring his community together.

"Afrika Bambaataa was a member of the Black Spades, a gang from the Bronx, when he had this idea of transforming gang culture into a more creative, social organization, moving away from street fighting to dance parties," said Baba Israel of the New York hip hop group Soul Inscribed. "He founded the Zulu Nation. While reality, of course, is never nearly as poetic as the mythology, he caused a significant shift in the gang activity in the Bronx. The transformation created an alternative social structure. Hip hop's origins did not start in the traditional music industry but with the block party where he set up turntables and a sound system and jacked into the electricity on the street. The Bronx in the seventies was not just on the outside of mainstream culture, it was on the outside of legality. There were certain neighborhoods that the police would not dare to drive through. After ten or twelve years of the scene building, the music industry came in very aggressively and co-opted hip hop culture. Afrika Bambaataa managed to stay out of that."

"Nothing stays the same, there were always renegades," Bam reminds us, as he namechecks everyone from Sitting Bull to Tom Payne, Martin Luther King, and Malcolm X to prove his point in his 1983 hit "Renegades of Funk."

"Renegades," he reminds us over a crush groove, "change the course of history." Knowledge, they say is power, and rather than duping his homeboys with decadent dreams of gold chains and a Caddy full of "bitches," guaranteed to bring them momentary satisfaction and fulfillment, Bambaataa offered an alternative, more practical path that involved no firearms. Like George Harrison and Bob Marley before him, he urged his fans to look within and seek inner peace by cultivating their inner worth.

Over the years, numerous musicians have crossed the border into outlaw territory, whether due to a proclivity for drugs, firearms, or adventure. Then, after receiving a slap on the wrist or an unjustly heavy sentence, many a bad boy has eventually done what the late comedian/standup philosopher Lord Buckley called "the great turn-around."

Although he served time for murder and attempted murder, Lead Belly, as his niece Tiny Robinson reminded me, "loved children," pointing out that her famous Uncle Huddie wrote and sang the perennial kids' song "Skip to My Lou."

While undeniably a tough bunch, the Neville Brothers of New Orleans' Thirteenth Ward never killed anybody, in contrast to Lead Belly. While his transcendental warble took songs like "Tell It Like It Is" and "Everybody Plays the Fool" to the top of the charts, Aaron Neville resembles the kind of guy you'd be foolish to mess with. An inhibiting presence, he stands approximately six feet tall and weighs over 200 pounds, with bulging biceps engraved with a smattering of jailhouse tattoos. (He also has the image of a sword scratched into his left cheek, a symbol for having committed murder, which his irate father once tried to make him remove with a Brillo pad.) Nonetheless, Neville is often described as "just a big pussy cat." He even recorded a tender, gospel-tinged version of "The Mickey Mouse March" (with Dr. John on piano) for *Stay Awake*, Hal Willner's 1988 album of Walt Disney songs.

Growing up in New Orleans' Calliope Projects, he and his brothers were always "ready to rumble," Neville told author David Ritz. "We'd carry knives—small cleavers I'd take from Mommy's kitchen that I'd sharpen at the grocery store. We'd cut someone every once in a while but only to show we didn't take no shit."

Neville's musical career began in 1954, singing with his brother Art in a band called the Hawketts, who scored a local Crescent City hit with their version of "Mardi Gras Mambo." Eventually he was nabbed for stealing cars and spent six months in Parish prison, with "eight people in a cell designed to hold four [and] rats running over everything," as he told an interviewer from *People* magazine. This would traumatize most people, but Neville shrugged the nightmare off, claiming it was "kind of fun. My brother Charlie had served time before me, so I had some idea of what to expect."

Half a year behind bars was hardly enough to make young Aaron change his ways. As it says in the words to "Junco Partner," a blues song that Neville undoubtedly knew well, "Six months, that ain't no sentence, and one year, that ain't no time." Back out on the street again "with goofballs popping off inside us, we'd get in barroom brawls, hitting everyone we didn't know. . . . Nothing scared us," Neville boasted.

The bend in the road came while he was shooting heroin in some dingy pad in Harlem. He claims he had a vision of a luminescent cross appearing before him on a dilapidated wall. Neville wisely took this as "a sign telling me, 'Get me out of there.'" But until he could free from himself from his smack habit, it didn't matter where he ran. Although in the throes of heroin addiction, Aaron still managed to hold down a number of menial jobs, from driving trucks, to digging ditches and working on the docks. His family, his son Aaron Jr. later revealed, subsisted off of mayonnaise sandwiches. Relocating to LA didn't help matters much, as Aaron soon wound up in the joint again for burglarizing clothing stores.

In 1967 Neville's singular voice, a perfect blend of country, gospel and soul, turned "Tell It Like It Is" into a national hit. Not helping matters any was the lousy deal he signed with his record company, which screwed him out of all future royalties after giving him a one-time flat fee for his chart-topping performance.

Neville has always been quick to credit his devoted wife Joel and his belief in St. Jude, the saint of lost causes, for helping him to regain control of his life again.

"I don't have no regrets about nothing or anything I did," he said. "Some of the things I've done give me compassion for people who've gone through it; maybe I can give them some worldly wisdom. I look at it as all the things I did, the world that I come from, has made me who I am."

Following his discharge from the Army, Aaron's older brother Charles garnered a solid reputation playing sax on the road for R&B and blues stars like James Brown, B. B. King, and Ray Charles. At home he could be found blowing soulfully on the bandstand with New Orleans's finest, including Huey "Piano" Smith, Allen Toussaint, and James Booker. But heroin would also wreak havoc with his life. Charles had been in and out of prison a number of times for petty theft when a judge, looking to make an example of him, slapped him with a severe five-year sentence for two marijuana joints. Released for good behavior after serving three-and-a-half years in the notoriously inhuman Angola prison, Charles split for New York City in hopes of finding a better life than he'd known in the racist South.

After the death of their mother, Amelia, in 1975, the brothers' Uncle George Landry, better known as "Chief Jolly" amongst the Black Mardi Gras Indian tribes, summoned his nephews to the studio to loan their sweet harmonies and funky rhythmic feel to an album of indigenous folk songs he was recording. Aaron likened Chief Jolly's beckoning to "a call from God." The resulting project, *The Wild Tchupitoulas* (produced by Allen Toussaint and released in 1976), included a pair of catchy numbers, "Meet De Boys On De Battlefront" and "Brother John," sonic portraits of Crescent City street life and the stiff competition that still exists around the annual Fat Tuesday carnival.

The subculture of the Black Mardi Gras Indian stretches back to the early 1700s, with its own cast of "maskers" (masqueraders), "flag boys" (who carry the tribe's colorful banners), and "spyboys," whose job is to report on the whereabouts of rival gangs and the details of their elaborate finery. While the Indians' unusual vernacular, heard in many Mardi Gras songs, is lost on most folks, that so-called "nonsense" is an intricate lingo composed of cryptic code words, derived from a combination of Creole French, English, African, and Native American languages.

According to James "Sugar Boy" Crawford, the origin of his 1953 song "Jock-A-Mo," usually known as "Iko Iko," was "a victory chant the Indians would shout." Its origin can be found in a Ghanaian dialect, as the word "Ayeko" translates to "well done," or "congratulations," while the well-known phrase, "Jockomo Feena Nay," as Dr. John explained in his slow jazzy drawl, means "something like 'kiss my ass or chew my drawers.'"

While eschewing physical violence, the tribes still compete with each other's custom-sewn costumes with the same fierce attitude they once held when they used to "stomp some rump" during neighborhood skirmishes.

The "itty bitty spyboy" who Chief Jolly toasts in "Meet De Boys On De Battlefront" possesses a "heart of steel." He may be small, but he means business. "(If his) shank won't get you, then his hatchet will," the Brothers sing. Apparently he has no fear of firing "his pistol at the jailhouse door," in hopes of freeing his fellow tribe members who wind up behind bars during the festivities.

The Wild Tchupitoulas often psyched out their rivals by singing about their supernatural powers, which included swimming through mud, snatching tail feathers off an eagle, and drinking panther blood. They were known as "Wild" for good reason. Like everyone else in Crescent City, they were famous for partying hard. On their album, they sing of "drink[ing] fire water till the sun goes down," until once more they "get back home" where they "kneel and pray," grateful to the loas (voodoo divinities) they worship (from Erzulie to Papa Legba) for having had "some fun on the holiday" and returning in one piece.

Written by the youngest brother, drummer Cyril Neville, "Brother John" recounts the story of "John 'Scarface' Williams, the vocalist for [R&B pianist] Huey Smith's Clowns, who was stabbed to death on Rampart Street." Neville told David Ritz, "There have been many songs about John. I hope mine expressed that weird mixture of violence and beauty that was part of our R&B street life."

Williams's violent death was not unusual for New Orleans–based musicians. Famous for late-night weekend shootings, the Crescent City is also known as "The Bucket of Blood." While most murders typically take place over drugs, gambling, and women, violence is all too commonly racially motivated, as in the case of Sugar Boy Crawford, who was forced to retire from his music career, having suffered head injuries after being repeatedly pistol-whipped by a pair of sadistic white cops.

"The image of the outlaw is at the very core of American culture," Andre Torres emphasized. "Look at respected establishment families like the Rockefellers and Kennedys, who made all their money doing their dirty work during the bootlegging era. It's been ingrained in the American psyche ever since this country began. You can't get around it. But I think the real outlaw in hip hop culture is the graffiti artist. They're out there, literally wearing masks and taking risks to express themselves. Kase2, the one-armed graffiti artist was legendary. The way he painted, you would've thought he had three arms!"

Kase2, or Jeff Brown, as his name appeared on his death certificate in August 2011, lost his right arm at the age of ten after he was severely burned in a subway accident. What might have seemed an insurmountable hurdle for most people could not thwart this single-minded underground outlaw from "bombing" the crumbling urban landscape with an arsenal of spray-paint cans. Transforming dingy trains and decrepit handball courts into a fluctuating museum of modern folk-art, the self-proclaimed "King of Style" (who was duly feted in the 1983 documentary *Style Wars*) devised a unique (and heavily imitated) "computer-rock" style of lettering that has become omnipresent across Manhattan's five boroughs since the mid-1970s.

Not surprisingly, one of the few places that graffiti artists have gleaned any respect in this world is from emcees. Over a chill groove, Rakim, who has refused to "work blue" and has never once cursed in a rap tune, elevates these "visual vandals" to the status of modern day prophets, whose message (as Paul Simon sang many years ago in "The Sound of Silence") is "written on the subway wall and tenement halls."

On "The 18th Letter," the title track from his 1997 album, Rakim (born William Michael Griffin) gives his perspective on this illegal and much-maligned art-form, putting it into historical perspective: "From the ancient hieroglyphics to graffiti painted pictures, / I study, I know the scriptures."

For many, the Bible remains a constant source of guidance in their lives. But when LL Cool J quotes "the book of James," in his string-laden epic "Dear Hip Hop," it is with his tongue firmly in his cheek: "Let there be light when I write graffiti on the train."

KRS-One's "Out for Fame" also gives props to graffiti artists by name-checking legendary writers "Phase2, Stay High, and Pre-Streets," among others, encouraging them to "grab [their] cans and hit the streets." Unlike rap, KRS-One pointed out back in 1995, "Graffiti isn't corporate so it gets no respect."

"It's all changing now," Andre Torres said. "The teens coming up now are breaking down the boundaries of what hip hop used to be and expanding on it. The Internet has opened the door for greater expression. You can just log on whenever you feel like it and watch someone like Young Thug from Atlanta, representing in women's clothes."

"The Best Rapper Alive," according to a Spring 2016 issue of *GQ*, Thug is the latest in a long line of disposable hip hop mega-stars, "a man-boy who'd been raised by wolves and suckled on Xanax and mushrooms and Lil Wayne, [who has invented] his own language."

Between Thug's appetite for cough syrup, heavy-duty weaponry, and an endless line of willing "bitches" of every variety, his former manager has predicted a tragic end for his ex-client, giving him ten years at best before he winds up "either dead or in jail."

Perhaps the Geto Boys summed up outlaw life best in their 1992 release "Damn, It Feels Good to Be a Gangsta." Over a laidback groove, with plenty of attitude to spare, the Houston-based hip hop trio comprised of Scarface, Willie D, and Bushwick Bill start out praising the usual trappings of gangsta life from "the flyest of the bitches" to their "drop-top Benz." But suddenly a few surprising twists appear. Beyond the hard-earned reward of living by one's own rules comes an inherent satisfaction from "feedin' the poor and hepin' out wit they bills." While shades of Robin Hood inform their rap, they urge all the "gangsta-ass niggas" to "think deep" and turn their lives around—not simply because it's the right thing to do, but as a plea for self-preservation. "This gangsta here is a smart one," the Geto Boys preach to the beat, "started living for the Lord and I'll last."

STAND AND DELIVER: AN AFTERWORD

What ultimately defines an outlaw? How do outlaws differ from pirates or gangstas? Is it the turf they lay claim to? Their choice of weapons? Or their fashionable outfits? Their swagger? The bottom line is that they all engage in some type of criminal activity or another, whether out of desperation or a taste for adventure.

For old school outlaws like Robin Hood and Jesse James, nature provided an impenetrable refuge whenever the heat was on. They took shelter within the maze of a dark forest or atop ominous mountains that lawmen, who were primarily city dwellers, feared or did not know.

Meanwhile, having had his fill of plundering and pillaging, the pirate made his getaway across the vast expanse of the ocean, where no landlubber could ever find him. On the other hand, gangbangers regularly find sanctuary in corners of the concrete jungle where no cop would ever dare set foot.

In the twenty-first century, the doors to a new frontier of opportunity and greed have been flung open with the advent of the Internet, where cyber brigands of all ages and backgrounds are free to loot when and whatever they wish, 24/7. There is no immediate danger to either the perpetrators or the victims, who aren't physically present while the hold-up takes place and most likely won't discover they've been robbed—whether of bankbook, privacy, intellectual property, or identity—until after the fact.

If Woody Guthrie had lived long enough he certainly would have added the computer to his famous lyric about Pretty Boy Floyd:

> *Yes, as through this world I've wandered,*
> *I've seen lots of funny men:*
> *Some will rob you with a six-gun,*
> *And some with a fountain pen.*

As fountain pens have fallen out of fashion, you are more likely to be hacked these days. Once again, it seems, the times—as Dylan foretold back in 1964—have changed. An outlaw has no need to don a mask and wield a weapon. Nobody needs to steer a getaway car through bustling city streets with precision and nerves of steel, hoping their tires don't get blown out by the hot lead of pursuing police. They can enjoy the comfort of their own homes while they burglarize with their laptops. With Russian hackers alleged to have meddled digitally with the outcome of the 2016 presidential election, perhaps the time has come for a new generation of cyber Robin Hoods. Whether they are rap stars, alt-country unplugged troubadours, or classic rock bands on the comeback trail, someone is sure to sing their praises.

SUGGESTED OUTLAW PLAYLIST

"The Adventures of Panama Red"—New Riders of the Purple Sage

"Bad Blood"—The Bonzo Dog Doo-Dah Band

"Bad Boy"—Carole King, the Holy Modal Rounders

"Bad Company"—Reverend Gary Davis

"Bad Sadie Lee"—The Incredible String Band

"Bad to the Bone"—George Thorogood

"Ballad of a Well-Known Gun"—Elton John

"The Ballad of Earl Durand"—Charlie Brown

"The Ballad of Easy Rider"—The Byrds, Richard Thompson

"Bandit Cole Younger"—Edward L. Crain

"Bankrobber"—The Clash, Hot Tuna

"Believer"—Eric von Schmidt

"Billy the Kid"—Ry Cooder

"Billy the Kid"—Billy Joel

"Black Jack David"—Dave Alvin

"Black Jack Davy"—The Incredible String Band, Taj Mahal, Bob Dylan

"Bonnie and Clyde"—Serge Gainsbourg and Bridget Bardot, Georgie Fame

"Branded Man"—Merle Haggard

"Brother John"—The Wild Tchoupitoulas

"The Buffalo Skinners"—Woody Guthrie, Ramblin' Jack Elliott

"A Bullet for Ramona"—Warren Zevon

"Burn and Rob"—Paleface

"Cocaine Blues"—Reverend Gary Davis

"Cop Killer"—Ice-T

"Country Death Song"—Violent Femmes

"Coming Into Los Angeles"—Arlo Guthrie

"Darling Corey"—Bill Monroe, Roscoe Holcomb, Bruce Hornsby and Ricky Skaggs

"Desperadoes Waiting for a Train"—Guy Clark

"Desperado"—The Eagles

"Dillinger"—David Olney

"Don't Take Your Guns to Town"—Johnny Cash

"Don't You Think This Outlaw Bit's Done Got Out of Hand"—Waylon Jennings

"Down by the River"—Neil Young

"Duncan and Brady (a.k.a. Been on the Job Too Long)"—Tom Rush, New Riders of the
Purple "Sage"—Bob Dylan, Dave Van Ronk

"Dupree's Diamond Blues"—Grateful Dead
"El Paso"—Marty Robbins
"Envy the Thief"—Eric von Schmidt
"For What It's Worth"—Buffalo Springfield
"Folsom Prison Blues"—Johnny Cash
"Frankie and Albert"—Mississippi John Hurt
"The Free Mexican Air Force"—Peter Rowan
"Friend of the Devil"—The Grateful Dead
"Fuzzy Was an Outlaw"—David Allan Coe
"G-Man Hoover"—Van Dyke Parks
"Gallows Pole (a.k.a., Gallis Pole, Hangman)"—Lead Belly, Led Zeppelin
"Gallows Tree"—Peter, Paul & Mary
"The Glendale Train"—New Riders of the Purple Sage
"The Harder They Come"—Jimmy Cliff
"Henry"—New Riders of the Purple Sage
"He's A Rebel"—The Crystals
"Hey Joe"—Jimi Hendrix, Love, the Byrds
"Heroin"—The Velvet Underground
"High Plains Drifter"—The Beastie Boys
"The Holdup"—David Bromberg
"Hoochie Coochie Man"—Willie Dixon
"If I Die 2Nite"—Tupac Shakur
"I Fought the Law"—The Bobby Fuller Four, the Clash
"Iko Iko"—The Wild Tchoupitoulas, Dr. John, the Grateful Dead
"Illegal Smile"—John Prine
"I'm So Bad, Baby I Don't Care"—Motörhead
"I'm Waiting for the Man"—Velvet Underground
"I Shot the Sheriff"– The Wailers, Eric Clapton
"Jailbirds in the Big House"—John Gorka
"Jawbone"—The Band
"Jesse James"—The Pogues
"John Sinclair"—John Lennon
"Johnny Too Bad"—The Slickers, Taj Mahal, UB40, Steve Earle
"Jumpin' Jack Flash"—The Rolling Stones
"Knockin' on Heaven's Door"—Bob Dylan
"Knoxville Girl"—The Louvin Brothers
"Leader of the Pack"—The Shangri-Las
"Let's Go Get Stoned"—Ray Charles, Joe Cocker
"Life in Prison"—Merle Haggard, the Byrds
"Little Criminals"—Randy Newman

"Little Sadie"—Bob Dylan
"Living on Borrowed Time"—Richard Thompson
"Loser"—Beck
"Lost Highway"—Hank Williams
"Love Child"—The Supremes
"Love Henry"—Judy Henske, Bob Dylan, Jolie Holland
"Machine Gun Kelly"—James Taylor
"Mama Tried"—Merle Haggard, the Grateful Dead
"Masters of War"—Bob Dylan
"Me and My Uncle"—The Grateful Dead
"Meet the Boys on the Battlefront"—The Wild Tchoupitoulas
"Mexico"—Beck
"Midnight Rider"—The Allman Brothers
"Minnie the Moocher"—Cab Calloway
"My Father's Gun"—Elton John
"The National Weed Growers Assoc."—Michael Hurley
"9mm Goes Bang"—KRS-One
"1952 Vincent Black Lightning"—Richard Thompson
"'03 Bonnie and Clyde"—Jay Z and Beyoncé
"Omie Wise"—Bob Neuwirth
"On the Road to Fairfax County"—David Massengill, the Roches, Joan Baez
"Outlaw"—Motörhead
"Panama Red"—Peter Rowan, New Riders of the Purple Sage
"Pancho and Lefty"—Townes Van Zandt
"Peg and Pete and Me"—Stan Ridgway
"Police and Thieves"—Junior Murvin, the Clash
"The Pope Smokes Dope"—David Peel
"Post Office Pin-Ups"—Paul K.
"Pretty Boy Floyd"—Woody Guthrie, the Byrds, Ramblin' Jack Elliott, Tom Rush
"Pretty Polly"—Judy Collins
"The Prisoner's Song"—Vernon Dalhart, Hank Snow, Bill Monroe
"Prodigal Son"—The Rolling Stones
"Railroad Bill"—Andy Breckman
"Railroad Bill"—Etta Baker, Mississippi John Hurt
"Raised on Robbery"—Joni Mitchell
"The Revolution Will Not Be Televised"—Gil Scott-Heron
"Ringo"—Lorne Greene
"Robert Ford and Jesse James"—David Olney
"Robbin' Banks"—Jeffery Frederick
"Rocky Raccoon"—The Beatles

"Roland the Headless Thompson Gunner"—Warren Zevon

"Sam Stone"—John Prine

"Send Me to the 'lectric Chair"—Bessie Smith, David Bromberg

"Shane and Dixie"—Richard Thompson

"Silver Dagger"—Joan Baez

"6 in the Mornin'"—Ice-T

"Sonora's Death Row"—Blackie Farrell

"Sovay"—Martin Carthy

"The Sound of the Police"—KRS-One

"Space Oddity"—David Bowie

"Stagger Lee"—Frank Hutchinson, Lloyd Price, Wilson Pickett, Dr. John, the Youngbloods, Taj Mahal, Dave Van Ronk

"Standing on the Corner"—The Four Lads

"Steppin' Razor"—Peter Tosh

"Street Fighting Man"—The Rolling Stones

"Superfly"—Curtis Mayfield

"Take Stuff from Work"—King Missile

"Take This Job and Shove It"—Johnny Paycheck

"Tania"—Camper van Beethoven

"They'll Never Lock Him Up"—Eugene Chadbourne

"Voodoo Chile"—Jimi Hendrix

"Your Flag Decal Won't Get You into Heaven Anymore"—John Prine

"Wake Up Niggers"—The Last Poets

"Walk on Gilded Splinters"—Dr. John

"Wanted Man"—Bob Dylan, Johnny Cash, Nick Cave, George Thorogood

"Wanted Man"—Jimmy Cliff

"Wanted Man"—Ratt

"What About Me?"—Quicksilver Messenger Service, Richie Havens

"What's Going On?"—Marvin Gaye

"Whiskey in the Jar"—The Dubliners, Thin Lizzy, Metallica

"Wild Colonial Boy"—Mick Jagger

"Willie, Waylon, and Me"—David Allan Coe

"Willin'"—Little Feat

ACKNOWLEDGMENTS

Thanks to everyone who generously gave their time to be interviewed for this project and/or granted me permission to use their songs:

Dave Alvin, David Bromberg, Bob Dylan, Steve Earle, Erik Frandsen, Kathryn Frederick, Gordon Gano, John Gorka, David Grisman, the Woody Guthrie Foundation, Mat Hagar, John S. Hall, Kip Hanrahan, Richie Havens, Judy Henske, Anne Hills, Jolie Holland, Michael Hurley, Baba Israel, Paul K., Lenny Kaye, Robert Earl Keen, Kirk Kelly, Danny "Kootch" Kortchmar, Victor Krummenacher, Massimo Liberatori, David Lowery, Taj Mahal, David Massengill, Anna McGarrigle, James "Seamus" Moginie, Danny O'Keefe, David Olney, Michael Ondaatje, Cáit O'Riordan, Paleface, Van Dyke Parks, Samantha Parton, Billy Payne, John Prine, Malcolm Rebbenack (a.k.a. Dr. John), Ishmael Reed, Stan Ridgway, Brian Ritchie, Suzzy Roche, Peter Rowan, Tom Rush, Jonathan Segel, John Sinclair, Peter Stampfel, Pat Thomas, Richard Thompson, Oliver Trager, Andre Torres, Stephen "Dogbowl" Tunney, Jeanene Van Zandt, Eric von Schmidt, Robin Williamson.

Thanks also to copyeditor John Morrish, Senior Editor of Backbeat Books Bernadette Malavarca, and the rest of the Backbeat Books team. Special thanks to Marilyn Cvitanic for watching my back for this long, wild ride.

BIBLIOGRAPHY

BOOKS

Bauldie, John. *Wanted Man: In Search of Bob Dylan*. New York: Citadel, 1991.

Brown, Cecil. *Stagolee Shot Billy*. Cambridge, MA: Harvard University Press, 2003.

Chang, Jeff. *Can't Stop Won't Stop: A History of the Hip-Hop Generation*. New York: Picador/St. Martin's Press, 2005.

Elegant, Simon. *A Floating Life: The Adventures of Li Po*. Hopewell, NJ: Ecco, 1997.

Erbsen, Wayne. *Outlaw: Ballads, Legends and Lore*. Asheville, North Carolina: Native Ground Music, 1996.

Feather, Leonard. *Biographical Encyclopedia of Jazz*. New York: Oxford University Press, 1999.

Grafman, Howard, and B. T. Manning. *Folk Music USA.* New York: Citadel Press, 1962.

Guralnick, Peter. *Lost Highway: Journeys and Arrivals of American Musicians*. Boston: David R. Godine, 1979.

Hoskyns, Barney. *The Band: Across the Great Divide*. New York: Hyperion, 1993.

Jennings, Waylon and Lenny Kaye. *Waylon: An Autobiography*. New York: Grand Central Publishing, 1996.

Kruth, John. *To Live's to Fly: The Ballad of the Late Great Townes Van Zandt*. New York: Da Capo Press, 2007.

Lomax, Alan. *The Folk Songs of North America*. Garden City, NY: Doubleday and Company, 1960.

Louvin, Charlie with Benjamin Whitmer. *Satan Is Real*. New York: Harper Collins Publishers, 2012.

Marcus, Greil. *Invisible Republic: Bob Dylan's Basement Tapes*. New York: Henry Holt, 1997.

Marcus, Greil. *Mystery Train: Images of America in Rock 'n' Roll Music*. New York: E. P. Dutton, 1975.

Ondaatje, Michael. *The Collected Works of Billy the Kid*. Berkeley, CA: Wingbow Press, 1970.

Palmer, Robert. *Deep Blues: A Musical and Cultural History of the Mississippi Delta*. New York: Viking Adult, 1981.

Palmer, Robert. *Rock & Roll: An Unruly History*. New York: Harmony Books, 1995

Rebbenack, Mac (a.k.a. Dr. John). *Under a Voodoo Moon*. New York: St. Martin's Press, 1994.

Reed, Ishmael. *Chattanooga*. New York: Random House, 1973.

Reed, Ishmael. *Conjure*. Amherst, MA: The University of Massachusetts Press, 1972.

Ridge, John Rollin. *The Life and Adventures of Joaquín Murrieta: The Brigand Chief of California*. San Francisco, CA: W. R. Cook and Company, 1854.

Ritz, David and Art Neville, Charles Neville, Aaron Neville, Cyril Neville. *The Brothers.* Cambridge: Da Capo Press, 2000.

Rogan, Johnny. *Timeless Flight: The Definitive Biography of the Byrds.* London: Square One Books, 1990.

Sandburg, Carl. *The American Songbag.* New York: Harcourt, Brace, and Company, 1927.

Scarborough, Dorothy. *On the Trail of Negro Folksongs.* Cambridge, MA: Harvard University Press, 1925.

Shelton, Robert. *The Face of Folk Music.* New York: Citadel Press, 1968.

Silber, Irwin and Earl Robinson. *Songs of the Great American West.* New York: Macmillan, 1967.

Streissguth, Michael. *Outlaw: Waylon, Willie, Kris, and the Renegades of Nashville.* New York: Harper Collins Books, 2013.

Torres, Ben Fong. *Hickory Wind: The Life and Times of Gram Parsons.* New York: St. Martin's, 1998.

Trager, Oliver. *The American Book of the Dead: The Definitive Grateful Dead Encyclopedia.* New York: Fireside/Simon & Schuster, 1997.

Trager, Oliver. *Keys to the Rain: The Definitive Bob Dylan Encyclopedia.* New York: Billboard Books, 2004.

Wald, Elijah. *Narcocorrido: A Journey into the Music of Drugs, Guns, and Guerrillas.* New York: Rayo/Harper Collins Publishers, 2001.

Whittaker, Adrian. *Be Glad: An Incredible String Band Compendium.* London: Helter Skelter Publishing, 2003.

Wilentz, Sean and Greil Marcus. *The Rose & the Briar.* New York: W. W. Norton and Company, 2005.

Wolfe, Charles. *In Close Harmony: The Story of the Louvin Brothers.* Jackson, MS: University Press of Mississippi, 1996.

Young, Rob. *Electric Eden: Unearthing Britain's Visionary Music.* New York: Faber and Faber Inc., 2010.

Zollo, Paul. *Songwriters on Songwriting.* New York: Da Capo Press, 1997.

MAGAZINES AND NEWSPAPERS

Cashman, Ray. "The Heroic Outlaw in Irish Folklore and Popular Literature." *Folklore* 111, no. 2 (October 2000): 191–215.

Cohen, John and Happy Traum. "Conversations with Bob Dylan." *Sing Out! The Folk Song Magazine* 18, no. 4 (October/November 1968).

Los Angeles Times. "Lancelot Pinard: Musician Brought Calypso to US." Obituary by *Times* staff and wire reports. March 18, 2001.

Rees-Mogg, William. "Who Breaks a Butterfly on a Wheel?" *The Times,* London, July 1, 1967.

St. Louis Globe-Democrat. "Negro Shot by Woman." October 16, 1899.

St Louis Globe-Democrat. "Shot in Curtis's Place." December 28, 1895.

LINER NOTES

Brown, Charlie. *Teton Tea Party*. Folkways Records, 1967.

Henske, Judy. *Judy Henske*. Elektra Records, 1963.

Rebbenack, Mac (a.k.a. Dr. John). *Dr John's Gumbo*. Atco, 1972.

Smith, Harry. *Anthology of American Folk Music*. Folkways Records, 1952.

ONLINE RESOURCES

"Jockomo Feena Nay." *Baltimore Diary* (blog), accessed May 4, 2017, http://baltimorediary.typepad.com/baltimore_diary/2011/06/jockomo-feena-nay.html.

Mannheim, James M. "Aaron Neville 1941–" *Encyclopedia.com*, accessed May 4, 2017, http://www.encyclopedia.com/people/literature-and-arts/music-popular-and-jazz-biographies/aaron-neville.

Powell, Azizi, ed. "Wild Tchoupitoulas: Meet De Boys On De Battlefront." *Pancocojams* (blog), accessed May 4, 2017, http://pancocojams.blogspot.com/2014/03/meet-de-boys-on-de-battlefront-mardi.html.

Smeeton, Chuck. "42 Musicians Who Spent Time in Prison." *The Cavan Project* (blog), accessed May 4, 2017, http://www.thecavanproject.com/42-musicians-who-spent-time-in-prison.

Spera, Keith. "Aaron Neville's Hardest Homecoming: He Returns to Bury his Wife." *Nola.com*, accessed May 4, 2017, http://blog.nola.com/keithspera/2007/01/the_hardest_homecoming_aaron_n.html.

Swenson, John. "Aaron Neville: One Man's True Story." *Offbeat Magazine*, accessed May 4, 2017, https://www.offbeat.com/articles/aaron-neville-jazz-fest-true-story.

Tamarkin, Jeff. "Aaron Neville's True Story." *Jazz Times*, accessed May 4, 2017, https://jazztimes.com/features/aarons-nevilles-true-story.

Younger, Cole. *The Story of Cole Younger, by Himself*. Project Gutenberg Ebook, http://www.gutenberg.org/ebooks/24585.

FILMS

The Ballad of Frankie Silver, directed by Tom Davenport, 1996.

Black Snake Moan, directed by Craig Brewer, starring Samuel L. Jackson and Christina Ricci, 2006.

Bloody Mama, directed by Roger Corman, starring Shelly Winters, Bruce Dern and Robert De Niro, 1970.

Bonnie and Clyde, directed by Arthur Penn, starring Warren Beatty and Faye Dunaway, 1967.

The Bonnie Parker Story, directed by William Witney, starring Dorothy Provine, 1958.

Butch Cassidy and the Sundance Kid, directed by George Roy Hill, starring Paul Newman and Robert Redford, 1969.

Easy Rider, directed by Dennis Hopper, starring Peter Fonda and Dennis Hopper, 1969.

The Harder They Come, directed by Perry Henzell, starring Jimmy Cliff, 1972.

Her Man, directed by Tay Garnett, starring Helen Twelvetrees, 1930.

Jesse James, directed by Henry Kings and Irving Cummings, starring Tyrone Power, 1939.

Lampião: O Rei do Cangaço [a.k.a. The King of the Highwaymen], directed by Benjamin Abraham 1937, 2007.

The Legend of Earl Durand, directed by John D. Patterson, starring Peter Haskell, 1974.

The Long Riders, directed by Walter Hill, starring Stacy Keach, Randy Quaid, and Dennis Quaid, 1980.

Machine-Gun Kelly, directed by Roger Corman, starring Charles Bronson, 1958.

The Man Who Shot Liberty Valence, directed by John Ford, starring James Stewart and John Wayne, 1962.

Mesrine, directed by André Génovès, starring Nicolas Silberg, 1984.

Monica la mitraille (Machine Gun Molly), directed by Pierre Houle, starring Céline Bonnier, 2004.

Ned Kelly, directed by Tony Richardson, starring Mick Jagger, 1970.

New Jack City, directed by Mario Van Peebles, starring Wesley Snipes and Ice-T, 1991.

O Cangaceiro, directed by Lima Barreto, 1953.

The Outlaw Josey Wales, directed by Clint Eastwood, starring Clint Eastwood, 1976.

Pat Garrett and Billy the Kid, directed by Sam Peckinpah, starring James Coburn and Kris Kristofferson, 1974.

The Postman Always Rings Twice, directed by Tay Garnett, starring Lana Turner and John Garfield, 1946.

Rebel Without a Cause, directed by Nicholas Ray, starring James Dean and Natalie Wood, 1955.

Robin Hood: Men in Tights, directed by Mel Brooks, starring Mel Brooks, 1993.

Robin and the 7 Hoods, directed by Gordon Douglas, starring Frank Sinatra and Bing Crosby, 1964.

Style Wars, directed by Tony Silver, starring Dondi, Kase2, and Zephyr, 1983.

Super Fly, directed by Gordon Parks Jr., starring Ron O'Neal, 1972.

Thelma & Louise, directed by Ridley Scott, starring Susan Sarandon and Gina Davis, 1991.

Violent Playground, directed by Basil Dearden, starring Stanley Baker and David McCallum, 1958.

The Wild One, directed by László Benedek, starring Marlon Brando and Lee Marvin, 1953.

Wyoming Outlaw, directed by George Sherman, starring John Wayne, 1939.

TELEVISION PROGRAMS

The Simpsons Halloween Special. "Treehouse of Horror VI," 1995.

The Twilight Zone, Episode 154. "Come Wander with Me," May 22, 1964.

The David Letterman Show. The Black Keys perform "Stack Shot Billy," January 5, 2005.

Seinfeld, Episode 141. "The Checks," November 7, 1996.

INDEX